Sins of
the Parents

The Politics of
National Apologies
in the United States

Brian A. Weiner

 Temple University Press
Philadelphia

Brian A. Weiner is Associate Professor of Politics at the
University of San Francisco.

Temple University Press
1601 North Broad Street
Philadelphia PA 19122
www.temple.edu/tempress

⊗ The paper used in this publication meets the requirements of the American
National Standard for Information Sciences—Permanence of Paper for Printed
Library Materials, ANSI Z39.48-1992

Library of Congress Cataloging-in-Publication Data

Weiner, Brian A., 1959–
    Sins of the parents : the politics of national apologies
in the United States / Brian A. Weiner.
        p.   cm. – (Politics, history, and social change)
Includes bibliographical references and index.
      ISBN 1-59213-317-7 (alk. paper) – ISBN 1-59213-318-5 (pbk : alk. paper)
      1. Civil rights – United States – History.   2. Reconciliation – Political
aspects – United States.   3. Japanese Americans – Civil rights.
4. Oneida Indians – Claims – History.   5. Apologizing.   I. Title.
II. Series.

JC599.U5W367 2005
323.1′0973–dc22

2004062560

10 9 8 7 6 5 4 3 2 1

Contents

In loving memory of my father and grandparents, whose presence remains. And to my mother, whose courage inspires.

Acknowledgments

This book has been a long time in the making (many of those close to me would say too long) and, along the way, I have amassed numerous debts of gratitude I take great pleasure in acknowledging.

The manuscript's first incarnation was as a dissertation written at the University of California, Berkeley under the direction of Norman Jacobson and Michael Rogin of the Political Science Department and Michael Smith of the Boalt Hall School of Law. Jacobson was an ideal dissertation chair: a source of calm encouragement, deep wisdom, and humanity, and a vast reservoir of reading suggestions. Rogin, whose death has left a deep hole in the field of American political thought, was an inspiring although at times humbling mentor. His mind worked so quickly, and his knowledge was so vast and varied, that discussions with him often left me feeling he could have written my dissertation in the time it took him to smoke one of his cigarillos. Michael Smith saved me from egregious errors in the law and encouraged me to more clearly and forcefully state my arguments. I am thankful for all of their contributions.

I have had the extreme good fortune to have studied as an undergraduate and graduate student with some of the most insightful and thoughtful political minds in the country: Amy Gutmann, Hanna Pitkin, and Sheldon Wolin. I thank them for the care and conscientiousness they displayed in their teaching and their generosity with their time.

I also was privileged to study with an extraordinarily talented and supportive cohort of graduate students. My sincere thanks for the help and encouragement of Dan Avnon, Graham Chisholm, Elizabeth Collins, Jeremy Elkins, Richard Ellis, Jill Frank, Joann Goven, Emily Hauptmann, Dennis McEnerney, Meta Mendel-Reyes, John Seery, Jackie Stevens, and Mark Tunick. Too many friends to mention also have been essential in helping me through graduate school and beyond. Three, however, deserve special mention for their sane and understanding advice in writing and other matters: Charles Hersch, Joshua Miller, and Michael Spolan.

Chapters of the book were presented at the American Political Science Association Annual Meetings and at the Law and Society Meeting, and my thinking was especially sharpened by the comments of Patricia Boling, Dana Villa, and C. Fred Alford. The Charlotte Newcombe Foundation generously awarded me a year-long fellowship to complete the dissertation, and the Phi Beta Kappa Association also provided me with financial assistance.

At the University of San Francisco, I have been fortunate to have found an immensely supportive environment for both teaching and research. In particular, my colleagues Robert Elias and Roberta Johnson read portions of my work with diligence, and Dean Jennifer Turpin read an earlier version of the work in its entirety and made numerous helpful suggestions. Robert Elias deserves special thanks for his friendly and considerate prodding for me to "send it out." I also thank the University of San Francisco Faculty Development Fund for their generous assistance. Through their means, I was able to hire a number of bright and conscientious research assistants, who I thank for their work: Dominic Caruso, Kevin Moss, Randy Torrijos, James Wade, and Noah Zimmerman.

Three other people, each in their own way, helped me to usher this book out into the light of day: Dorothy Duff Brown, Kristin Gager, and Annie Sweetnam.

I also want to recognize and thank the staff of Temple University Press for their kind consideration and competent editorial advice. Special thanks to Joanne Bowser, for shepherding the manuscript through the book process with professionalism and consideration, and to Lesa Shearer for her conscientious copy-editing. Also, particular thanks to Professor John C. Torpey, editor of the Politics, History, and Social Change series, and to Micah Kleit, senior editor at Temple University Press, for their early support of the manuscript and encouragement throughout. I thank them all for showing great patience in working with me.

Finally, my family has been a constant source of support and encouragement throughout. My parents and sister stood by me and continued to believe in me. Mischa put up with me, and Oggie stayed by my side during late night writing and editing sessions. Lily has been a constant reminder that there is much more to life than this book. Finally, were it not for the love, understanding, patience, intelligence and wit of Andrea Mock, I would be much less a person.

The Framers recognize that no one ought be condemned for his forefather's misdeeds—even when the crime is a most grave offense against the Republic.

> Justice Stevens, writing in dissent in *County of Oneida v. Oneida Indian Nation of New York*, 84 L.Ed.2d 203-4 (1985)

Time past is not believed to have any bearing upon time present or future out in the golden land.

> Joan Didion, "Some Dreamers of the Golden Dream"

Every generation, by virtue of being born into a historical continuum, is burdened by the sins of the fathers as it is blessed with the deeds of the ancestors.

> Hannah Arendt, *Eichmann in Jerusalem*

Introduction

Past Wrongs, Present Responsibilities?

INDIVIDUALS AND GROUPS claiming to be the victims or the inheritors of governmental misdeeds have stepped forward in increasing numbers and frequency since the end of World War II and demanded formal acknowledgment of wrongs done and rectification from governments around the world.[1] Provoked by charges of injustice and the accompanying demands for compensation, polities around the globe have been debating the merits of various claims and the rightfulness of current political bodies assuming responsibility for past political misdeeds. An official expression of remorse for past governmental acts, once unheard of, has become almost commonplace during the past decade or so. Accordingly, wrongs done to aboriginal and native peoples in Australia, New Zealand, Canada, and the United States have been acknowledged. Atrocities committed against political opponents by past authoritarian regimes in Argentina and Uruguay have been admitted and crimes committed under the apartheid regime in South Africa aired during Truth and Reconciliation hearings. Injustices committed by communist regimes in Eastern and Central Europe have been formally divulged and the Japanese army's harsh treatment of Korean comfort women revealed. The list of nations engaged in collective soul-searching over past actions could run for pages.

This book does not aim to explore the worldwide phenomenon of political *mea culpa* but rather offers a careful examination of the manner in which debates over rectification for past governmental injustices have been framed within the United States. The book strives to shed new light on the relationship between the individual citizen and the national collectivity by exploring the challenges that claims for rectification pose to American political practices and modes of thought, and the potential inherent in such claims to deepen and reinvigorate American citizenship. The book examines in depth two cases of claims for rectification and the renewed controversy over a national apology for slavery. The first case studied involves the land claims of the Oneida Indians of New York, Wisconsin, and Ontario. The Oneidas, like other Eastern Indian Tribes, have argued that land transactions completed in the late eighteenth and early nineteenth centuries, in which title passed from Indian tribes to states, and then to individuals, should be invalidated due to the failure of the federal government to live up to promises made to the tribes in treaties and laws regulating trade. The Oneida claim represents the largest (approximately 6 million acres of upstate New York have been at issue), lengthiest (the claims were first heard by the Indian Claims Commission in 1951 and remain unresolved at the time of this writing), and among the most contested (the claims have been heard before the Supreme Court twice). The land claims paint an unsettling portrait of American history and challenge key concepts of American political identity, most particularly the myths that America was a virgin "New World" discovered and civilized by our political ancestors and that contracts and promises were the primary means by which politics in early America were conducted.

The book then moves on to examine another contentious case—that of Japanese American claims for reparations for World War II injustices. Unlike the Oneidas, Japanese Americans, after more than forty years of struggle, succeeded in 1988 in convincing the U.S. government to apologize for the eviction, forced removal, and incarceration of almost 120,000 civilians of Japanese descent. The apology was accompanied by partial compensation: The United States provided $20,000 to each of the approximately sixty thousand surviving persons evicted from their homes pursuant to Executive Order 9066. The redress law provoked a hailstorm of attention, certainly much more than its relatively modest price tag of $1.25 billion can fully explain. The law's passage attests to the persistence of the movement, its political skill, and its good fortune in having four highly placed Japanese American sponsors in Congress.[2] The 1988 law was signed by Ronald Reagan contrary to earlier statements made by his Attorney General. Reagan's decision to sign rather than veto the law reflects the sea change in national and international sentiment regarding the appropriateness of governments offering reparations for past wrongs. However, the final law also reflects the taming of the more subversive elements of the early arguments raised for redress in the original 1979 bill introduced in Congress. Initial arguments likened the United States' internment camps to Nazi concentration camps and challenged the United States' identity as a law-abiding nation respectful of the individual rights of all, irrespective of race or ethnicity. The final law omitted these initial arguments, narrowly defined the victims of Executive Order 9066, and explicitly attempted to limit the law's precedential value for other groups arguably harmed similarly by the United States. After exploring the Oneida and Japanese American cases, the book considers the more recent calls for an apology and reparations for slavery, using the two prior cases to shed light upon this continuing controversy.[3]

In all cases, opponents of apologies and rectification have relied upon the injunction that the sins of the parents shall not be passed on to the children to defend the innocence of present-day American citizens. Proponents of rectification, in response, have had to make the case that the present generation of U.S. citizens should be held responsible for making amends for misdeeds committed by our "political ancestors." Struck by the prevalence of these exchanges, and believing, as political theorist Judith Shklar wrote, that one of the tasks of political theory "is to articulate and examine the half-expressed, political views that the various groups in any given society at any time come to hold," this book sets out to unearth and analyze the concepts that underlie this dialogue.[4] The injunction, seemingly based upon verses in Ezekiel that: "'The son shall not bear the iniquity of the father, neither shall the father bear the iniquity of the son: the righteousness of the righteous shall be upon him, and the wickedness of the wicked shall be upon him," encapsulates two fundamental political concepts relevant to the rectification debate.[5] The first concept, suggested in the Biblical injunction by the relation between parents and children, relates to political membership. The familial relation stands for the political relation between predecessors and present-day citizens. The second concept is tied to sin and innocence, which, in less religious and more political language, relates to issues of individual and collective guilt and responsibility.

The boundaries drawn between individuals and the polity, and between past and present, are at the root of much of the debate over past wrongs and present responsibilities. As members of a political collectivity that exists over time, we are identified with our political ancestors and, arguably, may be implicated by their deeds. While the original wrongdoers and their victims may have died, political misdeeds may live on in various forms, fostering group resentments against those identified with or perceived to be implicated in the initial wrong, and limiting political allegiance among many. The current exploration of national apologies and possible rectification is inspired by the conviction that diminishing the resentments that divide citizens and enhancing citizens' connection to the polity are worthy political goals. To that end, the book ultimately disputes the justness and the political practicality of the maxim that the sins of the parents shall not be passed on to the children. The work argues for a concept of political membership in which citizens recognize themselves as members of an intergenerational polity through which they have inherited both deeds and misdeeds, and in which they share responsibility for past wrongs as well as responsibility to a future less burdened by historical wrongs. The book concludes that national apologies, with or

without monetary compensation, may transform us as a citizenry
in our collective attempts to work through the ambiguous legacy
left us by our political ancestors.

The Post–World War II Context of National Apologies

Contemporary American debates over rectification for past political wrongs take place within the shadows of two events: the
Holocaust and the civil rights movement. As historian Elazar
Barkan makes clear in his broad comparative study of governmental attempts to rectify past wrongs, the 1952 voluntary agreement
by Germany to pay compensation to Israel, as the "descendant" of
the Jews they had victimized in the Holocaust, was "the moment
at which the modern notion of restitution for historical injustices
was born."[6] Barkan points out that the Versailles Treaty of 1919,
by stipulating harsh terms upon Germany, was consistent with the
practice of levying punishment upon the losers of wars—a practice dating back to Abraham's demands on the five kings.[7] The
Versailles Treaty, however, was roundly criticized for contributing
to the conditions under which World War II erupted. Accordingly,
in the aftermath of World War II, the Allies refrained from imposing war reparations upon Germany. Instead, the Marshall Plan
was put in place, freeing Germany from the customary obligations of compensating the winners of war. In this new paradigm,
Germany accepted responsibility for the Holocaust and attempted
to compensate some of its worst victims. Barkan contends the
Germans did so not only to reestablish its legitimacy in the eyes of
the international political community, but also "to facilitate self-
rehabilitation."[8] That is, reparations were conceived as not only
a remedy for the victims of the Holocaust, but also a means by
which those responsible for the injustices could atone for their evil
actions and reestablish integrity in their own eyes and in the eyes
of their victims—as well as the eyes of the world.

Not only did the German government's acts of contrition
provide a paradigm for later claims, but the philosophical debates prompted by "The German Question" framed almost all

later discussions regarding the responsibility owed by a polity's members—"innocent" or not—to victims of their polity's past injustices. Karl Jaspers and Hannah Arendt argue against notions of collective *guilt* but contend that Germans had a collective *responsibility* for crimes committed by their government.[9] Their arguments, as Chapters 4 and 5 will document, have significantly informed the debates over rectification in the United States.

World War II and the Holocaust haunt American efforts at rectification in another manner as well. The war provided an opportunity for minority groups that had been excluded and discriminated against by the United States to prove their loyalty to the country. And the wartime sacrifices made by American Indians, Japanese Americans, and African Americans, in particular, emboldened these groups to demand equal rights and an adequate hearing for grievances against the U.S. government. In turn, the U.S. government sought to differentiate itself as far as possible from the Nazis. Hitler himself had cited the United States' treatment of Western Indians during the nineteenth-century period of "manifest destiny" as justification for the Nazi invasion of Czechoslovakia and Poland.[10] The U.S. government, in all likelihood embarrassed by the analogy, began to treat Indian tribes with greater respect, and in 1946 Congress passed the Indian Claims Commission Act, establishing a method whereby any and all property claims Indian tribes wished to bring forward could be investigated and settled.[11] The Oneida claims explored in the next chapter began with a petition to the Indian Claims Commission.

It was also during World War II that President Roosevelt issued Executive Order 9066, which led the U.S. government to forcibly evict, remove, and incarcerate 120,000 civilians of Japanese descent. Though the distinctions between the Nazi death camps and the American "internment camps" must not be understated, it was true, as The National Committee for Redress bluntly stated in its first pamphlet (1978): "Both Germany and the United States persecuted their own citizens based on ancestry."[12] Japanese Americans' early calls for redress used the analogy between the internment camps and Nazi concentration camps to shame the American government and garner public attention. The fact that Germany had willingly paid reparations to some of the worst victims of the Holocaust also served to embarrass the U.S. government and provoked it to respond to persistent calls for justice by victims of Executive Order 9066. Finally, more than thirty years after Germany began to compensate victims of the Holocaust, the U.S. government issued a national apology and paid partial compensation to the victims of its wartime racist policy. The 1988 Act, in turn, inspired other groups to demand justice for past wrongs, and the Act became a model of how a historical injustice could be translated into an apology and compensation agreeable to both victims and the government assuming responsibility.[13]

The American rectification movements would be simply unimaginable without the cultural and political backdrop of the American civil rights movement of the 1950s and 1960s. The civil rights movement shattered the post–World War II liberal consensus in the United States, introduced the concept of group rights into American politics, and opened up the courts as a forum for collective grievances.[14] The liberal consensus, dominant in most accounts of American history, politics, and society up through the 1950s and early 1960s, portrayed the United States in a celebratory and conflict-free manner. According to this vision, Americans had been blessed with the opportunity to settle upon abundant "virgin land," creating the conditions under which a liberal egalitarian society was fashioned.[15] This theory held that plentiful land guaranteed an open society and that hierarchy could not take root where individuals could always pick up and move on. The political system allegedly mirrored the society at large: Free and equal individuals vied for spoils open to all in an environment where no one group dominated. Much of America's success was based upon the preternatural agreement that endured within the nation that held that conflict was unnecessary where all individuals basically agreed on fundamental values.[16] Class hardly figured in this depiction of American society, which was portrayed as without divisions and open to all. The liberal consensus also took little note of the "race problem," which was restricted in most consensus accounts to the South and to the pre–*Brown v. Board of Education* era.

The civil rights movement dramatically challenged this portrait of American history, society, and politics by ushering in a new model in which not all Americans were socially, legally or politically equal. It was no longer assumed that all groups had equal access to government decision making, and the U.S. government, rather than a guarantor of equal rights for all, was viewed as an oppressor of some. American oppression had a long if not well-known history. Celebratory or "mythic" accounts of American history were contested by new versions that highlighted (or at least took notice of), rather than whitewashed, the nation's treatment of American Indians and African Americans. The Trail of Tears appeared alongside the Mayflower Compact, and violence's place in American history received recognition alongside peaceful contracts.[17] In the wake of the civil rights movement, race and ethnicity moved to the foreground of American politics. As racial and ethnic categories became central to politics, the related concepts of group rights and what has become known as *identity politics* received greater theoretical attention.

Rectification movements may be understood as an outgrowth of identity politics inaugurated during the civil rights movement.[18] Political theorist Charles Taylor traces a politics based on identity or recognition (as opposed to distribution of goods) even further back—to Rousseau's and Hegel's notions of identity and authenticity. Taylor argues that "the spread of the idea that we are formed by recognition" has led to the situation that "misrecognition has now graduated to the rank of a harm."[19] He adds that, "The projection of an inferior or demeaning image on another can actually distort and oppress, to the extent that the image is internalized."[20] Taylor also observes that within this understanding, "the withholding of recognition can be a form of oppression" as well.[21] Among the ways recognition may be withheld is writing history from the perspective of the dominant majority, thereby excluding or misrepresenting the role of minorities within the collective's history.[22] One of the hallmarks of the civil rights movement was the revising of history; reparations movements built upon those revised accounts and in turn provoked further critical interpretations of America's history.[23]

A final crucial civil rights legacy for rectification movements involves the use of courts and the corresponding "legalization" of political arguments. *Brown v. Board of Education,* as well as later cases under the Warren and early Burger Courts, inspired minority groups aiming for greater social and political rights to look to the legal system to achieve their aims, especially when majoritarian politics seemed particularly unpromising.[24] The civil rights movement supplemented a political approach that sought new legislation (such as the Civil Rights Acts of 1964 and 1965) with a legal approach that sought court decisions calling for broad remedial measures.[25] U.S. movements demanding remedies in response to past political wrongs display a similar bifurcated approach, although the movements have not always effectively combined a political approach with the use of the courts. Taking root in the soil of the mid-1960s, minority groups began to pursue the possibility that justice could be achieved for the past political wrongs they had suffered, even if local, state, or national majorities seemed uninterested or opposed to their demands. The Oneidas, whose claims had languished in The Indian Claims Court, revived their claims in 1965 when Jacob Thompson, president of the Oneida Indian Nation of New York, approached an attorney to bring suit to recover its land.[26] The Japanese American redress movement dates from the same time period. A scholar of the movement writes that although difficult to date precisely, "In the late 1960s small groups of Japanese Americans in Southern California, San Francisco, and Seattle began agitating for some kind of compensation for the wrongs done to them and their people during World War II."[27] Not surprisingly, it was also during the mid- to late-1960s that legal arguments for reparations for slavery were formulated.[28]

American Modes of Thought

Rectification debates within the United States, while most proximately modeled after German reparations to Israel, and most immediately provoked and shaped by the American civil rights movement, assume their particular form within the broader context of American modes of thought. Martha Minow observes that when governments throughout the world have responded to past collective violence, the responses "lurch among rhetorics of history (truth), theology (forgiveness), justice (punishment, compensation, and deterrence), therapy (healing), art (commemoration and disturbance), and education (learning lessons)."[29] This range of responses is apparent in the American context as well. As Minow concludes, no single rhetoric is adequate, and I would add that each contains within itself its own problematic. Using terms drawn from Minow's work, in the American context, the theological, therapeutic, and juridical frameworks have predominated in most debates over recompense. These three rhetorics suggest different responses based upon varied understandings of what is to be achieved by responding to past governmental misdeeds.

The *theological* framework locates us in a world where justice ordinarily is associated with vengeance, although forgiveness exists as an extraordinary response to a wrong.[30] Whereas forgiving requires relinquishing vengeance (in fact, Arendt describes forgiveness as vengeance's very opposite),[31] it entails neither forgetting nor unwillingness to judge an act as wrong. A deed may be remembered and judged to be wrong, however, the forgiving party makes a conscious choice to forego vengeance, thus breaking the cycle of action and reaction. This decision ultimately keeps the wrong from permanently rupturing the relationship between the parties.[32] The ritual of apology in which one says, "I beg your forgiveness," suggests the relation between apology and forgiveness. One party admits its wrongdoing, acknowledges the effects of the wrong, and may accept the need to make amends. The party asked to forgive is then transformed from a victim of a wrong to an agent, for it is the forgiver who has the power to free the perpetrator from the guilt associated with the wrongful deed.[33]

Forgiveness, and the related concept of apology, is richly suggestive of the transformative possibilities for all parties involved. Parties cast by a wrongful deed into the roles of perpetrators and victims may be liberated from the wrong by offering and accepting an apology. However, the theological roots of forgiveness cast some doubt on whether such a concept is applicable to the political realm. Even when transplanted into the political realm, the theological rhetoric may still frame political misdeeds as sins and cast individuals in the roles of guilty or innocent. To apologize is to admit wrongdoing. Individuals who may not be individually guilty, but who, within the political understanding argued for in this book, stand as responsible for past political wrongs, may respond to calls for apologies with protestations of innocence. The theological rhetoric, then, may ultimately inspire a politics of self-righteous resentment among people implicated—although not actually guilty—of wrongful deeds.

The *therapeutic* framework tends to focus on the victims of wrongs rather than the doers of deeds. Within this framework, misdeeds are often characterized as traumas experienced and re-experienced by individuals in need of healing. This rhetoric rightly points to the ways in which past wrongs may intrude on the present, blurring the lines between past and present and ultimately obscuring the possibilities of a future untainted by past wrongs. The therapeutic rhetoric suggests that an appropriate response to a past wrong must focus upon the psychological well-being of the victims. This rhetoric suggests that "talk therapy" is called for, either through individual counseling or in public hearings, which at times have taken the form of truth commissions. Therapeutic-inspired responses may risk, however, depoliticizing political wrongs inasmuch as psychological healing could conceivably take place without the relationship between the wrongdoer and the wronged being altered, or without any changes whatsoever being made in the external world. Psychological healing from a trauma may enable individuals to act in new and different ways toward others and their environment, but it does not necessarily lead to political changes. And finally, the therapeutic rhetoric's focus upon the "traumatized" may ignore the "traumatizer" or others who coexist in the political world. The focus upon the victim may be supplemented by holding public hearings, but one would want to work toward meaningful changes in the political world in addition to publicly airing the effects of wrongful deeds.

As with so many political issues in the United States, issues surrounding present responsibilities for past wrongs have chiefly been framed by the *juridical* rhetoric.[34] In part, the prevalence of legal rhetoric is due to the leading role lawyers have played in debates over rectification.[35] And, as noted earlier, the courts have been a primary forum where advocates for compensation have made their arguments, necessitating the framing of their demands in terms recognizable and acceptable to the courts.[36] However, the "juridicalization" of the issues has extended beyond the courtroom, as American discourse in general, as noted by many observers, has become increasingly rights oriented and legalistic.[37]

Two juridical models have emerged in rectification discussions, one derived from the criminal justice system and the other from the civil justice system. Similar to the theological and the therapeutic frameworks, each model captures some essential components of the issue while mischaracterizing others. The first legal model aims for punishment, deterrence, and public vindication. In this model, wrongdoers deserve to be punished and victims are owed public condemnation of the wrong done to them. Ideally, the punishment will deter future wrongdoing. However, in cases where the original wrongdoers and wronged have died, the aims of punishment and deterrence may be misdirected as applied to present political actors and citizens. And similar to the manner in which the theological framework paints an oversimplified picture of sin and innocence, here the world is peopled by the guilty or the innocent. This division obscures the possibility that individuals may be "innocent," yet responsible, as citizens, for addressing their polity's misdeeds.

The second legal model focuses on compensating victims for wrongs suffered. Here, a number of legal methods suggest ways in which victims may be compensated. Three terms, in particular, are used to refer to the process of making amends for a wrong: restitution, reparations, and redress. *Restitution* tends to refer strictly to the restoration of what has been taken from the legal owner, such as the return of land or particular material goods.[38] *Reparations* and *redress* typically refer to financial compensation for that which cannot be returned, such as lives lost, communities destroyed, or rights violated.[39]

All three of these compensatory methods suggest a "backward looking" approach, in which the primary goal is to return the wronged, and possibly the wrongdoers, to the conditions that existed prior to the wrong. This "backward looking" approach is most clearly associated with restitution—where objects wrongfully taken are returned—but also is suggested by reparations and redress, where money typically compensates for losses incurred. Reparations and redress may be most logical in the world of *things*—where objects have been wrongfully taken and where an economic value can be fairly straightforwardly attached to the wrong.[40] However, where the wrong in question cannot so easily be translated into economic terms—for example, the violation of rights, the destruction or diminishment of a community, or the death of loved ones—the payment of cash may appear crude, callous, and unsatisfactory. In cases where a great deal of time has passed, returning people to the position they would have occupied, had it not been for the wrong done, becomes an almost hopeless task inasmuch as it is impossible to know what this "prelapsarian" world would look like had it not been for the wrong.[41] And, the attempt to remedy some may be likely to cause harm to others, including those not even alive at the time of the original wrong. In this civil justice model, the relationship between the parties is framed by the notion of a debt; the wronged are owed compensation by those who have unjustly enriched themselves or have been unjustly advantaged.[42] While possibly not as combustible a charge as "guilty," the demand that one pays compensation for deeds not individually undertaken has still proven quite capable of provoking a politics of resentment.

What is sorely missing in the debates regarding past wrongs is a *political*, rather than a theological, therapeutic, or juridical framework. Unlike the theological approach, a political framework would attend to the consequences of wrongs in this world rather than in the afterworld and would call for the judgment of human beings rather than relying on God's judgment. Unlike the therapeutic approach, a political framework would necessitate a public discussion rather than the intimacy of a therapeutic setting and would supplement discussion by focusing on material changes to the political world. Finally, unlike the legal approach, a political framework would consider the present and future consequences of a response rather than being primarily concerned with compensating for past wrongs. As I argue, though, principally in the later chapters of the book, not just any political framework will do, as the three primary political perspectives evident in most scholarly discussions of the issues surrounding present responsibilities for past wrongs either attend insufficiently to history, overemphasize the dangers resulting from airing political misdeeds, or have retreated from imagining a nation-state that aims to do right.

The political framework suggested in *Sins of the Parents* presumes that action concerning public issues necessarily occurs in a context shaped by history, and charged with difference, inequalities, and conflict. At its best, though, within the political realm, by using our human capabilities of speech and judgment, we create a collective capable of responding to the concerns of the diverse individuals who comprise the polity. The political framework proposed here, then, is best for addressing past wrongs in that by recognizing the historical wrongs that may burden, albeit unequally, present citizens, and by encouraging citizens to respond to the wrongs that may stand between them, it may orient the polity toward the future with recovered hope in the possibilities of what common political action can realize.

Underlying Theoretical Questions

The primary theoretical issues concerning present political responsibilities for past wrongs assume their distinctive shape in relation to the four frameworks (theological, therapeutic, juridical, and political) outlined above. The issues, most basically, are composed of three questions: What is the nature of the alleged wrong and who or what has been wronged? Who should be held responsible for the wrong? And how far back in history should the present generation go to respond to wrongs?

Defining the Wrong and the Wronged

Most claims raised against the U.S. government in the post–World War II period center around three pivotal encounters between the government and indigenous nations or minority groups. The first set is rooted in encounters occurring during the seventeenth to the nineteenth century between the American settler nation and indigenous peoples. The claims unearth the violence, fraud, and deceit that permitted much of the expansion of the United States across the North American continent and beyond, incorporating the Hawaiian Islands.[43] These claims demand that the government recognize (limited) sovereignty for indigenous groups or nations, return land unjustly taken or compensate the nations for the unjust takings, and repatriate human remains and sacred objects.[44]

The second case entails the United States' long history of slavery followed by legal segregation.[45] Calls to make amends for this history of oppression speak not only to the uncompensated labor, but also to the loss of human rights and the continuing burdens—economic, psychological, physical, and cultural— placed upon African Americans. America's system of Jim Crow bears eerie resemblances to South Africa's apartheid system. While South Africa has engaged in a much-publicized process of "truth and reconciliation," in response to the apartheid experience, the United States has not yet formally apologized for slavery or legal segregation, nor has it offered reparations.[46]

Finally, the third primary case that instigated calls for reparations was the wartime policy imposed upon citizens and permanent resident aliens of Japanese ancestry during World War II. Here, the U.S. government, acting under Executive Order 9066, stipulated that "wartime emergency" justified the forcible evacuation, relocation, and internment of approximately 120,000 civilians. A commission established in 1980 to study the events precipitating the executive order concluded that rather than wartime emergency, "race prejudice, war hysteria, and a failure of political leadership" were the "broad historical causes which shaped" the decisions.[47]

If colonialism and conquest, slavery and segregation, and racism and relocation are the initial deeds later judged to be unjust, then how should these large-scale acts be translated into specific wrongs (that is, what is the nature of the wrong), and who is the rightful party to make claims based upon them? The Oneida land claims, as well as many other American Indian claims, focus upon the property losses suffered by the tribes. Primarily, these claims seek to pierce the cloak of legality veiling the transfer of great portions of the North American continent from American Indian tribes to the U.S. government, state governments, and private individuals.[48] Rather than basing claims upon the violence that accompanied much of the dispossession of the continent, American Indian claims use the legal promises (in the form of treaties and laws) that sought to regulate the treatment of American Indians and seek redress from the government for its failure to live up to those promises.[49] In most cases, the claims are brought by tribes rather than individuals. The tribes then determine for themselves the requirements for tribal membership. If U.S. law recognizes the existence of the tribe, the accepted legal theory is that the present members of the tribe constitute the proper claimants for the original wrongs done to past generations of tribal members.[50]

The internment of Japanese Americans presents another model of translating wrongs into legal claims and claimants. Here, the forcible evacuation and confinement of civilians was eventually deemed a constitutional violation of due process rights inasmuch as individuals were rounded up and sent off to internment camps with neither a trial nor even criminal charges filed against them. These wholesale violations were eventually recognized, but not before approximately sixty thousand ex-internees had died. Their deaths, as Chapter 2 documents, prompted heated debate over the question of whether claims can be passed down to the next generation, or if they are to be buried along with the original victims. In addition, the debate over Japanese American reparations provoked renewed attention to the issue of group rights. Many proponents of reparations contended it was not simply individuals of Japanese descent who were harmed, but the entire Japanese American community. They argued further that these broader communal harms should be ameliorated as well.

These two contested issues have resonance beyond the debate over Japanese American reparations. A great deal of the argument for reparations for slavery and segregation rests upon the related claims that the harms associated with slavery or segregation did not vanish with their legal termination, and that African Americans as a group, and not just as separate individuals, have been harmed by these historical wrongs. A major obstacle toward inducing the U.S. government to formally apologize as a first step, and then to provide compensation for slavery and segregation, is to persuade most Americans that there are continuing harms flowing from "the ancient" wrong of slavery and the less remote wrong of segregation. Americans must be persuaded that African Americans alive today (or some segment of the population), continue to be disadvantaged by this history and deserve an apology and possibly a more tangible admission of remorse.

Defining the Responsible Party

The identification of the responsible party proves just as challenging. The difficulties here are rooted in the same issues that complicate identifying the proper claimants: the passage of time and the difficulties determining the responsible parties when groups or collectives are involved. The mainstream American approach has been to focus upon the specific individuals involved in the acts under question. Yet, the individuals whose actions or inactions contributed to the expropriation of American Indian land (or the enslavement of African Americans) have long since died. And while some individuals who played a part in or benefited from the internment of Japanese Americans (or the legal segregation of African Americans) may still be alive, holding them individually responsible for deeds done in the name of the government, or with the legal imprimatur of the government, seems to unduly inflate their responsibility and deflate those in whose name they acted. For some, the deaths of the individuals who perpetrated misdeeds mark the end of the trail of responsibility. As we have seen, in both the theological and criminal justice frameworks, the sins or guilt of the parents must not be visited upon the children. Further, some reparations opponents defend their innocence by virtue of their ancestry's innocence. Camille Paglia, for instance, writes that "All four of my grandparents were born in Italy; my mother did not arrive here until the 1930s. My people had nothing to do with the African slave trade, nor did most Asian immigrant groups."[51] Other opponents derisively calculate the "reparations" owed to them for their ancestors' sufferings.[52] These arguments presume that responsibility is either purely individual (i.e., only the people who intended and performed an act should be held responsible for it) or familial (i.e., that deeds flow through the generations of families). Convinced that the latter scenario is specious, and with the original perpetrators dead and buried, many Americans feel secure in their "innocence" and thus decry any responsibility for the wrongs done to American Indians, African Americans, and Japanese Americans.

Proponents of apologies and possible rectification, then, attempt to counter this complacency by making connections between the original wrongdoers and contemporary citizens. The links tend to be crafted in one of two ways: either through an argument of "unjust advantage" or of "collective implication/ identification." The first argument underscores the ways present-day citizens profit from the past expropriation of land from American Indians, or the past discrimination against African Americans.[53] The connections, however, are often attenuated (think here of the position of recent immigrants to the United States, for instance). Additionally, the attribution of unjust advantage often provokes resentment, rather than remorse. The second argument, often applied to racial or ethnic categories, tends to declare rather broadly and bluntly that all whites are guilty and hence responsible for the crimes committed against racial and ethnic minorities.[54] This argument sharpens racial and ethnic divisions rather than pointing a way to greater unity. All white Americans, or all Americans, are neither necessarily "innocent" nor "guilty." The central thesis of the present book holds that the responsibility of contemporary citizens should not be held to be rooted in their individual deeds, family history, or racial and ethnic make-up, but rather in their political identity as citizens—both implicated by the deeds of political ancestors and identified with those deeds.[55] This concept of political responsibility rests upon the possibility of citizens imagining their connections to political ancestors and their deeds in a particular manner: willing to acknowledge the presence of past wrongs as part of the legacy, yet not the whole of it. Clearly, if political wrongs are not recognized, then there is no need to respond. Conversely, however, if the legacy is rotten to the core, then present citizens will not be inclined to identify with it or to sense any responsibility stemming from it. Identification with past political actors and their deeds is required for political responsibility to take root. Yet, the identification must provoke both pride and shame. Too much pride may prompt defensive denials of past wrongs; too much shame may prompt detachment, rather than attachment, to political ancestors and their legacy.[56]

The Passage of Time

The third theoretical concern relates to the passage of time and its effects upon past wrongs. Opponents of apologies and possible rectification in all three historical cases often point to the passage of time as a compelling argument against present-day responsibility. For critics of present-day political responsibility, the passage of time and the passing of the original perpetrators and victims justifies the erasure of the initial wrongs. In addition, the inevitability of changing circumstances may erase perceived injustices and the need to respond to them.[57] However, when we assess the issue of the passage of time in the theological, therapeutic, juridical, and political frameworks discussed above, it becomes clear that time alone cannot conclusively resolve grievances.

The inability of time alone to resolve grievances is most apparent within the therapeutic framework. The therapeutic framework is premised upon the conviction that "time does not heal all

wounds"[58] and reminds us that a traumatic past, rather than evap-
orating, will continue to encroach upon the present. Arguments
asserting the need to "come to terms with the past," are rooted
in the therapeutic insight that even if the past appears hidden or
buried, it is not powerless.[59] Hannah Arendt was fond of quoting
William Faulkner, one of whose characters said, "The past is not
dead and gone; it isn't even past."[60] The therapeutic insight also
suggests that a traumatic past, if not properly resolved, may be
reawakened, and, as horror stories tend to suggest, past crimes
may return to haunt the present.[61] Indeed, it is a central premise
of the present book that "coming to terms with the past," entails
an active grappling with the past, reminding individuals of their
power to act (differently).[62]

Two contrasting interpretations of the meaning of the passage of time are conceivable within the theological framework.
As the book's title suggests, one interpretation explicitly argues
for an ethic of individual responsibility in which sins should not
be passed down through the generations. However, an opposing
ethic appears in the Hebrew Bible as well, in which "the iniquity
of the fathers" is visited "upon the children unto the third and
fourth generation."[63] The theological framework also suggests
the mandate that human beings remember past deeds through
moral lenses—that the present generation should judge past and
present events, and by doing so, actively relate past to present
rather than leaving the past behind.[64]

The legal framework similarly suggests two possibilities regarding the wisdom and practicality of bringing forth claims based on
past wrongs. Critics of rectification have seized upon the phrase
"statute of limitations" to oppose reparations claims, arguing
that the prescribed number of years within which actions may
be brought have been established by the legal system for good
reasons. In terms of criminal justice, memories may fade over
time, thus undercutting the possibility of recapturing the truth.
Similarly, in terms of civil justice, background circumstances may
change so dramatically as to render claims based upon one set
of historical circumstances almost meaningless in a different set

of circumstances. Finally, innocent third parties may develop settled expectations, and rights based upon those expectations, that should not be upset.[65] Statutes of limitations are one means by which the legal system embodies the maxim, "let sleeping dogs lie." On the other hand, it is important to note that statutes of limitations are enacted by legislatures, and thus subject to political will. Legislatures bar statutes of limitations for certain crimes such as murder in order to underscore core principles that are not diminished by the passage of time.[66] The passage of time can also have a positive effect for claimants: At times it is essential for some time to pass before a polity is able to hear certain historical truths.[67]

The legal system's concept of statutes of limitations, then, reveals that polities determine the time horizons within which wrongs may be vindicated. Polities may hold that there exist wrongs that might so rupture the polity's sense of order and challenge its sense of meaning as to demand a response even after a lengthy passage of time. We can even go so far as to assert that a polity's historical identity is itself a political artifact rather than an organic creation. Benedict Anderson's *Imagined Communities* has brought attention to the political processes whereby the coherence of nation-states are constituted. Unable to rely upon shared descent, language, or religion, nation-states must create or impose national identity. To the extent that the nation-state exists as a coherent temporal entity, that coherence is the result of politics rather than national identity somehow predating politics.[68] To that end, polities construct narratives to tie the particular memories of individuals and groups into a larger national narrative. This process is a political construction in which those in power choose to remember, ritualize, and highlight certain acts while choosing to forget or bury others.[69] Calling this a political process points to the fact that it is open to challenges by individuals and groups who may hold contrary ideas about which deeds are worthy of remembrance and which should be forgotten. In particular, political misdeeds such as colonization and conquest, slavery and segregation, and racism and relocation occupy sites of contestation where governmentally sanctioned narratives typically presenting a "winner's history" in which political wrongs are justified, minimized, or erased vie with alternative histories presenting accounts of the deeds from the perspectives of the "losers" or victims. Precisely how, or even *if,* the oftentimes violent and coercive struggles of the past appear within contemporary constructions of the polity's history is itself a political struggle engaged in by diverse peoples with unequal means at their disposal. Official accounts often marginalize or silence accounts that place the history of deceit, violence, and racism closer to the core of American national identity than at its margins.

Examining the passage of time's effect on past wrongs through the political lens outlined in *Sins of the Parents* highlights the active and contested process by which a polity's temporal horizons are demarcated. The political perspective advanced here, as opposed to the therapeutic, theological, or legal framework, underscores the multiple, overlapping, and sometimes conflicting perspectives that individuals and groups within a nation-state have regarding the content, contemporary meaning, and significance of the polity's past. It is not only the historical narratives that are contested, but also the very sense of time itself—its speed or pace.[70] That is, within the American nation-state, there may be neither a shared history nor a shared sense of time's tempo. As political theorist Sheldon Wolin has written, "There is no single shared 'political time,' only culturally constituted different times. Their self-conscious character produces the equivalent of a different time zone that contributes to a disruption and undermines the possibility of a common narrative structure and, along with it, a common identity."[71]

The primary tempo within the contemporary American nation-state, as Wolin argues, is set by the economy and culture—one that is "dictated by innovation, change, and replacement" and "governed by the needs of rapid turnover."[72] The breakneck pace dictated by the American economy and culture quickens the passage of time, thus turning the relatively recent past into "ancient history." Thus, proponents of redressing past wrongs have had to make their argument within a "time zone" grown accustomed to the disappearance of the past rather than its continuing presence. And yet, paradoxical as it may appear initially, the erosion of the past may create a hunger for the apparent safety of a nostalgic rendition of the past.[73] Such nostalgic renditions were most evident in the various bicentennial celebrations of our revolutionary and constitutional founding moments.[74] Proponents of rectifying past wrongs have had to contend with both the erosion of the past and its nostalgic recreation to obtain justice for past political wrongs. Countering the erosion of the past, rectification supporters have had to convince courts, Congress and the public of the presence and relevance of past wrongs to present politics. Moreover, contending with versions of the reconstructed past that glorify or downplay past injustices, they have had to argue for the relevance of their own versions of historical truth.

The Case for National Apologies

National apologies, with or without material compensation attached, have become a remarkable contemporary development across the globe, including in the United States. Since the wake of World War II, new questions have entered political debate and a new political lexicon has developed. Polities now debate under what circumstances it is appropriate to offer an apology, whether to accept an apology, and if so, when it is fitting to display a willingness to reconcile with past enemies. President Reagan, for instance, in 1985, by laying a wreath in the Bitburg cemetery, where former SS officers were buried, was lambasted by many for forgiving too soon, thus displaying an inadequate regard for the totality of victims and for American Jews in particular.[75] In this new lexicon of national apologies, fine shades of distinction have been drawn between apologizing, expressing remorse, contrition, or sorrow. President Clinton, for instance, in traveling to Africa in 1998, declined to apologize for America's history of slavery, although he did express regret and contrition.[76] The new politics of national apologies requires an attuned sensibility and a rich vocabulary.

The novelty of national apologies has led some to question whether apologies and the related concept of forgiveness belong in the political realm. Others dismiss apologies as empty symbolic politics; still others see ordinary interest group politics lurking beneath. *Sins of the Parents* argues that apologizing and forgiving may be political acts, while recognizing that the political realm does strain a human capacity most at home in the personal realm. Unequal power relations endemic to politics may mean that the responsible party feels no need to apologize. The political realm's representative institutions and the passage of time may obscure who should apologize to whom, and the political realm may prove to be a difficult environment within which to convey the required sincerity for an apology to be accepted. The book argues that a national apology, under the right circumstances and performed in the right manner, can be meaningful and transformative, while also recognizing that under different circumstances similar words may appear to be insincere and hollow. Finally, while it would be naïve to neglect the material aspects that accompany some calls for national apologies, an interpretation that focused solely on costs and benefits would be equally incomplete. As political theorist Hanna Pitkin writes, "Because we are simultaneously both distinct and connected, politics always simultaneously concerns both the distribution of costs and benefits among competitors, and the nature and direction of their shared community."[77] The calls for national apologies, the book argues, have just as much to do with the nature and direction of the polity as they do with who is to bear the greatest burden of past wrongs and how past wrongs can be translated, if at all, into tangible terms.

The justness and practicality of national apologies cannot be evaluated in the abstract, but must be examined in the specific context within which the call for an apology and a response arise. Even given the difficulties involved in the political practice of apologizing and forgiving, the book contends that national apologies offer a meaningful approach to responding to past wrongs as well as the possibility of transforming peoples' political identities. Implicit to the book's argument is that the present state of American political identity is less than ideal: The relationships between individual American citizens can and should be improved; the relationship between individuals and the nation-state be made more meaningful; and the relationship within individuals amongst their various identities (e.g., racial, ethnic, political) could become less problematic. Although September 11, 2001 reportedly unleashed an outpouring of American patriotism, we are now being warned that the American polity may be slipping back into its pre–September 11, 2001 malaise. The contemporary literature on the "decline of citizenship" or "disappearance of patriotism," in somewhat simplistic terms, may be divided into three primary camps. The first, the *liberal* camp, seems to have given up on the project of cultivating close allegiances amongst citizens and instead contents itself with a legalistic notion of citizenship based upon procedural norms. The second, the *neo-conservative* camp, attempts to recreate political unity by holding onto coherent traditions and myths in the face of divisiveness and difference. Finally, the third camp, the *postmodern*, looks upon the project of political unity within the nation-state with skepticism and fear. My own work is animated by the conviction that none of the three perspectives provides sufficient insight to help us navigate through the present-day dilemma of what we should do regarding past wrongs. The liberal argument tends to fail to acknowledge the contemporary relevance of our nation's past wrongs, nor does it provide the depth of attachment needed to justify sacrifices that may be required to adequately apologize for them. The neo-conservative argument, in its fear of national fragmentation, fails to acknowledge either the wrongs or their present-day relevance. And the postmodern argument, while sufficiently understanding of the consequences of difference, seems insufficiently attuned to the need to create a measure of political unity and a sense of political identity from which political responsibility may derive. The book strives to bring to light an alternative vision, one in which a polity consciously chooses to respond to the presence of past wrongs to move toward a more just present and future rather than forgetting or repressing troubling moments that may haunt the hearts and minds of many of our fellow citizens.

1

The Promises of Great Nations

The Oneida Land Claims Cases

For a nation famously unconcerned with its history, the last third of a century has seemed almost like an uninterrupted indulgence of mythmaking and nostalgia creation. The bicentennial of our revolutionary birth was commemorated; the bicentennial of our constitutional foundation celebrated; the bicentennial of the Bill of Rights feted. These celebrations coexisted uneasily with another kind of return to the early history of the United States. American Indian tribes also have been returning to North America's history, albeit with a markedly different intent. From the late 1960s to the present, American Indian tribes have stepped up their efforts to convince U.S. Courts and Congress, as well as state courts and legislatures, to invalidate land transactions completed in the late eighteenth and early nineteenth centuries and to return huge tracts of land to the original and, as the tribes contend, rightful owners. Among the most contested land claims have been those brought by Eastern Indian tribes, relying upon the federal government's promises made to them, in the form of treaties and laws regulating trade, that appear to contravene land transactions in which title passed from Indian tribes to states, and thence to individuals.

The American Indian land claims threaten to undermine central components of American political identity. The land claims pierce the myth of the "newness" or "virginity" of the New World, and put in its place a more troubling portrayal of deceit, conquest and extermination, suggesting that the United States is not an exception to the tainted roots of virtually every nation-state. The early history of violence, deception, and fraud documented by American Indian tribes also calls into question the centrality to our political and legal identity of treaties and contracts. If deception and coercion accompanied treaties and contracts, and promises were not kept, then our faith in the power of promising to cement political and legal relationships, a fundamental tenet of American political thought, appears naive or duplicitous. Finally, our very sense of "at-homeness" is at risk, for implicit (and at times explicit) to Indian land claims is the troubling conclusion that present-day owners are but strangers on the land, squatting without rightful legal title.

This chapter follows the largest and oldest set of land claims in the United States, that pursued by the Oneida Indians of New York, Wisconsin, and Ontario against the federal government, New York State, upstate counties of New York, and at times, individual landowners. The chapter analyzes the manner in which legal and political questions have been framed, partly in order to minimize the threats to American identity and interests. As noted in the Introduction, three primary issues must be clarified in thinking through the existence and nature of present political responsibilities for past wrongs. The wrong and the wronged must be defined, the responsible party identified, and how far back in history the present generation should go to respond to wrongs determined. This chapter, as it focuses on deeds done in the eighteenth and nineteenth centuries, must consider the import of the passage of time on the land claims. If New York State did, indeed, secure title to the Oneida Tribe's lands illegally approximately two hundred years ago, should the intervening history and change of circumstances diminish the rights of the Oneidas or the responsibilities of present political bodies? Finally, the chapter briefly examines which institutions of government are best positioned to craft a suitable remedy that would take into consideration the interests of the various Oneida tribes, the U.S. government, New York State, the local counties, and private individuals who firmly believe they hold legal title to the land. Ultimately, the chapter suggests there is a political responsibility at both the state and national levels to address the Oneida land claims, although with so many competing interests, and such thorny past and present legal and political complexities, a resolution that all parties can agree to appears unlikely.

The past thirty years or so have seen a dramatic surge in the number of Indian land claims filed in state and federal courts across the country. The increase is due partly to Indian tribes' responses to legal and political actions by the federal government. Federal courts have lifted a number of legal barriers that had impeded tribal access to the courts, and the U.S. Congress, attempting to remove conclusively any future threat of land claims, passed legislation in 1966 giving Indian tribes six years to file suits for damages resulting from trespass.[1] The original six-year limit was extended to 1977, then to 1980, and finally to 1982.[2] With each advance of the deadline, Indian tribes protected their legal rights to sue by initiating lawsuits.[3] During the past thirty years Eastern Indian tribes filed land claims in Maine, Massachusetts, Connecticut, Rhode Island, New York, South Carolina, and Louisiana, covering somewhere between 16 and 17 million acres.[4]

Settlements have been reached in many of these claims, including an agreement with the Passamaquoddy and Penobscot tribes in Maine that granted them 350,000 acres of land and approximately $80 million,[5] and a $50 million settlement with the Catawbas of South Carolina.[6] The claims of the Oneidas of New York, Wisconsin, and Ontario, however, as of this writing, remain unresolved, even though the Oneidas have carried their arguments from the Indian Claims Commission in the 1950s to the Court of Claims, from the U.S. District Court to the Court of Appeals, and twice have been heard before the Supreme Court. After nearly fifty years of litigation, negotiation, and legislation the claims remain unsettled. In February 2002, the New York Oneidas and the state of New York announced, prematurely, that they had reached a tentative settlement that would pay the Oneidas of New York, Wisconsin, and Ontario $500 million in return for the tribes' dropping their land claims. Under the terms of the proposed settlement, half of the money would come from New York State and half from the federal government. However, neither federal officials nor the Oneidas of Wisconsin and Ontario supported the settlement. The Wisconsin and Ontario Oneidas opposed it because they wanted land, not money, and the federal government claimed they were not consulted about the terms of the settlement prior to its announcement. Most recently, in December 2004, Governor Pataki announced a far-reaching tentative agreement with the Oneidas of Wisconsin, in which the tribe would agree to drop its claim to 250,000 acres in upstate New York in exchange for the rights to build a casino in the Catskill mountains as well as the rights to buy 1,000 acres in the tribe's ancestral homelands. The agreement would represent a dramatic policy shift in Indian affairs, for it would mark the first time that the federal government would allow out-of-state tribes to obtain land beyond their current reservation state. The proposed settlement, however, faces a number of significant obstacles, including the fact that only one of the original three Oneida tribes have agreed to the terms. The settlement would require passage of legislation at both the state and federal level. Its fate remains uncertain, as of this writing.[7]

Actually, three sets of claims comprise the overall Oneida claim, all of which are rooted in treaties signed between 1785 and 1842 between the State of New York and the Oneida Indian Nation. The first and second land claims concern actions taken after 1790 (and thus after New York had adopted the U.S. Constitution) and the third concerns actions that predate the Constitution, and required courts to base their rulings on interpretations of the Articles of Confederation. The treaties in total transferred approximately 6 million acres of land from the Oneidas to New York State. The first lawsuit, filed in 1970 and intended by the Oneidas as a test case, concerned portions of land transferred from the Oneidas to New York by a 1795 lease. The suit alleged that the 1795 agreement violated the 1790 Trade and Non-Intercourse Act, as well as the federal Constitution. This first suit called only for damages representing the fair rental value of land presently owned and occupied by the counties of Oneida and Madison for the period from January 1, 1968 through December 31, 1969.[8]

A second lawsuit was filed in 1974 in which the Oneidas challenged purchases made between 1795 and 1842. The second claim, building upon the arguments enunciated in the first, encompassed a much larger tract of land (approximately 250,000 acres), and asked for the restoration of the lands, an award of fair rental value for the entire period of dispossession, a declaration of dispossession, and an award of all costs and attorneys' fees. In 1978 the Oneidas brought a third claim, alleging that land purchases that took place in 1785, prior to the adoption of the U.S. Constitution, violated the 1784 Fort Stanwix Treaty and the Articles of Confederation. This third claim, asking for restoration of approximately 4.5 million acres, has been dismissed (*Oneida Indian Nation v. New York,* No. 78-CV-104, slip op. [N.D.NY Nov. 19, 1986]).[9]

The Original Promise and Purchase

At the time of the American Revolution, the Oneida Indian Nation was part of the powerful Six Nations or Iroquois Confederacy. The Oneidas held aboriginal title to more than 6 million acres of land in central New York (see *Oneida Indian Nation of NY v. County of Oneida,* 434 F. Supp. 527, 533 [N.D.NY 1977]). The Oneidas traditionally had been allies of the British, but during the American Revolution they split from the pro-British Confederacy and allied themselves with the colonists. After the war, the newly formed United States sought to reaffirm its alliance by entering into a series of treaties in which the United States formally recognized the Oneidas and promised that they would be secure in the possession of their lands ("Treaty with the Six Nations," Oct. 22, 1784, Art. III, 7 Stat. 15) unless they sold their land to the United States. The treaties stipulated that if a state wished to purchase land from the Oneidas, federal consent would have to be obtained.

Many states, however, refused to recognize federal supremacy in the area of Indian affairs. New York was particularly brazen in this regard. Aware of the federal treaties with the Oneidas that outlawed outright purchase of the Indian land by states, New York State resorted to deception to meet public pressure to open up the Oneida's land for white settlement (*Oneida,* 434 F. Supp. at 533). In 1788, New York secured a lease with the Oneidas, assuring them that the lease would allow them to keep their land, and would allow New York to "extend its protection over their property, against the dealings of unscrupulous white land speculators."[10] Historian Jack Campisi explains why the Oneidas would enter into such an agreement:

> The New York commissioners . . . led them to believe that they had [already] lost all their land to the New York Genesee Company, and that the commissioners were there to restore title. The Oneidas expressed confusion over this since they had never signed any instruments to that effect, but Governor Clinton just waved that aside . . . Thus the Oneidas agreed to the lease arrangement with the state because it seemed the only way they could get back their land. The state received some five million acres for $2,000 in cash, $2,000 in clothing, $1,000 in provisions, and $600 in annual rent.[11]

The Oneidas retained a reservation of approximately 300,000 acres at this point.

In 1790, Congress, at the behest of President Washington and Secretary of War Knox, passed the first Indian Trade and Non-Intercourse Act.[12] The Commander-in-Chief and Secretary of War, realizing that the United States was at this time militarily weak compared to the bordering Indian nations, sought to reduce the possibility of warfare by prohibiting all settlement until the federal government negotiated a treaty with the Indian tribes. If the federal government regulated all trade with the Indians, it was thought that Indian land could be taken over in a relatively peaceful and orderly manner.[13] The 1790 Act declared that "no sale of lands made by any Indians . . . shall be valid to any persons or

person, or to any state, whether having the right of pre-emption
to such lands or not, unless the same shall be made and duly exe-
cuted at some public treaty, held under the authority of the United
States."[14] When the 1790 Act expired, a revised and more detailed
version was passed in 1793 that called for criminal penalties for
violation of its terms. The 1793 Act allowed states to negotiate
with Indian tribes, although it stipulated that:

> No purchase or grant of lands, or of any title or claim thereto, from
> any Indians or nation or tribe of Indians, within the bounds of the
> United States, shall be of any validity in law or equity, unless the
> same be made by a treaty or convention entered into pursuant to
> the Constitution . . . [and] in the presence, and with the approba-
> tion of the commissioner or commissioners of the United States
> [appointed to supervise Indian land sales.][15]

President Washington, soon after the 1790 and 1793 Acts were
passed, explained their import to the Seneca Indians of New York:

> No state, nor person can purchase your lands unless at some public
> treaty, held under the authority of the United States. The General
> Government will never consent to your being defrauded, but it
> will protect you in all your just rights . . . [w]hen you may find it in
> your interest to sell any part of your lands, the United States must
> be present, by their agent and will be your security that you shall
> not be defrauded in the bargain you make.[16]

Neither President Washington's promise nor the Trade and
Non-Intercourse Acts could withstand the eastern states' hunger
for Indian land, however. Eastern states methodically acquired part
or all of tribally held lands, blatantly ignoring the law's requirement
to gain federal authorization. In fact, New York's Governor Clinton
and later Governor Jay were warned by Secretary of War Pickering
that the Non-Intercourse Act required that their negotiations with
the Oneidas be attended by federal commissioners to supervise any
land transaction.[17] Both governors ignored these warnings, and
New York finalized an agreement in 1795 in which the Oneidas
conveyed virtually all of their remaining land to New York for
annual cash payments of $2,952.[18] Evidence introduced during

the initial Oneida trial revealed that, contrary to the dictates of the Non-Intercourse Act, the transaction was not approved by the federal government nor was any agent of the United States present during the negotiations. This 1795 transaction stands at the heart of the initial Oneida land claim case.

The Oneida Land Claims Reach Federal Court

Through the nineteenth and much of the twentieth century, the Oneidas periodically struggled, albeit unsuccessfully, to dispute the legality of the 1795 land transaction.[19] In 1951, the Oneidas filed a petition against the United States before the newly instituted Indian Claims Commission.[20] The commission, as noted in the Introduction, had been established in 1946 with a broad mandate "to settle finally any and all legal, equitable and moral obligations that the United States might owe to the Indians."[21] The Oneidas sought judgment against the United States, as trustee, for the fair market value of their lands sold to New York since the eighteenth century.[22] The Oneidas argued that the United States had fallen short in its fiduciary duty toward them, and thus was responsible for damages. Twenty-seven years later, the Oneidas did finally prevail, in 1978,[23] although the tribe decided afterward to dismiss the case, for fear that obtaining monetary damages might prejudice their land claim.[24] Under the provisions of the Indian Claims Commission, only monetary damages could be awarded, and damages were limited to the value of the land *at the time of the illegal taking*, without interest. The Oneidas decided to drop their case against the United States and pursue two suits against counties of New York, various state agencies, and New York State itself. Private landowners were not named in these original suits.

The Oneida's initial forays into the federal courts were repulsed by the New York counties' argument that the damage suits did not present a federal question, and thus the suits must be pursued in state courts. Defeat in New York state court was all but guaranteed, owing to the state's sovereign immunity and various time-based limitations on claims.[25] The Oneidas persisted, however, and the

Supreme Court, in a unanimous 1974 decision, reversed the lower federal courts' decision. Justice White, writing for the Court, explained that "federal law, treaties, and statutes protected Indian occupancy and that its termination was exclusively the province of federal law."[26] The Court conclusively put to rest the notion that the original thirteen states had preserved their sovereignty over Indian lands, and that disputes regarding these lands must be resolved in state courts.[27] The Supreme Court remanded the case to the District Court for trial on the merits. There, Judge Edmund Port expressed his displeasure that the courts, and not Congress, had been called upon to resolve the dispute.[28] Rather than ducking the substantive issues, however, Judge Port decided that the 1795 transaction between the Oneidas and the State of New York was contrary to the Non-Intercourse Act and thus void. Although this decision "may seem harsh," wrote Port, "by the deed of 1795 the State acquired no rights against the plaintiffs . . . consequently, its successors, the defendant counties, are in no better position."[29] The Oneidas were entitled to fair rental value of the land presently owned by the counties. In a later hearing Judge Port determined the fair rental value to be $16,694.00 plus interest for the years 1968 to 1969 covered in the initial, narrowly defined, complaint.

The defendant counties, anticipating that the consequences of Judge Port's decision could go much beyond the $16,694.00 award, promptly appealed. The U.S. Court of Appeals, Second Circuit, in a two-to-one decision, affirmed the lower court's ruling that the counties were liable for damages.[30] The dissenter, Judge Meskill, voiced the fears of the counties, the state, and private landowners when he wrote that "nothing in the Court's opinion would prevent tribes from suing for the full value of all land taken from them at any time during our nation's history in contravention of federal law—to say nothing of an action for ejectment."[31] Where was the limiting principle, he worried? The counties, buoyed by Meskill's dissent and alarmed at the potential ramifications of the case, appealed the Court of Appeals decision to the Supreme Court. The Supreme Court agreed to hear the case "to determine whether an Indian tribe may have a live cause of action for a violation of its possessory rights that occurred 175 years ago."[32] Oral argument was scheduled for the opening day of the 1984 Supreme Court's fall term.[33]

Oral Arguments at the Supreme Court

Allan van Gestel represented the counties of Oneida and Madison. Van Gestel opened his oral argument by placing before the Court the specter of Indian land claim cases let loose across the land. An affirmance of the lower court ruling, van Gestel warned, would encourage other Indian tribes to proceed with their claim cases now pending in the lower courts. If the Oneidas were to prevail, van Gestel predicted that they would sue for ownership of the land, which would imply sovereignty. The private landowners residing on the contested 100,000 acres of land would find themselves living under Indian sovereignty (related claims were later consolidated with this claim, and thus currently the acreage under dispute stands at 250,000).[34] Indian sovereignty would throw into doubt all matters of governmental services and taxation.[35] Having shared these fears with the justices, van Gestel then proceeded to his core legal arguments.

Van Gestel presented three primary arguments before the Court. First, he contended that the Non-Intercourse Act of 1790 and 1793 did not entail a private right of action—that is, if action is to be taken to enforce these Acts, it was up to the federal government to do so, and not private citizens. Second, if the Oneidas did have a private right of action, surely it was no longer live after 175 years. Reciting the time-based defenses that failed to convince the lower courts, van Gestel argued that state statutes of limitations should be applied where the federal law was silent; that the action had abated since the 1793 Act expired; and that the federally approved treaties of 1798 and 1802 represented a subsequent ratification of the earlier land transactions. Finally, providing the Court with a graceful means of sidestepping the thorny issues raised by the Oneida claims, van Gestel argued that this case presented a non-justiciable political question, and that the Court should defer to Congress on this matter.[36]

Whereas the counties' attorney attempted to place before the justices' minds the potential future consequences of their decision, Arlinda Locklear, the Oneida's attorney, tried to make the past come alive again. She began her oral argument by reminding the justices of the precariousness of the United States' revolutionary struggle and the pivotal role played by the Oneidas to that struggle. The Iroquois Confederacy was a powerful military force in the eighteenth century, sought after as an ally by both the British and the Americans. While four of the six tribes of the Confederacy sided with the British, the Oneidas gave active military support to the Americans. During and after the war, the American Congress assured the Oneidas that "[W]hile the sun and moon contrive to give light to the world, we shall love and respect you. As your trusty friends, we shall protect you; and shall at all times consider your welfare as our own."[37] Promises such as these, Locklear implied, should be honored if a nation considered itself honorable.

Locklear then turned to refuting the counties' arguments. Responding to the argument that the Oneidas did not have a private right of action, Locklear first established that the United States, as the guardian of most Indian resources, plainly could take action for the benefit of the Oneidas in the present case. She then posed before the Court the question of whether the wards, the Oneidas, should be able to do in their own name what their guardian, the United States, could do if it so chose.[38] Then, marshaling various legal doctrines that display solicitude for Indians, Locklear answered the counties' time-based defenses by arguing that to apply here state statutes of limitations would be inconsistent with the underlying federal policy, as expressed by Congress on various occasions from 1952 to 1982, to enable Indians to pursue land claims. Reminding the justices of the canons of construction dictating that treaties be construed liberally in favor of Indians, and that if the Court is to find that Indian title has been extinguished, then congressional intent must be "plain and unambiguous," Locklear countered the counties' theory that the land transactions implicitly had been subsequently ratified by later treaties.[39] And although the 1793 Act may have expired, Locklear directed the Court's attention to subsequent versions of the Act, including 25 USCS 177, now in force, that contain substantially the same principle—a sovereign act is required to extinguish Indian title.

The record of the oral argument before the Supreme Court suggests that two primary issues had to be addressed to make possible an Oneida legal victory. The first was evident in the Court's order granting certiorari: the 175-year gap between the alleged wrong and the filing of the Oneida's suit. The passage of time, and the concerns encapsulated by the legal doctrines of statutes of limitations and laches, as well as the related issues attending to the passage of time (What had transpired during those 175 years? Hadn't the wronged party died? Hadn't the responsible party died? Hadn't innocent third parties developed settled expectations and rights to the land in question? Hadn't the background circumstances changed so dramatically that it no longer made sense to claim the Oneidas had possessory rights to the land?) vexed the justices.[40]

The second principal issue was apparent in a question bluntly put to Locklear by a Supreme Court justice: "How many millions of dollars are involved here?"[41] If the Oneida's claim were in fact still live, and the Court were persuaded that the Oneidas had been wronged, then how expensive would it be to remedy the wrong, and were courts institutionally equipped to implement a remedy? The justices assumed, as van Gestel had predicted, that if the Oneidas prevailed in this case, they would sue for ownership of the 100,000 contested acres (if not more); the Court wanted to know the financial consequences of an Oneida legal victory. It is worth noting that the justice who posed the question, "How many millions of dollars are involved here," seemed to assume that the case boiled down to money rather than the return of land. Locklear spoke of Congressional action in similar Indian land claim cases and of the Oneida's preference for a negotiated settlement. The Court, Locklear argued, rather than becoming entangled in the Oneida case for years, would be spurring Congress to live up to its constitutional duties with regard to Indian affairs by upholding the lower court's decision.

The 1985 Supreme Court Decision

One commentator described the Court's decision as a "shock-wave." ("The Supreme Court sent a shockwave through the eastern United States by holding that the Oneidas could maintain an action for violation of their possessory rights based on federal common law."[42]) The Court held, in a five-to-four decision, that while "one would have thought that claims dating back for more than a century and a half would have been barred long ago," there is no "applicable statute of limitations or other relevant legal basis for holding that the Oneida's claims are barred or otherwise have been satisfied."[43] The Supreme Court did not settle on the legal remedy, but remanded the case to the Court of Appeals for a determination of the damages to be awarded. (Nearly twenty years later, and countless court battles hence, a final legal determination as to damages has yet to be finalized.)[44]

Statutes of limitations and other time-based rules are intended to bar stale legal claims. Locklear succeeded in persuading five justices (Powell, Blackmun, O'Connor, Brennan, and Marshall) that the Oneida claims were not stale, and that the long delay in bringing these suits was due to the fact that until recently federal courts were practically closed to the Oneidas. The Oneida's attorney argued that the courts, until recently, had been effectively closed to American Indian tribes due to the use of the political questions doctrine,[45] the 1863 requirement that Indians seeking justice in a treaty dispute needed special legislation giving the Court of Claims jurisdiction over its claim,[46] and the unsettled legal question as to whether Indian tribes had the capacity to sue in their own names, separate from their trustee, the federal government.[47] The lower court had found these arguments persuasive, and had noted that the Oneidas "never acquiesced in the loss of their land, but have continued to protest its diminishment up until today."[48] Rather than sleeping on their rights, the Oneidas had shown remarkable perseverance.

For the four dissenting justices, however, the Oneida's claim was "barred by the extraordinary passage of time."[49] In dissent, Justice Stevens, joined by then Chief Justice Burger, and Justices

White and Rehnquist, reminded the majority of "the historic wisdom in the value of repose."[50] In an intriguing distinction between that which is historic and that which is ancient, the dissenters called upon "historic wisdom" to defend the irrelevance of what they deemed an "ancient wrong."[51] Footnoting Blackstone's and Kent's *Commentaries on Law*, quoting Justice Story and Chief Justice Marshall, and concluding by likening the Oneidas to those whom "Abraham Lincoln once described with scorn [as sitting] in the basements of courthouses combing property records to upset established title,"[52] the dissenting justices deemed the various quoted authorities (written at approximately the same time the Oneida's title to their land was extinguished contrary to the dictates of the Non-Intercourse Act) as historic, whereas the wrongs done the Oneidas were "ancient." Remembered words of the past were cited to legitimate forgetting past illegal deeds.

Justice Stevens's dissent focuses on the economic consequences of the Court's decision upon counties and private landowners in the area. "Nothing so much retards the growth and prosperity of a country as insecurity of titles to real estate," Stevens quoted from an 1831 Supreme Court decision.[53] Stevens argued that the settled expectations of the present landowners had to be enforced rather than an "ancient" Indian right to the land.[54] Additionally, the counties could not be considered "responsible for their predicament," nor were "the taxpayers, who will ultimately bear the burden of the judgment in this case . . . in any way culpable for New York's violation of federal law in 1795."[55] For Stevens and the three other dissenting justices, the case offered a fundamental choice between burdening innocent counties and private landowners, or allowing past illegal governmental actions to go unrectified. The latter was deemed preferable, for, even if the original land transactions were invalid under the Non-Intercourse Act, as the framers recognized, Stevens wrote that, "no one ought to be condemned for his forefathers' misdeeds."[56]

Stevens's dissenting opinion reflects stark "either/or" thinking in which the alleged innocence of present non-Indian residents leads to the conclusion that the Oneidas should be barred from having their land claims respected. But that conclusion does not necessarily follow. Even if present-day residents are innocent (and one could question this innocence, given the fact that, as A. John Simmons writes, "We all know the history of theft, broken agreements, and brutal subjugation on which our holdings in land and natural resources historically rest,"[57] or as Martha Minow suggests, all of us have benefited from the expropriation, and thus are less than completely innocent[58]), the innocence of present-day inhabitants does not wipe away the damage done to the Oneidas. It could be argued that the Oneidas have been wronged, and that the (partial?) innocence of present-day upstate New York residents suggests that they should not alone bear the burden of making amends to the Oneidas for wrongs chiefly done by New York state officials in the late eighteenth and early nineteenth centuries. Ultimately, if there is present responsibility to make amends to the Oneidas, then it must be determined whether the brunt of that responsibility lies with local, state, or federal governmental entities. Connected to that question is which body of government is best equipped to respond to claims such as these that take us back to the early history of the nation and encompass hundreds of thousands of acres of land and entangle hundreds of thousands of lives.

Legislative or Judicial Remedy?

If the more than thirty year history of the Oneida land claims can teach us anything, it is the utter difficulty of developing a remedy to which all parties can agree. When the 2002 settlement agreement fell apart, officials from New York State and local counties, and the Oneidas of New York, Wisconsin, and Ontario had agreed to a number of points: government payments of $500 million to the Oneidas of New York, Wisconsin, and Ontario; the sale of approximately 1,000 acres of land in New York to the New York Oneidas; and the promise that current residents would not be ejected from their homes. However, as earlier noted, the Wisconsin and Ontario Oneidas wanted land as well, and the federal government claimed it had not agreed to pay half of the $500 million settlement. A number of other issues remained unresolved as well, including disputes over sales taxes and property taxes on Indian land, and related controversies concerning the New York Oneida's lucrative Turning Stone casino.[59]

It remains uncertain how Governor Pataki's December 2004 settlement proposal will fare. As noted above, it too faces considerable hurdles, including the fact that only one of the tribes, the Oneidas of Wisconsin, has agreed to its terms. Neither the Oneida tribes of New York and Ontario, nor a third tribe recently joined to the claim, the New York Brothertown Indian Nation, have signed on to the settlement. Both the New York Oneidas and the Brothertown tribe have stated that they will contest the settlement being imposed on them.[60] In addition, Pataki's proposal calls for five casinos in the Catskills of New York, two of which have yet to be authorized by the state legislature. Pataki's plan to add two more casinos than currently allowed faces resistance from upstate residents, some legislators, as well as the gaming interests that would face added competition. The plan will surely face opposition at the state legislature and in Congress, and then may be met by legal challenges by the three tribes who have not yet agreed to its terms.[61]

The seeming near-impossibility of resolving the Oneida land claims brings into sharp relief the question of which institutions of government are best equipped to resolve complex claims of this sort. During the course of the protracted litigation, several judges have voiced frustration that they, rather than legislative bodies, have been asked to resolve the dispute. Even the five justices of the Supreme Court who sided with the Oneidas in their historic 1985 decision seemed to ask Congress to step in and take the lead in resolving this dispute. In a final footnote to their decision, the majority wrote:

> The question whether equitable considerations should limit the relief available to the present-day Oneida Indians was not addressed by the Court of Appeals or presented to this Court by petitioners. Accordingly, we express no opinion as to whether other

considerations may be relevant to the final disposition of this case should Congress not exercise its authority to resolve the far-reaching Indian claims.[62]

The Court here seems to be suggesting that Congress is best-positioned to resolve this dispute in that they would be able to consider all relevant factors in crafting a remedy to suit all the parties. Legislative bodies, the Court suggests, have greater leeway in crafting a compromise that all parties could agree to and are better able to create a non–zero-sum resolution. Congress also may be more legitimate than courts to settle disputes of this sort, particularly if a resolution is to include a large compensatory payment from the state and federal government to the Oneidas, or involve a major change in policy such as additional casinos in a state. Legislatures, more accountable and arguably more representative of the people than judges, should initiate policy with regard to far-reaching disputes of this type. Of course, the representativeness of legislative bodies and their greater responsiveness to majority interests pose classic problems for minority interests. The intensity of many private landholders' objections to the Oneida claims has been evident both within and without the political system. Incidents of racial hatred greeted the Oneida's claims, and a local group, Upstate Citizens for Equality, as well as a national organization, the Interstate Congress for Equal Rights and Responsibilities, formed to oppose Indian claims, and are still actively opposing them.[63] The U.S. Congress responded to this pressure, and both the House and Senate held hearings in 1982 on a bill designed to extinguish the land claims, ("The Ancient Indian Land Claims Settlement Act of 1982," HR 5494 and S 2084). The bill was introduced in the House by Representative Gary Lee (R., NY) along with four other New York congressional cosponsors, and in the Senate by Strom Thurmond (R., SC) and Alfonse D'Amato (R., NY). The bill, written to address directly the Oneida claims, would have solved the claims problem by prohibiting Indian tribes from regaining their lands and strictly limiting any monetary compensation.[64]

This is neither to argue that judges are immune to public pressure, nor that they necessarily will be sympathetic to the claims of

American Indian tribes. In fact, legal scholar Joseph Singer has observed that judges have open to them a distinctive style of thinking that allows them to decide against American Indian land claims while abjuring responsibility for their decisions. Singer notes that:

> Courts continue to cite, or rather to miscite, the older cases as a way to remove responsibility from themselves.... To the extent they are read to authorize unjust expropriation of Indian lands, they provide a convenient scapegoat. They shift responsibility from current judges to a Court led by perhaps the most respected of all Chief Justices [John Marshall].... To the extent that the process entails injustice, it is safely relegated to the past.[65]

The long and, at this point, still unresolved history of the Oneida land claims attests to the myriad obstacles along both the legislative and the judicial routes of resolution. In most cases where resolutions of American Indian land claims have been reached, both legislative and judicial bodies have been involved, and both state and federal officials involved. Legal victories by American Indian tribes have pressured typically recalcitrant legislative bodies (as well as governors) to attempt to craft non–zero-sum resolutions in which both the settled expectations of current residents are recognized as well as the rights of American Indian tribes to be rectified for past wrongs.[66]

Passage of Time

One way to view the Oneida's land claims cases is as a fundamental conflict between a dominant culture's and a minority culture's understanding of the relationship between past and present, fought out on a playing field the boundaries of which have been established by the stronger party. From this standpoint, the claims present the question: To what extent will the dominant culture take into consideration the perspective of the minority culture? The Oneidas argue that the land, theirs by original acquisition, and never rightfully relinquished, still belongs to them and must be returned, or some rectification made. The intervening history has not diminished their rights to the land. Promises made by the federal government to their ancestors have not been eviscerated by the passage of time, for the tribe exists over time, as does the state and federal government, and thus neither the wronged nor the wrongdoer are dead, which, in turn, implies that the promises are still binding.[67] Legislative action to extinguish their claims, and legal judgments that fail to recognize their claims, represent yet another indication that the state and federal governments reject the dictates of fair play to placate the majority's hunger for land.[68]

The New York counties, on the other hand, attend not to past promises, but to the present occupants of the land, and to the present circumstances of the Oneidas, arguing that the rights of current residents are paramount. If there were wrongdoing, it is as Justice Stewart wrote, "ancient history," and sometime over the past 175 years, custom and settled expectations created new rights to the land.[69] The counties and private landholders contend that they are not responsible for any past wrongdoing, and as innocent parties, should not bear the burden of remedying past wrongs. Theirs is a discontinuous political collectivity, in which obligations do not devolve upon future generations. The counties also call into question the Oneida's status as "successors in interest" to the wrongs done to their ancestors. In this view, neither responsibilities nor wrongs outlive a generation.

New York state officials also had declared in 2002 that they would refuse to continue negotiations unless the Oneidas agreed to also discuss disputes surrounding the New York Oneida's immensely profitable Turning Stone casino. This position underscores the fact that within the long period between the alleged wrongs and the present much has happened; not only has time passed, but circumstances have changed. The Oneidas of New York are no longer a poverty-stricken American Indian tribe, and no longer is it accurate or honest to represent a response to the Oneida land claims as an attempt to both rectify past wrongs and reduce present inequities. If the Oneidas are due land and or money, their claims must stand on the independent basis of rectifying past wrongs, rather than any present redistributive impulse. Though I do think that rectification alone suggests that a response to the claims is due, I would add that I do not think that the New York Oneida's recent financial success diminishes their present claims. Such an argument would seem to have perverse implications. The lower courts as well as the Supreme Court found that the Oneidas did not sleep on their rights, but rather that the courts had been effectively closed to them. And, until very recently the Oneidas were severely handicapped in pressing their claims in the American political and legal environment due to financial limitations and political and legal inexperience. It was only when certain background circumstances changed—that is, when the Oneidas developed financial resources which enabled them to obtain political and legal resources—that they had a realistic chance to effectively pursue their claims. To contend that the change in the Oneida's financial circumstances argues against their claim seems to suggest that the Oneidas should not be able to vindicate their claims only because they finally stand a chance of doing so. This perspective implies that only when practical considerations dictate that the Oneidas would be unable to mount an effective political and legal campaign should their claims be recognized.

The Oneida land claim cases disclose the disquieting possibility that "ancient crimes" have tainted our history. What is at issue here is both a conflict between a dominant culture's and a minority culture's understanding of the relationship between past and present, as well as different versions of that past; one celebratory, and the other more ambivalent in which ancient crimes have tainted not only our past, but continue into the present. The Oneida cases present competing visions of the relationship between past and present, conflicting versions of the content of the American past, and of the very nature of our collectivity and of what responsibilities we may owe to others. The Oneidas contend that their claims are not only a part of the American past, but of the present, and that present-day citizens have a responsibility to right a historic wrong. New York counties respond that the Oneida claims are more akin to the dusty property records in the basements of courthouses, referred to by Justice Stevens in his dissenting opinion. The past is buried, and better left to collect dust. Present-day citizens, in this portrayal, innocent of any wrongdoing themselves, bear no responsibility to address ancient crimes. Chapters 3 and 4 more fully examine these competing visions of political identity and political responsibility. Before we move on to these broader issues, we now move on to explore another case history, that of Japanese Americans interned during World War II.

2

Explaining (away) the Misdeeds of Political Ancestors

The Civil Liberties Act of 1988

THIS CHAPTER examines the 1988 Civil Liberties Act, a crowning moment in the short history of post–World War II claims for reparations. In addition to explicitly acknowledging the fundamental injustice of the government's actions pursuant to Executive Order 9066 and apologizing for them, the law provided reparations to U.S. citizens and permanent resident aliens of Japanese ancestry who were forcibly evacuated, relocated, and/or interned during World War II.[1] More than forty-six years after the internment began, the U.S. government agreed to provide $1.25 billion to compensate Japanese Americans harmed by Executive Order 9066. The 1988 law marked the first time the U.S. government provided redress to compensate a group of citizens for the violation of their constitutional rights. This Act has been the most significant event in contemporary reparations politics. It has inspired other groups within and without the United States to press claims for compensation for wrongs done to them or to their ancestors, and it has provided a model of how past governmental wrongs may be translated into redress legislation acceptable both to victims and the government.[2]

Certainly, one story worth telling about the 1988 Act is a tale of legislative success over long odds. Japanese Americans at the time of the bill's passage were neither a numerically significant political minority nor a politically active "interest group." They comprised less than 1 percent of the U.S. population, and, at least partly, if not primarily, owing to the scars caused by the internment experience, had remained politically quiescent.[3] Nor was the general political climate conducive to spending bills that seemed non-essential and earmarked for "special interest" groups. The ballooning federal budget deficit of the 1980s led to increasing calls for fiscal restraint, and even the relatively modest $1.25 billion price tag of redress payments posed an easy target for fiscal conservatives. In addition, advocates of reparations struggled for the bill's passage under the looming threat of a presidential veto. President Reagan's Attorney General, Edwin Meese, had publicly stated his opposition, and President Reagan was certainly no fan of ostensibly liberal civil rights legislation.[4] And yet, on August 10, the Civil Liberties Act of 1988 was signed into law by Ronald Reagan and by October 1993 most ex-internees or their immediate heirs received letters of apology signed by George H. W. Bush along with checks for $20,000.[5]

A comprehensive story of the bill's success must take into account the extraordinary persistence of the Japanese American redress movement, its political acumen, and its good fortune in having four highly respected, strategically placed, and politically skillful Japanese American sponsors in Congress, some who could speak personally (and movingly) of the suffering caused by the internment.[6] Leslie Hatamiya's study on the passage of the Civil Liberties Act also brings to light the importance of institutional factors within Congress. The 1986 midterm elections returned Senate control to the Democratic Party, allowing the Democrats to seize leadership positions formerly held by Republican opponents of redress. And in the House, committed redress supporters (Speaker Jim Wright, Majority Leader Tom Foley, Majority Whip Tony Coehlo, and Judiciary Subcommittee Chair Barney Frank) assumed positions of power. Thus, in both houses of Congress institutional hurdles were cleared for the bill's passage.[7] More generally, Hatamiya argues that the redress movement's ability to stem large-scale, effective public opposition to the Act allowed most members of Congress to vote on the bill's merits without fearing political backlash and electoral costs. As she writes, "This allowed members to vote their own preferences, follow their party leadership, or return favors done by other members."[8]

What resulted from this combination of factors may be termed extraordinary politics, rather than interest group–driven electoral politics as it is ordinarily practiced in the United States.[9] The Act's extraordinariness is signaled immediately by the symbolic touches Congress lavished on the bill—it was numbered HR 442 in honor of the Japanese American regiment that fought courageously in Europe during World War II, and was brought to the floor for final consideration on the two hundredth anniversary of the signing of the Constitution. An examination of the bill's supporters also indicates that this was not politics as ordinarily practiced; party lines as well as ideological ones were broken in support of the bill. Newt Gingrich (R., GA) joined Ron Dellums (D., CA) in the House and Orrin Hatch (R., UT) joined Paul Simon (D., IL) in the Senate supporting the bill's passage. This is not to say that all supported the bill (a final version passed in the House by a vote of 243–141 and in the Senate by 69–27), that it passed in the form that its early supporters had hoped for, or that it sped through Congress upon its introduction (an initial redress bill was introduced in 1979). However, one could argue that much more than most bills, party and ideological lines were broken, and while the vote for some representatives, as Hatamiya argues, was "free," other representatives were atypically willing to pay a cost to back the bill. In many districts, constituent mail was overwhelmingly opposed to the redress bill, yet many representatives remained unswayed by popular opposition and voted for its passage anyway.[10]

One could still argue, however, that beneath the symbolic flourishes of the Act and the somewhat surprising bedfellows amongst its supporters, the give and take of ordinary legislative politics still lurks. Although the Japanese American community was relatively politically insignificant and was not in a position to apply much electoral pressure, one could reason that individual legislators voted for the bill as part of the typical reciprocal workings of the legislative system. However, the congressional record suggests otherwise. A careful reading of the congressional debates demonstrates that the 1988 Act signified more than simple appeasement of a "special interest" group or typical pork barrel politics. Rather, what emerges in the congressional debate is an unusually principled examination of the issues concerning the present government's responsibility for redressing the wrongs inflicted upon Japanese Americans evacuated, relocated, and/or interned during World War II.[11]

This chapter focuses on those debates. Most of my inquiry is limited to the issues that arose only after Congress had accepted the conclusion that the forcible evacuation, relocation, and incarceration of U.S. citizens and permanent resident aliens were unjustified. By focusing on these issues I do not mean to belittle the efforts of those who for so long strove to convince the government and the public of the injustice, but rather to accurately portray the Congressional debate in which almost all opponents of the redress bill conceded that internment was a misguided policy.[12] Opponents rejected the conclusion, however, that an apology and reparations as a material sign of the apology's sincerity, both as a matter of principle and policy, was the proper present response to the government's 1942 forced evacuation and relocation. Three principal questions emerged in the legislative debates: Who should be recognized as the proper claimants for the wrongs done; Who should be held responsible; and What is the appropriate response to these wrongs?

The ethical seriousness with which the 1987 redress bills were considered may be explained partly by the debate's resonance to other debates raging in the United States at the time, most notably the controversy over affirmative action. That debate, still with us, also features claims for compensation for past acts of collective injustice.[13] The relation between redress for Japanese Americans and affirmative action points up the need to explain why many steadfast opponents of affirmative action supported the Civil Liberties Act of 1988, and one of affirmative action's most hostile foes, Ronald Reagan, agreed to sign the Civil Liberties Act into law. Moreover, as noted earlier, because the 1988 Act has inspired other groups to press claims, and has become a benchmark for resolving claims arising over past governmental wrongs, an understanding of the bill's success can shed light on the prospects for resolving contemporary standing claims by American Indians and African Americans. I argue in this chapter that the bill's passage can, in large part be attributed to the supporters' framing of the issue in constitutional and legal terms, and to Congress' taming of the potentially more subversive ideas that inspired the initial redress movement. The legislative debates ultimately leading to the passage of the Civil Liberties Act of 1988 reveal the political and legal traditions in which responses to demands for apologies and rectification are grounded in the United States. The calls for rectification by Japanese Americans, African Americans, and American Indians pose troubling tests for these traditions. The debates provide a vivid chronicle of the possibilities for apologies, as well as forgiveness, within the dominant modes of American political thought—and its limitations. Ultimately, I read the Civil Liberties Act of 1988 as an extraordinary political achievement, although the Act's more subversive implications were tamed by Congressional supporters acceding to a narrow definition of personal and political identity, as well as to an attenuated understanding of the past's relevance to present political reality.

A Brief History

On February 19, 1942, two months after the attack on Pearl Harbor, President Roosevelt issued Executive Order 9066, authorizing the Secretary of War and designated military commanders "to provide military areas (in such places and of such extent) from which any or all persons may be excluded" (Executive Order 9066). The California congressional delegation, General DeWitt, and California Attorney General Earl Warren had been lobbying

Roosevelt to take actions against people of Japanese ancestry on the West Coast. The reasoning provided in Executive Order 9066 justifying the exclusion was to supply "protection against espionage and against sabotage to national defense material, premises, and utilities" (Executive Order 9066). Lt. General John L. DeWitt, the Military Commander of the Western United States, and an early and vocal supporter of exclusion, seized upon his newly established authority to denote the entire Pacific Coast a military area. Congress ratified the Executive Order by passing Public Law 77-503, stipulating that anyone who entered or stayed in the prescribed military areas could be subject to a civil penalty of $5,000, up to one year of imprisonment, or both. DeWitt, ultimately authorized by the president, and further empowered by Congress, then forcibly removed more than 120,000 persons of Japanese ancestry, including more than 77,000 American citizens from the West Coast and western Arizona, to assembly centers, and then on to confinement in internment camps established in remote areas in seven interior western states.[14]

The policy was not without its critics. FBI Director J. Edgar Hoover opposed the exclusion and internment, contending that it was being implemented due to "public and political pressure rather than factual data."[15] The attorney general of the United States, Francis Biddle, advised President Roosevelt that the policy was unconstitutional.[16] However, overall, there was little public outcry against the policy and much popular support from newspapers and western local and state politicians.[17] The Japanese American Citizens League (JACL), the foremost national Japanese American organization, ultimately decided to urge their members to comply with the order, concluding that not doing so would be confirming the government's doubts about their loyalty, and fearing that non-compliance would lead to violence and bloodshed.[18] For the most part, Japanese Americans went along with the JACL recommendation and complied with the government's orders. Not all did so, however. More than one hundred Japanese Americans engaged in acts of civil disobedience. In response, the U.S. government chose to prosecute three. Fred Korematsu, charged with refusing evacuation; Minoru Yasui, with violating curfew; and Gordon Hirabayashi, with violating curfew and failing to report for detention. All were convicted in federal courts and appealed their convictions to the Supreme Court. The Supreme Court agreed to hear these three cases, as well as a fourth, in which Mitsuye Endo, who cooperated with government orders, filed a habeas corpus petition, which was denied, and she too appealed to the Supreme Court.[19]

The Supreme Court had the opportunity in 1943 and 1944 to review the constitutionality of the curfew orders, as well as the exclusion and detention of Japanese Americans. A majority of the Court, while establishing that "all legal restrictions which curtail the civil rights of a single racial group are 'immediately suspect,'" still upheld the constitutionality of the curfew orders and the exclusion and detention of Japanese Americans.[20] Deferring to Congress and the Executive Branch, and relying upon the government's arguments of "military necessity," the majority of the Court permitted placing under curfew, expelling from their homes, and detaining in camps a group of people defined entirely by ethnic ancestry. Dissenting in the Korematsu case, Justices Roberts, Murphy, and Jackson assailed the majority decision, pointing to the "legalization of racism," the undermining of the principle of individual guilt, and the almost unlimited discretion given to the government and military during claimed emergencies.[21] As the dissenters and some legal scholars argued at the time, constitutional guarantees of equal protection of the laws, freedom of movement, protection of property, due process of law, and the presumption of innocence until proven guilty were all brushed aside in the name of "military necessity."[22]

However, on the same day the Court handed down the Korematsu decision, upholding the government's exclusion order, they also announced their decision in the Endo case. Mitsuye Endo, unlike the other appellants challenging the curfew, exclusion and detention policies, had followed the government's orders, reporting to an assembly center at a converted racetrack. She was then moved to the Tule Lake War Relocation Center and later to an internment camp in Topaz, Utah. In July 1942, she sought a writ of habeas corpus, which the northern California district court turned down a year later. Endo, however, then received official clearance from the War Relocation Authority to apply for a permit to leave the Topaz internment camp. The Topaz internment camp officials, however, refused to release her, claiming that local resettlement problems in Utah stood in the way of her release. Because the government conceded in her case that Endo was a loyal American citizen, and she had broken no laws, a unanimous Supreme Court ruled that Endo had to be released.[23]

What followed from this decision was that only those Japanese Americans whom U.S. government officials proved to be disloyal could be detained in internment camps. Aware of the far-ranging effects of the Court's decision (the decision no longer permitted the detention of individuals without due process of law), Chief Justice Stone notified President Roosevelt in November 1944 of their impending decision. Scholars have uncovered that Roosevelt did not want to end the internment policy until after the November 1944 elections, and the chief justice agreed to delay the announcement of the Endo decision.[24] The War Department, secretly notified of the Court's pending decision, revoked the exclusion and detention orders on December 17, the day before the Supreme Court handed down the Korematsu and the Endo decisions. The War Department announced that all the internment camps would be closed within a year.[25] All Japanese Americans were free to return to their homes on the West Coast by January 2, 1945. On March 20, 1946, Tule Lake, the lone remaining internment camp, was closed, putting an end to the government's ill-advised and unjust policy.

Post–World War II Responses to Executive Order 9066

In the aftermath of World War II, the U.S. government did begin the process of addressing the wrongs committed during the internment. In 1948, the government partially compensated Japanese Americans for their real and personal property losses suffered because of Executive Order 9066 through the American-Japanese Evacuation Claims Act.[26] The Act provided $37 million to compensate for property losses. However, this figure represents only one-quarter of the $148 million claim put forward by ex-internees. And as the commission authorized by Congress in 1980 to study the internment notes, the 1948 Act was not intended to compensate for the broader range of injuries that had been recognized by the 1980s: "The stigma placed on people who fell under the exclusion and relocation orders; the deprivation of liberty suffered during detention; the psychological impact of exclusion and detention; the breakdown of family structure; the loss of earnings or profits; physical injury or illness during detention."[27] As noted earlier, in 1946 the United States also had established the Indian Claims Commission to hear claims regarding the abrogation of tribal or other property losses that had occurred prior to 1940. The post–World War II period seemed to hold out the promise of the U.S. government meeting past obligations.

The 1950s brought two changes that would eventually enhance the political clout of Japanese Americans. In 1952, Congress passed the McCarran-Walter Act, which removed racial and ethnic bars from naturalization statutes.[28] Although Europeans were still favored under the immigration quotas (that would take until 1965 to change), "no longer were Issei aliens ineligible to become citizens."[29] Then, in 1959, Hawaii achieved statehood, and elected Asian American representatives to Congress. From that point on, Japanese Americans would have a visible presence in American politics, and by the 1970s when two California districts elected Norman Mineta (first elected in 1974) and Robert Matsui (first elected in 1978) to Congress, the Japanese American community would have four effective representatives to defend their interests.

As noted earlier, the civil rights movement of the 1960s inspired some within the Japanese American community to begin to press the U.S. government to publicly apologize and provide reparations for the internment. At this early stage, this was neither a large nor a unified movement; one historian of the redress movement estimates that in its early stages, "a third of the Japanese Americans supported redress, a third objected to it, and the rest were unconcerned with it."[30] In 1967, the first academic conference was called to analyze the evacuation and its consequences.[31] Three years later, redress advocates were able to pass a resolution at the national convention of the predominant Japanese American organization (the JACL) acknowledging redress as an issue of concern for their organization.[32] While not an endorsement of redress, the 1970 resolution marks the overcoming of shame that some within the Japanese American community felt over their internment, as well as a new sense of security within the United States, and a growing sense of political efficacy.[33]

During the 1970s, those advocating a governmental apology and compensation pursued various strategies, some aimed at gaining further support within the Japanese American community, and others to begin to educate the American public and governmental officials about the internment and its lingering effects. These efforts were first rewarded in 1976 when President Ford, marking the anniversary of the issuance of Executive Order 9066, formally apologized for the Order and formally proclaimed "that all the authority conferred by Executive Order 9066 terminated" with the end of World War II. "The American Promise"—Ford's proclamation—stated, "We now know what we should have known then—not only was that evacuation wrong, but Japanese Americans were and are loyal Americans."[34]

Heartened by their ability to elicit a formal governmental acknowledgment of the injustice of the internment, advocates turned to the more daunting task of achieving reparations. In 1974, the JACL had created a National Redress Committee, and four years later, just prior to the annual JACL convention, the committee published a blunt, provocative statement likening the experience of Japanese American internees to that of the model World War II victims—German Jews in Nazi concentration camps: "Both were imprisoned in barbed wire compounds with armed guards. Both were prisoners of their own country. Both were there without criminal charges, and were completely innocent of any wrongdoing. Both were there for only one reason—ancestry."[35]

The comparison seemed intended to press the argument for reparations—if Germany has admitted its wrongdoing and made reparations, then the United States should as well. At the JACL national convention that year, the organization authorized the redress committee to work toward securing compensatory payments of $25,000 to individuals interned as well as a trust fund to benefit the Japanese American community at large.[36] That year in addition marked the first "Day of Remembrance" in which ex-internees returned to the site of their internment and publicly engaged in remembering their experiences, working to overcome any lingering shame and further educating the public about the unjust governmental acts committed against them.

By the late 1970s, the JACL National Committee for Redress was actively engaged in a two-pronged approach toward achieving redress: public education to build broad popular support, and lobbying political leaders who could introduce and usher legislation through Congress. As noted earlier, the committee was fortunate to have four Japanese American legislators in Congress, two of whom had been evacuated and interned as children (Representatives Mineta and Matsui) and two of whom had fought with the richly decorated 442nd Regimental Combat Team during the war (Senators Inouye and Matsunaga).[37] Their presence in Congress, their power within it, and their willingness to risk political capital certainly influenced the JACL's choice of pursuing a legislative strategy rather than a judicial one toward achieving redress. Members of the National Redress Committee met with the four Japanese American members of Congress in 1979. At this meeting, Senator Inouye proposed that rather than immediately introducing redress legislation, the congressional sponsors first introduce legislation to form a commission to examine the government's actions during World War II and to issue a report. Inouye argued that this approach was less likely to provoke a political backlash and that the commission would educate the American public about the internment experience. While two members of the National Redress Committee opposed any strategy that did not call for immediate redress, they were outvoted and the Committee agreed to pursue Inouye's commission strategy. By the end of September 1979, bills had been introduced in both houses to establish the Commission on Wartime Relocation and Internment of Civilians (CWRIC).[38] By July 31 of the following year, both houses had passed legislation and President Carter signed into law an act creating the commission.

The Act called for a commission of nine people, three each selected by the president, the House, and the Senate. Inouye, sensitive to the charge that redress was strictly a Japanese American issue, wanted to make sure that the commission could not be dismissed as captured by a "special interest." The commission membership included former members of Congress, the Supreme Court, and the cabinet, only one who was Japanese American. In 1981, the commission held twenty days of hearings in nine cities and in December 1982 they released their report, *Personal Justice Denied*. The report's thoroughness, the respect with which its authors were held, and the fact that all commission members—Democrats and Republicans alike—signed on to the report's findings lent it a great deal of legitimacy. The report concluded that Executive Order 9066 "was not justified by military necessity. . . . The broad historical causes . . . were race prejudice, war hysteria and a failure of political leadership.[39] Rather than including its recommendations for remedies, the commission first published its findings and waited six months before publishing its recommendations. This two-stage approach was purposeful: In this way, rather than public attention being immediately drawn to the aspect of the report most likely to provoke a political backlash, the six month hiatus between the release of the findings and its recommendations allowed the public to focus upon the government's past unjust acts. In June 1983, the commission came forward with its recommendations, including the recommendation that redress advocates had set their sights on for a decade: that Congress provide compensation of $20,000 (though $5,000 less than the JACL proposed) to individuals who had been evacuated or interned. A hint that the seeming straightforwardness of the recommendation for redress obscured some underlying dilemmas was made apparent by the majority's inability to muster unanimity on the redress recommendation. Republican congressman Dan Lungren dissented from this recommendation, foreshadowing his active opposition on the floor of the House. The next step would be to introduce legislation in Congress to implement the commission's recommendations.

While the JACL had been pursuing a legislative approach aimed toward receiving moderate redress payments, a more radical wing of the original movement, frustrated over the decision to follow Senator Inouye's two-step strategy, formed the National Council for Japanese American Redress (NCJAR). The NCJAR favored a judicial approach to achieving redress and sought much more than the relatively moderate figure proposed by the JACL—$25,000 per living detainee and a small community trust fund. In 1983, the NCJAR filed a class action lawsuit against the U.S. government asking for $27 billion in damages. Similar to the Oneida land claims cases, for the next four years, the NCJAR and representatives of the U.S. government sparred in various federal courts, primarily over questions of sovereign immunity and statutes of limitations.[40] Ultimately, in 1987, the U.S. government prevailed in court and the class action lawsuit was thrown out, although the federal courts did formally exonerate the Japanese Americans who had been convicted of violating curfew and exclusion orders during the war. The NCJAR lawsuit, however, also may have provided a helpful "bad cop" backdrop for the lobbying efforts to push the redress legislation through Congress and past the president's desk.

While the commission's findings and recommendations entered the public and legislative debate with a certain amount of legitimacy, the effort to pass redress legislation still faced significant opposition both outside and inside Congress. Soon after the CWRIC issued their recommendations in June 1983, legislation was introduced in both Houses of Congress to accept and implement the report's findings.[41] This legislation failed to clear the congressional committee hurdles to passage, as did similar legislation introduced in 1985. These earlier failures accentuate the extraordinariness of the eventual passage of HR 442, the Civil Liberties Act, in 1988.

Four primary objections were raised against redress in the public debate provoked by the CWRIC's hearings and report. Some people, including two surviving high-ranking officials who participated in the decision to relocate Japanese Americans and its implementation, continued to defend the policy against the charge that it was not justified by military necessity. A related objection raised held that the commission's findings essentially exemplified "twenty-twenty hindsight" and that the original decision should be judged by what decision-makers knew at the time rather than from the security of the present. A third objection present in public debate was that in a time of war almost all citizens are required to make sacrifices and that the relocation and internment was akin to sacrifices made by U.S. soldiers. The final primary objection raised was fiscal—that with a ballooning federal budget deficit, to provide lump sum payments to a group of people who, on the whole, were not suffering economic woes, was imprudent public policy.

Although public objections to redress were voiced, an effective, organized opposition failed to materialize. One group, calling itself Americans for Historical Accuracy, was the creation of a right-wing ideologically driven historian, Lillian Baker. While this group actively opposed redress by writing letters, holding rallies, and submitting testimony before congressional committees, it had minimal effectiveness due to the extremism of its founder. Congressman Mineta recounts that Baker's opposition did not pose an obstacle to redress, for after hearing her arguments, people "would realize what a kook she is."[42] Veterans' groups, who may have opposed any criticism of the war effort, posed a more serious potential obstacle to redress. Japanese American veterans, however, could point to the storied achievements of the 442nd Regimental Combat Team, the 100th Infantry Battalion, and the Military Intelligence Service, thus foreclosing arguments that Japanese Americans posed subversive threats to the country. The national organizations of the two primary veterans' groups—the American Legion and the Veterans of Foreign Wars—actually passed resolutions supporting redress.[43] Thus, when Congress fully considered the merits of the redress legislation from 1987 to 1988 they did so relatively free from large-scale public opposition. In this context, Congress had the opportunity to conduct a principled examination of the merits of redressing a past act of governmental injustice.

Congress Debates the Civil Liberties Act

The first question that Congress had to confront in their deliberations over rectifying the U.S. government's actions arising out of Executive Order 9066 was whether the actions were, in fact, ill advised and unjust. While President Ford's 1976 Proclamation stated, "We now know what we should have known then—not only was that evacuation wrong . . ."[44] and while the CWRIC report concluded that the internment policy "was the result of racism, war hysteria, and failed political leadership,"[45] some Republican members of Congress were reluctant to accept the initial critical premise. In the House's Subcommittee on Administrative Law and Governmental Relations, and its parent Judiciary Committee, a few continued to defend the government's actions as just; others criticized what they regarded as the rewriting of history forty years after the fact. However, these objections were overcome through the combined efforts of Congressmen Mineta and Matsui, and HR 442 made it to the House floor.[46]

Defining the Wrong and the Wronged

To agree broadly that a wrong had been done was easier, however, than to define its precise nature. While the congressional debates did not require the level of specificity called for in a court of law, members of Congress still sought to define carefully the nature of the wrong and the identity of the wronged, as these definitional matters would affect the choice of remedies. To the extent that the wrong was defined in terms of property damage, opponents of redress could argue that the 1948 American-Japanese Evacuation Claims Act already compensated people for their losses. The CWRIC report noted that the 1948 Act was not intended to compensate for the non-material losses suffered, including the

deprivation of civil and constitutional rights. Congressional supporters of redress emphasized the violation of civil liberties perpetuated under Executive Order 9066, and advocates crafted a narrative in which the internment experience was framed in terms
of the violation of constitutional rights. While framing the evacuation, relocation, and internment as "fundamental violations of
the basic civil liberties and constitutional rights of those individuals of Japanese ancestry"[47] appealed to conservative Republicans and liberal Democrats alike, it also raised the question of
how and why these violations should be translated into monetary
terms.

Another troubling issue raised by introducing the language
of constitutional rights was that the generality of the language
of constitutional violations made apparent that the internment
was not a unique instance of U.S. governmental injustice. Much
of the legislative debate was devoted to consideration of how
other groups wronged in the past by the U.S. government would
react to the bill's passage. Most congressional opponents of the
bill cited a concern for the precedent it would set as one, if not
the major, reason for their opposition. Opponents assumed that
many other groups wronged by the U.S. government would now
demand equal treatment (i.e., compensation). The vision of the
past coming back to haunt the present vividly played before the
eyes of Congress.

Opponents of the bill seized upon the language of equal treatment in the debate on the floor of Congress. Congressman Dan
Lungren of California, the lone dissenter from the CWRIC's
recommendation for redress, stated, "The principles of equity
involve more than the satisfaction of wrongs in this specific
case. Rather, similar treatment for those with similar grievances
is required."[48] Interestingly enough, it was those members of
Congress most stridently opposed to the redress bill who spoke
movingly of the "countless other groups of Americans who have
suffered because of actions of the U.S. Government."[49] Congressional opponents contended that the number of other groups
gravely wronged by the U.S. government, particularly American
Indians and African Americans, diluted the claims of Japanese

Americans. Rhode Island senator John Chafee's statement exemplifies this response:

> What will passage of this measure say to the American Indians whose ancestors were brutally removed from their lands? Surely, argument can be made that the reservations on which so many Indians were placed, and continue to live today, and the federal programs in place to assist American Indians, have not sufficiently redressed the wrongs committed against them. Should we calculate a rough monetary figure for the value of the property American Indians might own today if they had not been displaced, and add to it the income they might have earned over the years if they had been able to work that land? . . . What about Black Americans? Think of those, their families, their predecessors who were in slavery in this nation, not temporarily but permanently in slavery? How are we going to make a redress to them and their descendants? It is not just those of many years gone by of the Black population of this country. They suffered the most outrageous discrimination in this nation right up to the mid-sixties when some of the civil rights were passed. Are we going to make some kind of redress to them?[50]

The American history of uncompensated wrongs and the accompanying fear of opening the floodgates to claims from all sides were used to pit some victims against others in the attempt to gain redress. Senator Malcolm Wallop (R., WY) posed the question: "If we are compelled to offer redress to Japanese-Americans, should we not also offer some monetary atonement for the sins of our forefathers, for those on the Trail of Tears, for those forced back to the Nations?" Wallop, if we are to take him at his word, considered proposing an amendment that stipulated, "No funds shall be appropriated under this title until the U.S. Government has also fairly compensated the descendants of the victims of the Trail of Tears."[51] Wallop stated that he had drafted an amendment to compensate the descendants of the Cherokees forced to walk the Trail of Tears, although an amendment was never offered. Notice that the amendment that Wallop referred to, rather than offering compensation to certain American Indian tribes, would have barred appropriations to Japanese Americans until the much larger, and much less likely, redress to descendants of the Trail of Tears was made. Congressional opponents hoped to use the unlikelihood of rectifying wrongs done to some to undermine doing justice to others.

Congressional sponsors of Japanese American redress legislation were compelled to address the fear of past wrongs coming back to haunt the present, and especially the fear of American Indians and African Americans turning to the courts to obtain compensation for the past wrongs perpetuated against them. Proponents chose a strategy that promised the greatest prospects for success, although the strategy had its costs. Senator Daniel Inouye of Hawaii, responding to an amendment to strike monetary compensation from the bill, asserted, "The internment experience is unprecedented in the history of American civil rights deprivation."[52] If the internment experience, however, was conceived of as a case of violations of civil liberties of a group of people singled out by the federal government because of their race or ethnicity, then, rather than unprecedented, it was but a chapter in a longer story that certainly included the U.S. government's treatment of American Indians and African Americans. It was not, then, the internment *experience* that was unprecedented; but rather redress proponents claimed that the *victims* of the evacuation, relocation, and internment, compared to other victims of U.S. governmental policies, were unique. Senator Spark Matsunaga's (D., HI) statement during Senate debate makes explicit the extent to which redress supporters felt compelled to quell the fear that the redress legislation would inspire other groups to bring forward even larger claims:

> It should be noted that under the provisions of S.1009, payments are to be made only to those living individuals who were victims of the federal government's wartime policy. No payments are to be made to heirs or descendants of the former internees. S.1009 would, therefore, not open the door for claims by descendants of former slaves or the descendants of Native American victims of the federal government's nineteenth century policies with respect to American Indians. When we look for cases of people alive today who were themselves directly injured by the federal government because of their race or ethnicity, the incarceration of Japanese Americans is unprecedented.[53]

To stand in contrast to the potentially more far-reaching claims of American Indians and African Americans, the claims recognized under the redress legislation for Japanese Americans evacuated, relocated, and interned were limited to those of individuals alive at the time of the bill's passage.[54] To define the class of claimants in this narrow manner accomplished two things: It limited rightful claimants to those who were still alive, thus suggesting that harms pass away when individual victims die, and it almost exclusively defined the victims as individuals, thus limiting governmental responsibility for any wrong that may have been done to Japanese Americans as a cultural and ethnic group.

The decision to limit eligibility to redress to survivors only, and not to compensate heirs of victims of the government's policy, had profound practical and theoretical implications. A 1979 bill championed by the more radical wing of the redress movement calling for compensation of $15,000 for each internee, plus $15 for each day in camp, specified that heirs of deceased victims of the internment be paid as well.[55] By 1988, when the Civil Liberties Act was nearing passage, approximately half of the individuals interned had died. Thus, the economic implications of compensating heirs were substantial; reparation payments of $20,000 to an additional sixty thousand claimants would add another $1.2 billion to the already-controversial bill. Yet, as was pointed out by an opponent of the bill, Congressman Shumway (R., CA), if one of the stated purposes of the bill was to demonstrate that the government did something wrong, "then there ought to be the ability to inherit on the part of those heirs of those who were unlawfully incarcerated."[56] Moreover, if the bill aimed to deter future injustices—it stated that one of its purposes was to "discourage the occurrence of similar injustices and violations of civil liberties in the future"—then a strong case might be made for heirs to be compensated.[57] If the claims of the dead were forgotten, then the deterrent was weakened and the sincerity of the government's apology could be questioned. The legislative debate makes clear that the decision not to compensate heirs of the victims of the government's internment policy was consciously driven by the desire to distinguish the redress legislation from similar claims that may be brought by American Indians or African Americans.

In a similar manner, the apparently commonsensical definition of the victims of the government's internment policy as "individuals of Japanese ancestry who were interned," had weighty implications for other groups wronged by the U.S. government. Rather than also recognizing the wrongs done to the broader Japanese American community, Congress, in conference committee, ultimately limited claimants to individual victims of specific discriminatory acts of the U.S. government. The Senate version of the bill had authorized funds to be available for "the general welfare of the ethnic Japanese community in the United States."[58] Under the Senate bill, funds would have been available to establish cultural and historical programs and to build community and research centers. Such programs and centers would have served as tangible and lasting reminders of the government's unjust deeds and the resilience of the Japanese American community. In turn, such programs and centers would have encouraged the continuing vitality of the Japanese American ethnic community.

By authorizing funding, albeit a modest amount, for programs to benefit Japanese American communities (approximately $100 million out of the $1.3 billion was to be allotted for the general welfare of the ethnic Japanese American community), the Senate bill implicitly acknowledged that defining the victims of the internment solely as individuals did not faithfully capture the events of 1941 to 1946. Those who had been excluded, relocated, and/or interned were not simply individuals who happened to be Japanese American. They were singled out by the government because of their race, ethnicity, and culture (neither German Americans nor Italian Americans as a group had been treated in this manner). Responsible members of the U.S. government perceived and treated individual Japanese Americans as members of a particular racial, ethnic, and cultural group. Their membership in that group accounted for their victimization, and to redress the wrong done as if it were only separate individuals who had been injured ignores the harms suffered by Japanese Americans as a group.[59] The stigma unjustifiably attached to Japanese Americans extended beyond those who were actually detained, relocated, and/or interned, and the resulting shame also was shared by those both directly and indirectly harmed by the government's actions. Although the government's apology and redress to individuals may do much to remove the stigma and shame attached to the group as a whole, and a sense of justice may be shared by all members of the group, aid to the group at large, such as funding cultural and historical programs and community and research centers, may better remedy the group harm.

The Senate, in so recognizing group claims, also wrestled with the question of who would best represent the needs and desires of the ethnic Japanese American community. If money was to be allotted for the "general welfare of the Japanese American community," who should sit on the board to disburse the funds, deciding what was in the best interests of the ethnic Japanese American community? An initial version of the Senate bill established that at least five of the nine directors of the fund "must be of Japanese ancestry."[60] Senator Orrin Hatch (R., UT) objected to the clause, and an amendment to strike it was agreed to without debate.[61] The clause itself was stripped of much import when, in conference, House and Senate managers of their respective bills agreed to follow the House version that did not allot any funding for programs specifically aimed to benefit the ethnic Japanese American community.[62] Although the final law did establish a Civil Liberties Public Education Fund in addition to compensatory payments to individual Japanese Americans harmed by Executive Order 9066, the harm done to the ethnic Japanese American community, and the very existence of such a group, was not reflected in the ultimate Civil Liberties Act of 1988.

Once again, the specter of claims by other groups wronged by the U.S. government loomed in the background of the congressional debates. If the internment of Japanese Americans not only harmed the particular individuals relocated, evacuated, and interned, but also the broader ethnic Japanese American community, then arguably it would follow that slavery's effects, or the effects of the dispossession of American Indian lands, would be felt by members of those groups who were not themselves immediately harmed. Even a minimal recognition of group harms, and an accompanying right to group remedies, created a too-dangerous precedent for some members of congress who were willing to support the Civil Liberties bill as long as it remained strictly defined as an attempt to rectify wrongs done to specific individuals by an overbearing government.

If the final version of HR 442 failed to include recognition of the harms done to the larger Japanese American community, it did, however, necessarily reflect the harms caused by the internment to the larger American citizenry. Japanese Americans, particularly those who were citizens of the United States (others interned were permanent resident aliens), under the law were supposed to be treated as equal members of the American polity; the internment made their exclusion from American political society all too evident, however. Possibly the most emotionally charged moment of the congressional debate occurred when Senator Jesse Helms (R., NC) proposed an amendment to block appropriations for the Civil Liberties law until the government of Japan compensated the families of those killed at Pearl Harbor on December 7, 1941. When word reached the House of Helms's amendment, Congressman Mineta exasperatedly pointed out that the meaning of the internment experience and the redress bill was lost on those who would support such an amendment: "This bill has nothing to do with the nation or people of Japan. It deals with how the U.S. Government treats its own citizens."[63] If the larger Japanese American community shares in the harm done to the particular individuals detained, relocated, and or interned in that they can identify with those unjustly treated, then so too— to the degree that the larger American society can identify with the ex-internees—do they share in the harm.[64] However, even more fundamentally, the Civil Liberties Act of 1988 presumes that the American citizenry at least partially identifies with the government that performed the unjust deeds, and thus shares in the responsibility to apologize and make reparations. Sponsors of the redress legislation repeatedly emphasized that the Act, rather than directed at a "special interest," was intended for all Americans. What was due all Americans, in the minds of the Act's sponsors, was the opportunity to apologize, make amends, and implicitly, be forgiven. The insight that "we owe it to ourselves" to make amends, voiced by Speaker of the House Jim Wright (D., TX) immediately preceding a vote on an amendment to strike the clause authorizing reparations, makes sense only if American citizens at least partially identify with the government that performed the harmful deeds and imagine themselves part of a larger political collectivity.[65] The concepts of political identification and imagination were at issue, as well, on the floor of Congress.

Defining the Responsible Party

As well as precisely who deserved an apology and reparations, debate took place in Congress over whether the Japanese American evacuation, relocation, and internment should be considered unjust violations of civil liberties. The identity of who had been responsible for the unjust deeds was much less in question, though. Clearly, Executive Order 9066 was a matter of "state action," as local, state, and federal governmental officials from 1941 to 1946 all played a part in conceiving and implementing the policy. The commission authorized to study the internment concluded that a failure of political leadership, along with war hysteria and racial prejudice, were the broad historical causes of the internment. In the commission's judgment, many local and western state political leaders failed to exercise leadership in that they lobbied for the exclusion order and were able to convince President Roosevelt, over the opposition of both Attorney General Biddle and FBI Director Hoover, to issue Executive Order 9066.[66] The President failed in that he ignored the constitutional objections of Biddle as well as the objections of Hoover, who perceived the exclusion as driven by "public and political pressure rather than factual data."[67] The failure was not only that of political leaders, but also of much of the public, who especially in the western states expressed support for the exclusion in newspapers and through citizens' associations.[68] Unquestionably, American political leaders, and the larger American political society of 1941 to 1946 were responsible for the injustices suffered by Japanese Americans excluded, relocated, and interned.

A much thornier question on the floor of Congress was whether the American political collectivity of 1987 to 1988, as well as into the future, was responsible for the injustices. Did responsibility for political misdeeds pass from generation to generation? Did present citizens inherit responsibility for the misdeeds of their political ancestors? And could they, and should they, pass part of that responsibility along to their children and grandchildren? The supposition that present-day American citizens could be held responsible for deeds over which they had no control and to which they did not consent rankled numerous congressional and public opponents of the Civil Liberties Act. The remarks of Representative William Frenzel (R., MN) gave voice to this resentment catapulting him into the limelight. Excerpts of Congressman Frenzel's speech were oft quoted in the Senate and proved very popular with editorialists opposed to the bill:[69]

> What a funny way they ask us to rub ashes on our heads. . . . The committee is asking us to purge ourselves of somebody else's guilt with another generation's money. . . . We are going to put the hairshirt on somebody else and that somebody else is our children and our grandchildren. And remember, they did not make the decision and neither did we make the decisions.[70]

Through his use of religious metaphors, Frenzel suggests that "rubbing ashes on our heads" is an inappropriate aim of governmental action. While this argument remains implicit in his speech, the explicit one relies upon the notion of a virginal birth to profess the innocence of present and future generations. German chancellor Kohl gave these sentiments their most notable post–World War II expression by anointing those born after the Nazi atrocities with "the grace of being born late."[71]

These sentiments take us to the heart of the dominant American conception of the relationship between individuals and the political society in which they are born. Within this conception, individuals are born innocent, and their birth or entrance into a political society maintains if not reaffirms that innocence. As Congressman Frenzel's statement exemplifies, as well as the enthusiastic reception it received from newspaper editorialists, the imposition of either guilt or responsibility (and oftentimes these are mistakenly equated) for deeds done by others in the past engenders political resentment. If we were not alive when the deeds were done, then we had neither control over nor could we have consented to the enactment of the evacuation, relocation, and internment. Thus, within this understanding what necessarily follows is that we are innocent and undeserving of guilt or responsibility for the deeds.[72]

A contrary conception of political identity and political responsibility, however, was also voiced during the congressional debates. Within this alternative understanding, rather than starkly distinguishing between generations, members of the present generation look upon the acts of predecessors as somehow their own, and assume some responsibility for them. Congressman Matsui's response to Frenzel's argument on the floor of the House suggests a conception of political identity and responsibility at odds with Frenzel's generational demarcation: "I do not look upon America in terms of generations. We must look upon this country as a continuous flow and ebb. We are not talking about a generation in the 1940s and a generation today."[73] Within this contrary understanding, even though most members of the present generation were not alive when the U.S. government evacuated, relocated, and interned approximately 120,000 U.S. citizens and permanent resident aliens of Japanese ancestry, and thus neither had control over nor consented to the deed, they still, in their identity as American citizens, may be responsible for righting this past wrong.

Devising an Appropriate Response

Section I of the final Act states Congress's multifaceted purposes in passing the legislation. In specifying seven purposes of the Act, Congress implies that all seven can be achieved in harmony with one another, although the congressional debate suggests otherwise.[74] Section I states that the Civil Liberties Act was intended to:

> Acknowledge the fundamental injustice of the evacuation, relocation, and internment . . .; apologize on behalf of the people of the United States . . .; inform the public about the internment . . . so as to prevent the recurrence of any similar event; make restitution . . .; discourage the occurrence of similar injustices and violations of civil liberties in the future; and make more credible and sincere any declaration of concern by the United States over violations of human rights committed by other nations.[75]

Principally, the Act seems intended to serve compensatory, educational, and expressive functions.

Although various reasons were voiced by some members of Congress who resisted passage of the Act, the chief source of contention during congressional debates was whether monetary compensation should to be paid to Japanese Americans who had been interned. In both chambers, amendments were offered to withdraw the authorization of funds for payments to former internees. Whereas sizable majorities had agreed that a wrong had been done; that it had yet to be addressed adequately; and even that they, as representatives of the U.S. government of 1987 to 1988, were willing to assume responsibility for the acts taken between December 7, 1941 and June 30, 1946; there was much less agreement that monetary compensation was an appropriate response to the wrong. Within a compensatory model of justice, remedies may achieve three primary purposes: make the victim whole again, deter similar harmful action, and punish the wrongdoer. As the indefatigable Senator Helms (and the almost equally untiring Congressman Lungren) argued, however, arguments for monetary compensation based on deterrence or punishment are weakened "when most, if not all, of the people responsible for the decision have long since left government service . . . [and] most are probably no longer alive."[76]

Monetary compensation, however, had been a principal element from the beginning of the movement by both the fairly mainstream Japanese American Citizens League and the more radical National Council for Japanese American Redress. These early calls, however, varied immensely in the amount of compensation envisaged, the method of determining the amount due, and who would be paid. Some early proponents of redress called for aid to the larger Japanese American community rather than payments to individuals. Most, however, imagined some form of individual payment, although some supporters called for an equal amount to be paid to each internee, while others advocated a more individualized approach based upon the German Federal Compensation Law that allowed for different categories of claims based upon the extent of the harm suffered.

Not all, however, within the Japanese American redress movement believed monetary compensation was the most appropriate form of redress. Shiro Shiraga contended that remembrance of the injustice was most essential, and to that end, proposed that the U.S. government erect monuments the size of the pyramids of Egypt at each of the ten camp sites.[77] Jitsuo Morikawa argued against the whole enterprise of suggesting to the government proper forms of redress. Deciding upon a rightful form of redress was not the proper burden of the victims, but of the perpetrators of the wrong. If, as Morikawa insisted, "the acts of redress must be as costly as the pain and agony of the injustice," then monetary compensation was too cheap a form of redress, no matter what the amount.[78]

The CWRIC (established by Congress in 1980) recommended monetary compensation, with Congressman Lungren the lone dissenter, and thus the call for monetary compensation entered the congressional debate with a presumption of legitimacy. Clearly, some members of Congress who had voted to authorize the commission thought that its creation would delay and/or discourage demands for monetary compensation—Senator Hayakawa (R., CA), in fact, endorsed the commission bill on the condition that no monetary reparations would be asked.[79] Congressman Lungren later attempted to convince his colleagues that Hayakawa's stance was representative of Congress's understanding of the commission bill and that monetary compensation should be struck from the 1988 redress bill to remain true to the 1980 bill establishing the commission. His argument failed, though, as redress advocates pointed out that Hayakawa's view was not necessarily representative, and that as members of Congress in 1988 they were not bound to the wishes of their predecessors.

The commission had justified their recommendation that Congress provide a one-time payment of $20,000 to each of the approximately sixty thousand surviving persons excluded from their homes pursuant to Executive Order 9066 by focusing on the economic losses suffered by the Japanese Americans for which they had not received compensation:

> It is estimated that, as a result of the exclusion and detention, in 1945 dollars the ethnic Japanese lost between $108 and $164 million in income and between $41 and $206 million in property for which no compensation was made after the war under the terms of the Japanese-American Evacuation Claims Act. Adjusting these figures to account for inflation alone, the total losses of income and property fall between $810 million and $2 billion in 1983 dollars. It has not been possible to calculate the effects upon human capital of lost education, job training and the like.[80]

The commission seems to have reached the figure of $20,000 to each of the approximately sixty thousand surviving victims by calculating a reasonable range of the economic losses suffered by all those excluded and detained, picking a rough midpoint in that range, and dividing it evenly among those still surviving. Such attempts at mathematical niceties certainly leave redress proponents open to the charge that the $20,000 figure is an arbitrary one that will overcompensate some and undercompensate others. The commission anticipated such responses and did not base its recommendation for personal redress solely upon the economic losses suffered by Japanese Americans. "The injury of unjustified stigma," "the deprivation of liberty," "the psychological pain," and "the weakening of a traditionally strong family structure," were all cited as less tangible yet no less real injuries suffered by those excluded and detained.[81] And while these injuries could not be neatly translated into dollar figures, they too de-manded compensation. The $20,000 amount, then, within the commission report, symbolized compensation both for material and intangible losses.

On the floor of Congress, however, some opponents of redress were not persuaded by the commission's argument that equal pay-ments be made to surviving victims of the internment. Congress-man Shumway (R., CA) objected to the redress law's lump sum approach, and offered an amendment that called for the age of the victim and the amount of time spent in the internment camps to be considered in determining the amount of compensation paid. Adults were to be paid more, due to their higher earning power, and all internees were to be paid on a per diem basis, reflecting Shumway's conviction that the more time spent in the camps, the more compensation one deserved.[82] Earlier, during commit-tee hearings, representatives considered differentiating among the various material and nonmaterial harms suffered, and compen-sating individuals differently based on the harms endured. Advo-cates of these more individualized approaches to compensation contended that they may better make individual victims whole again, and that these approaches remove the stigma of arbitrariness attached to the amount of compensation. An approach that distin-guishes among the harms suffered may also remind the public of the many rights the government violated during the internment experience. Similar to a class action lawsuit, the listing of the rights infringed by the government, and the claims arising from those violations, may better inform the public about what happened and remind citizens more forcefully of the value of rights commonly taken for granted.[83]

However, the individualized approach was never seriously con-sidered by congressional redress sponsors. The practical difficul-ties involved with presenting evidence and the costs involved in the assessments were said to be enormous. An individualized ap-proach that more accurately reflected the particular harms done to victims would cost, redress sponsors warned, much more than the $1.2 billion figure supposed under the equal sum approach.[84]

The equal sum approach also precluded disparities in settlement amounts among claimants, and the possibility that the variations would sow resentment amongst the ex-internees. The equal sum approach signified the group's solidarity. Victimized as a group on the basis of shared ancestry, the equal sum approach would maintain group ties and not splinter the citizens and permanent resident aliens of Japanese ancestry into subgroups.[85]

Advocates of monetary compensation underscored the extent to which the payments were in accord with our legal tradition. Even in this case of an intergenerational collective wrong, support-ers contended that deterrence and punishment both were appro-priate. Proponents maintained that acknowledging and making rectification for the government's wrongdoing would discourage similar violations in the future. They also cited the fairly recent "constitutional tort" concept employed by the courts in cases in which individuals' constitutional rights have been violated by gov-ernment agencies.[86] These members of Congress did not look upon the $20,000 payments as reimbursement for the loss of in-come or property; rather, the money was partial compensation for the violation of civil rights and a punishment meted out to the wrongdoers. Rather than compensation for material losses, here money acted as a surrogate for the loss of constitutional rights. Whereas an argument for compensation based upon economic losses demanded a detailed and complex accounting of the wages and property lost by more than 120,000 Japanese Americans (or of the approximately sixty thousand still alive), and a conversion of that figure into current dollars, the argument for compensation for constitutional violations called for an even more challenging—and subjective—conversion of rights into dollars. Conceding that this conversion was less than scientific, but insisting that $20,000 vastly underrated the value of the rights violated by the govern-ment, proponents contended that compensation was due when the government breached peoples' rights. Responding to the argu-ment that the monetary valuation of rights demeans their value, Congressman Mineta asserted, "It is absurd to argue that because constitutional rights are priceless, they really have no value at all.

Would you sell your civil and constitutional rights for $20,000? Of course not. But when those rights are ripped away without due process, are you entitled to compensation? Absolutely."[87]

Ultimately, those advocating reparations had to confront the limitations as well as the benefits of monetary compensation. Proponents allowed that a payment of $20,000 would not make the victims whole again—no amount of money could undo all of the harms inflicted forty years earlier. However, the goal of restoring victims to as good a position as they would have been if no wrong had been done remained implicit in their argument and is reflected in the law.[88] To restore that which was lost turns the gaze backward in time and presumes an original innocence before the harm. Legislative or legal action conceived of as acts of restorative justice aims to recapture a condition that existed before a wrong was done. In a narrow and distinctly economic sense, that is certainly called for here. But, considered in the larger political context, the desire to return to the past historical conditions seems mistaken, for it was precisely those conditions that allowed the internment to occur. It was Japanese Americans' political powerlessness and their near complete exclusion from political society that permitted the racism and war hysteria fueling the internment to proceed relatively unimpeded. Rather than restoring these conditions, a better goal would be to transform the conditions whereby Japanese Americans and others similarly situated are empowered and fully included in political society. The Civil Liberties Act lists "making restitution" as one of its primary goals. Some of the older meanings of the word *restitution* may be instructive here. In English ecclesiastical law, a suit brought by either a husband or wife whenever either of them lived apart without sufficient reason was known as a suit of restitution of conjugal rights. Similar suits existed within ecclesiastical law to restore a man to the church.[89] The connotation that restitution could close communal ties that had been sundered is suggested by these older meanings. However, if those ties did not exist originally, then the political or legal task is not to return, but to create the conditions in which such ties are possible.

If inclusion in political society and the transformation of the relationship between Japanese Americans and the larger political society are fitting goals of restitution, then the expressive function of the law assumes as much significance as the compensatory. How can the Act best give voice to the desire to include within political society those formerly excluded and wronged? Can an apology on behalf of the people of the United States lead to a transformed relationship between ex-internees, the larger Japanese American community, and the broader American political society? Can the passage of the law enhance the ex-internees' trust in the American political society and their desire and willingness to participate within it? Much of the legislative debate was devoted to the meanings attached to the payment of money, and whether money was an appropriate means to acknowledge the injustice of and apologize for the forced evacuation, relocation, and internment of Japanese Americans. Did money express the sincerity of the government's apology or demean it?

Proponents of monetary compensation argued that an apology alone would not convey the full intent of Congress. The payment of money would "make it very clear that we are in effect imposing a penalty on ourselves to show and to demonstrate in fact how sincere we are."[90] Supporters of redress struggled with the predicament of how to express sincerity when official words were distrusted and had lost their power to convey meaning. Within this political–cultural context of distrust, words alone were inadequate:

> In America we all know that we deal also with things valued with money, and the willingness to pay compensation in dollars speaks about how absolutely clear we want to be about what is at stake . . . We as a nation are going to make a small sacrifice, to make what amounts to a small payment; but what we are going to say with that payment is not only that our words are behind our apology and our recognition of the wrong, but our resources are, too.[91]

Advocates asserted that in America, dollars spoke more loudly than words. If a crucial purpose of the law was to acknowledge and apologize for the wrong done by the U.S. government, then money was an essential component of any expression.

Many members of Congress balked at the payment of money, however, troubled by the lack of trust in the government and its pronouncements therein implied. They argued that the payment of money cheapened both the government's apology and the redress recipients. For opponents of monetary compensation, the proper response to the prevailing political–cultural distrust was not to relent to it by speaking the language of money, but to hold onto the mode of expression that employed words alone. Senator Nancy Kassebaum (R., KS), who ultimately voted for the bill, voiced her reservations in asking whether "monetary payment is necessary to ensure the sincerity of a formal apology?"[92] Senators Helms (R., NC), Hollings (D., SC), Symms (R., ID), and Simpson (R., WY) all objected to what they called the logic of materialistic reductionism in which "unless money is exchanged, the sincerity of our expression is brought into question."[93] For these senators, the formal apology of the U.S. government was meaningful in itself. Nor were all opponents of monetary compensation on the political right. Earlier in the public debate over reparations, the *New York Times'* editorial board opposed monetary redress, maintaining that even if the "lasting resentment" of Japanese Americans was "legitimate," a symbolic "gesture of atonement" such as a "fund offering scholarships" was more appropriate than monetary redress.[94] For redress critics on the political right and left, money symbolized ordinary interest-group politics, and the extraordinariness of the government's apology would be obscured in the language of dollars and cents. The dilemma of how to express an extraordinary political concept within the ordinary context in which American politics typically functions runs right through the Civil Liberties Act of 1988.

Extraordinary Politics

On September 21, 1987 the Civil Liberties bill, hailed by congressional supporters as the perfect gesture to mark the two hundredth anniversary of the Constitution, passed the House of Representatives. Yet, the precipitating events of 1941 to 1946 that the law addressed, and much of the initial impetus behind the movement for its passage, call into question fundamental legitimizing beliefs of the government established by that Constitution. Rather than the perfect gesture to mark the bicentennial of the Constitution, the congressional debate leading up to the law's passage—and the ultimate law—may better be seen as reflecting an extraordinary, if not subversive, understanding of political identity, political responsibility, and the possibility of political forgiveness partially tamed by the ordinary context in which American politics is practiced and conceived.

The Civil Liberties Act of 1988 truly was unprecedented within American politics. The Act marked the first time the U.S. government apologized for and provided redress to compensate a group of people for the violation of their constitutional rights. Intrinsic to the Act was the assumption of responsibility by present representatives of the U.S. government for the misdeeds performed by past representatives. Intrinsic as well was the meaningfulness of an apology within the political realm, and the understanding that shame, as well as pride, may be felt by citizens about the deeds of their government, even if they neither consented to nor were even alive at the time of their enactment.

These extraordinary meanings threatened to extend beyond the specific acts of 1941 to 1946 under discussion. The Act's precedent applied to the United States' ignominious history with other racial and ethnic minorities, most particularly with African Americans, American Indians, and Mexican Americans. Indeed, at various points during the bill's travels through the House and Senate, the Act was impeded by members of Congress who feared it would create a dangerous precedent that would inspire other groups similarly wronged to seek an apology and possible reparations. To the extent that the story told about the acts under question resembled the stories of other racial and ethnic groups who had been wronged by the U.S. government, the Civil Liberties Act's apology and redress seemed to invite replication.

In the narrative constructed by the commission established by Congress to study the events of 1941 to 1946, "race prejudice" as well as "wartime hysteria and a failure of political leadership" led to the internment. In the commission's telling of the story, one can note the beginnings of a de-emphasis of the centrality of racial prejudice directed against a group of people. Coupling race prejudice with wartime hysteria seems to explain the conscious steps directed against Japanese Americans taken by all three branches of the U.S. government from 1941 to 1946 as an incidence of hysteria that has little relevance to everyday reality or the reality of other racial and ethnic minority groups.

The commission entitled their report, *Personal Justice Denied,* and the report emphasized the violation of individual rights. On the floor of Congress, Republican supporters of the law seemed most receptive to interpretations of the events of 1941 to 1946 that accentuated the lesson that a too-powerful national government poses an ever-present threat to individual rights. Within the narrative as well, discriminatory state action results when the state takes note of the race or ethnicity of individuals. Notice that this narrative can be used to support reparations for Japanese Americans while simultaneously opposing affirmative action or reparations for African Americans or American Indians. The wrongs done to Japanese Americans are framed as individuals who had been treated as members of a racial or ethnic group; the story told is that the U.S. government violated their rights by treating their race or ethnicity as significant. Thus the lesson, as T. Alexander Aleinikoff writes about the post–World War II civil rights era in general, is that "the category had to be overcome and made invisible in order to eradicate its harmful uses."[95] The state should not use race or ethnicity in any governmental action, even when they were attempting to remedy past wrongs. Within this conception, only individuals—not groups—had a right to request an apology and redress for past wrongs committed by the government.

Understood in this light, it may be said that the Japanese Americans who were still alive in 1988 and who had been evacuated, relocated, and interned did stand in an exceptional position relative to others unjustly harmed by U.S. governmental state action. However, to frame the victims and the events of 1941 to 1946 as unique may diminish their political and legal significance. Senator Jesse Helms, tirelessly combating the legislation, offered three amendments to the bill. Two crippling amendments were defeated, but a third, unopposed by sponsors of the bill, was appended to the legislation.[96] The accepted amendment attempted to impose a restricted reading of the bill's import and to dissuade other groups wronged in the past from taking heart in its passage. As Helms explained, his amendment was "intended to preclude . . . this legislation from being used as a precedent in the courts or elsewhere to give standing to any precedent or future claims on the part of Mexico or Mexicans or any other citizen or group claiming to have been dealt an injustice by the American Government at some time in the past."[97] Helms's amendment, which became Title III of the Act, was the counterpart to the sponsors' argument of the uniqueness of their claims.[98] If the claims were unique, they had no precedential value—and little value as a means of illuminating America's past or present. This narrative allowed the acts of 1941 to 1946 to be dismissed as grotesque aberrations of the national character provoked by wartime hysteria, with little connection to the present, and from which little could be gleaned regarding the U.S. government's treatment of African Americans, American Indians, and other racial and ethnic groups.

However, contrary to the best efforts of Senator Helms and to the stated intent of the Act, as amended by Helms's Title III, the Civil Liberties Act has provided inspiration and political, if not legal, ammunition for other groups aggrieved by the U.S. government. As Harvard law professor Charles Ogletree Jr. has said, a proponent of an apology and some sort of redress to African Americans, "The elephant's nose is under the tent."[99] Even tamed by Congress, in that the Act does not allow the claims of those who had died before the law's passage to be inherited by their heirs, nor does it attempt to remedy the harms done to the ethnic Japanese American community, the Act's boldness eclipsed the strictures placed on it. The Act opens up questions of political identity and political responsibility typically neglected, or answered in a narrow fashion, within American political thinking. Underlying the apology and reparations of the Act is the premise of connections that entangle members of a political collectivity, and that tie past, present, and future together. Rather than personifying individual citizens as detached from others and from the historical continuum into which they are born, the Act is predicated upon the contrary insight that part of an individual's identity is inherently connected to the particular political society, with its particular histories, in which they live. The Civil Liberties Act implicitly expressed the hope that shame in the government's actions and in one's identity as a citizen, long-simmering resentment of the government, and mistrust amongst various groups within American political society, could be remedied, if not resolved, by the expression of a sincere apology. The following chapters explore these underlying concepts of political identity and political responsibility, as well as the promise and limitations of national apologies.

3

The Birth and Death of Political Memories

As we have seen in the two preceding chapters, contemporary calls for national apologies, with or without material compensation, and the fiery debates within the United States provoked by these calls, exhibit a tension in American political thinking regarding the relation of the present to the past. This tension, typical of a revolutionary nation, has deep roots in American thought and continues to complicate our relation to political ancestors and their deeds. Our political identity—that is, who we imagine ourselves to be politically—typically is conceived in two dimensions: space and time. Defining oneself as a member of a political collectivity in spatial terms calls for locating or situating one's self in relation to geographical boundaries. An individual establishes oneself as an American, for example, by establishing one's birth or present location in relation to the border between the United States and Canada or Mexico, for instance. Mobility destabilizes this relation. In thinking about membership and space, the primary issues that arise are the political consequences of human mobility. An individual may confront uncertainties regarding identity when moving across a border, and a political collectivity must consider whether and how many immigrants (or emigrants) to allow and whether and how new-comers (and which of those newcomers) may become members of the collectivity.[1]

An analogous set of issues arises in defining membership in terms of the temporal dimension. Once again, membership must be defined in terms of boundaries, but in this case, the boundaries separate past, present, and future. And, once again, movement may prove to be destabilizing. Here, however, the movement is continuous and the boundaries less secure and less well defined. Whereas spatial boundaries are permeable and changeable, we still can point to the geographical border between the United States and Mexico with greater confidence than we can point to any sharp division between the past, present, and future. The nebulous divisions between past, present, and future, and their political consequences largely have been overlooked by contemporary political thought. According to Peter Laslett and James Fishkin, coeditors of *Justice between Age Groups and Generations*, contemporary political theory has, on the whole, "taken place within the grossly simplifying assumptions of a largely timeless world." This observation provides an excellent starting point for an overview of contemporary political thought. Laslett and Fishkin go on to write that the world within which political theory now operates is "limited, at most, to the horizons of a single generation who make binding choices, for all time, for all successor generations."[2] Although contemporary political theorists may have constructed theories of justice oblivious to the temporal dimension of politics, as the last two chapters have demonstrated, demands for justice reaching across time have become increasingly common in the political world. This chapter focuses on the temporal dimension of politics, most particularly on the relation between present and past, and its connection to concepts of political membership, as they effect the question of whether present-day members should be held responsible for the deeds of political ancestors.

Remembrance and the Construction of Political Unity

Membership is a perennial political issue, as all collectivities strive to create commonality out of difference and maintain unity in the midst of disintegrative forces. The root word, *member*, in its etymological connection to *re-member*, suggests intimate connections between belonging and re-call or re-collection. To re-member seems to presuppose an earlier *dis-membering*, and highlights the effort involved in memory and the ever-present possibility of forgetting. *Re-membering* may be defined, then, as bringing together anew that which has become dismembered, disunited, or forgotten.[3] The etymological connection between member and re-member suggests the possibility, or the very necessity, of the active recreation of a political collectivity's identity through time, and the essential role that re-membrance plays in the process.

If a political collectivity is to exist through time, then it must negotiate the relation between past, present, and future. Memory's role in creating and sustaining a sense of commonality and unity has long been recognized within the republican tradition of political theory. Thinkers such as Machiavelli, Burke, and de Tocqueville considered memory an essential element of political unity; the republic itself was pictured as a vessel of remembrance.[4] Typically, the contents of the vessel were recollections of the great deeds of the founders, regularly invoked before the members of the republic, known as *citizens* or *patriots*.[5] One's very identity as a patriot, as John Schaar explains, is defined by remembrance of and gratitude toward one's political predecessors:

> To be a patriot is to have a patrimony; or perhaps more accurately, the patriot is one who is grateful for a legacy and recognizes that the legacy makes him a debtor. There is a whole way of being in the world, captured best by the word reverence, which defines life by its debts: one is what one owes, what one acknowledges as a rightful debt or obligation. The patriot moves within that mentality. The gift of land, people, language, gods, memories, and customs, which is the patrimony of the patriot, defines what he or she is.[6]

Political thinkers beyond the republican tradition have also recognized that a common legacy may go a long way toward solving the dilemma of how to tie disparate individuals together and create commonality out of difference. Walter Lippmann wrote that traditions "are the public world to which our private worlds are joined. This continuum of public and private memories transcends all persons in their immediate and natural lives and it ties them all together. In it there is performed the mystery by which individuals are adopted and initiated into membership in the community."[7] It is, in some senses, a mystery by which individuals acquire political memories. Anne Norton notes, "Little of what we remember as a nation lives in our separate memories. Most of what we take for our history is foreign to our private memories and personal experiences. . . . In becoming citizens we acquire a form of being that extends beyond the limits of our separate bodies. Our private memories are supplemented by public and political histories. Insofar as we are citizens, we take those histories for common memory."[8] As the first two chapters have demonstrated, since the 1960s, the relationship between private memories and public and political histories has become increasingly problematic and "politicized." It has become ever more apparent that the process by which individuals are initiated into political membership may involve not only remembering certain things, but also forgetting, or repressing, others. What we should do about the less-proud moments of our collective past has become a pressing dilemma. A less consensual and more conflictual relationship between private memory and political membership is best suggested by Milan Kundera's memorable line, "The struggle of man against power is the struggle of memory against forgetting."[9] Contemporary American politics makes plain that remembering does not necessarily engender political unity. Much depends upon who is doing the remembering, what is being remembered, in which context, and against what forces.[10]

Although political theorists long have recognized the power of the past on contemporary imagination and emotions, the effect of a past tainted by wrongs and failings is a relatively novel concern in the history of political theory. What are we to do if public memory does not serve as a cohesive, but rather as a divisive, force? This question is particularly acute in diverse collectivities such as the United States, where individuals and groups have very different memories that provoke present political conflict. Part of the perplexity regarding the political meaning of private and public memory is that the past itself is elusive and must be captured metaphorically. Thomas Jefferson and Abraham Lincoln, central figures in American political theory and action, thought deeply about the relationship between memory and political membership, and offered alternative visions that continue to shape American political discourse. Their theories offer contrasting visions of the relationship between past and present and contrasting answers to the question of whether "the children" have a responsibility to make amends for the "sins of the parents."

American Alternatives

Typically, a collectivity negotiates its existence through time in an unspoken, if not relatively unconscious, manner. During moments of political crisis, however, issues formerly thought to be unproblematic become open to questioning. Certainly, in North America during the Revolution, the founding of the U.S. Constitution, and the Civil War, central questions regarding the nature and preservation of the American political collectivity were debated. Thomas Jefferson's and Abraham Lincoln's writings display their concern with the practical and theoretical dimensions of altering the prevailing relation between present and past and the effect of an alteration upon their visions of political membership. The two actors' different conceptions of the present's relation to the past establish an important backdrop for current debates about the present polity's responsibility for past wrongs.

Thomas Jefferson: The Birth and Maintenance of the New

In reading Jefferson, one is struck by his nearly lifelong preoccupation with the relation between past and present. In a 1789 letter to

James Madison written from Paris in the midst of the French Revolution, Jefferson wrote, "The question, whether one generation of men has a right to bind another . . . is a question of such consequences as not only to merit decision, but place also among the fundamental principles of every government."[11] Jefferson continued to reflect on the question of generational continuity, amending his calculations of the lifespan of a generation in letters written in 1813, 1816, and 1823.[12] Jefferson's private and public writings, ranging over issues such as the American Revolution, the establishment of political and legal institutions, and the institution of slavery, share a concern with the lasting power of institutions, habits, and thoughts. The shadows cast by the past posed dilemmas for Jefferson's political thinking. The manner in which Jefferson resolved those dilemmas has marked much current American political thinking on the relation between past and present.

Certainly, those participating in a revolution that intended to overthrow the institutions, laws, and customs of the British monarchy would be attentive to the binding force of the past. Jay Fliegelman has shown that in revolutionary America, the predominant metaphor used to express the relation between Great Britain and America was the familial one: Great Britain was the parent and America the child.[13] Fliegelman's point is evident in a pamphlet urging revolution in which Tom Paine writes, "To know whether it be the interest of the continent to be independent, we need only ask this easy, simple question: Is it the interest of a man to be a boy all his life?"[14]

King George III posed a threat to the autonomy of revolutionary men by preventing them from growing up and assuming unchallenged responsibility for their world. The King, in the eyes of the revolutionaries, refused to recognize that the colonists had matured and were prepared to be autonomous. Similarly, parents, by their simple presence, deny that children are completely independent. And, even in death, the memory of parents may remain an obstacle to the autonomy of children. A character in an unfinished Nathaniel Hawthorne story expresses this frustration: Because "the sire would live forever . . . the heir [would] never come to his inheritance, and so he would at once hate his own father, from the perception that he would never be out of his way."[15] The relation between parent and child also reveals that individuals neither choose nor create the particular time, place, and circumstances of their birth. The world simply is not of our making. Yet the American revolutionaries seemed fervently to believe, or to wish, that the world could be reborn in America. One of the American Revolution's more memorable declarations holds that, "We have it in our power to begin the world over again."[16] The metaphors of birth and death play principal roles in the political writings of American revolutionaries, especially Jefferson and Paine. Jefferson's political thinking starts from the proposition that "the earth belongs in usufruct to the living," and "that the dead have neither powers nor rights over it."[17] Birth grants one the right to face the world as if it were new; this principle demands that once dead, the deceased must depart without leaving a trace.

The recurring metaphor of natality in Jefferson's and Paine's political writings expresses a confluence they perceived between an individual's birth and the birth of the World: "Every child born into the world must be considered as deriving its existence from God. The world is as new to him as it was to the first man that existed, and his natural right in it is of the same kind."[18] Each individual birth recreates the potential of the World. Birth places individuals on the stage of life, and any debris left by past characters impedes their right to make themselves and the world what they choose.

Two fundamental terms of American political discourse—*freedom* and *equality*—were honed in the revolutionary context in which the past was experienced as an obstacle to autonomy. Paine declared that, "Every age and generation must be as free to act for itself in all cases as the age and generations which preceded it."[19] Political equality was a relationship not only among contemporaries (at the time, defined only as white male property owners) but also among generations. Both freedom and equality were determined by a need to alienate one's self from the past. Jefferson and Paine had little patience with the historical circumstances into which people were born: In their concern with individual autonomy, the past was perceived as a continual threat to the autonomy of the present.

These thoughts on the autonomy of the individual and the dangers posed by the past grew into the distinctive American ideology of the self-made man that fully flowered in the nineteenth century. Judith Shklar, in her examination of the American concept of citizenship, argues that the ideal of the self-made man epitomizes the democratic American:

> Nothing was more democratic than the ideal of the self-made man—not necessarily the man who builds a fortune by hard work only, but more expansively the model of a perfect human character, of what was called "Young America." This truly new man, whom Emerson idolized, is a youth who has no fixed place in society, nothing inherited, who does not stick to a single role in life and who rejects all efforts to restrict and bind him to a place and status. He is self-reliant because he is socially unfettered, immensely self-created, and the master of many skills.[20]

One can only believe oneself to be self-made by denying the significance of one's parents and of the circumstances and events into which one was born and from which one becomes who they are.[21] In other words, to sustain the belief in being self-made, one must deny the power of the past both consciously and unconsciously. This denial does not necessarily leave one autonomous, though. Rather, it may simply leave one hypothetically free to choose other parents.[22]

To the earlier fiction of "the New World," Jefferson and other revolutionaries added this fiction of the self-made man. To sustain the twin fictions of America as the New World and the English colonists as self-made, Jefferson and other revolutionary and postrevolutionary Americans looked to recreate the original emigration across the Atlantic by moving west across the continent. The West sustained the fiction that the past could be left behind. As Frederick Jackson Turner wrote, "Each frontier did indeed furnish a new field of opportunity, a gate of escape from the bondage of the past."[23] The continual westward movement, fueled by

Jefferson's lifelong efforts to encourage the exploration of the trans-Mississippi area and his Louisiana Purchase, served as a constant reminder of the movement from the Old World to the New, and from past to present.[24] The movement west also may have inspired the desire to forget the carnage of the near extermination of American Indians left in its wake. Forgetting the past, then, may not only have held out the possibility of freeing Americans from their English parents, but also from guilty deeds.[25]

Space and time were very much linked in the minds of Jefferson and his peers. The transatlantic crossing and the continual westward movement suggested that the past could be left behind. Yet, Jefferson's writings also suggest the realization that physical movement could not completely erase reminders of the past. Jefferson, in his initial draft of the Declaration of Independence, urged his readers to jettison memories of affectionate relations between Britain and America. Jefferson hoped to convince the colonists that British insults "have given the last stab to agonizing affection. . . . We must endeavor to forget our former love for them."[26] The past, in the form of memories, was also within us, thus physical movement alone was inadequate to the task of transcending the past's presence.

The persistence and elusiveness of memories partially explain why space alone was inadequate to safeguard against the potential tyranny of the past. As long as the past remained elusive, it could not be guarded against. Jefferson, an exemplary Enlightenment thinker, sought to define scientifically the parameters of the past and present. If he could precisely locate the past, then he could protect the present from it. If, however, the past intermingled with the present, then it would be impossible to ensure the "sovereignty of the present generation," as Daniel Boorstin labeled Jefferson's ethic.[27] In his 1789 letter to Madison, Jefferson puts his mind to setting clear boundaries between the past and present. Reasoning from his first principle, which he supposes "to be self-evident, that the earth belongs in usufruct to the living; that the dead have neither powers nor rights over it," Jefferson goes on to consider the political ramifications of his principle.[28] For Jefferson, applying a principle true for individuals to a political society at large entails no great complexity, "since the rights of the whole can be no more than the sum of the rights of individuals."[29] Jefferson here displays his liberal stripes, conceiving of a collectivity as a simple amalgam of individuals, without an identity or existence of its own. In this view, to apply a principle true for individuals to a collectivity merely requires addition.[30] Yet, as Jefferson acknowledges, reasoning about the ramifications of life and death, present and past, for a collectivity is more complicated than it is for an individual, for collectivities do not live and die in unison. To contend with this complexity, Jefferson supposes "a whole generation of men to be born on the same day, to attain mature age on the same day, and to die on the same day, leaving a succeeding generation in the moment of attaining their mature age, all together."[31] Employing this fiction allows Jefferson to think from the supposition that "each successive generation would . . . come and go off the stage at a fixed moment, as individuals do now."[32] Jefferson, having consulted mortality tables and discovering that a person's average lifespan was fifty-five years, and asserting that individuals reach political maturity at twenty-one years, concludes that each generation has thirty-four years of sovereignty.[33] To ensure that each generation receives the world "clear of the debts and incumbrances [sic]," Jefferson suggests to Madison that he propose a preamble to the first law for appropriating the public revenue in the United States, establishing that the public can only engage debts within thirty-four years of the date of engagement. Likening the public debt to constitutions and laws, all simple expressions of the will of the present generation, Jefferson also argues, "Every constitution . . . and every law naturally expires at the end of thirty-four years."[34]

For Jefferson, the present generation could be analogized to a spatial entity with clear boundaries that should be respected by others. The others are past generations, who, to follow the analogy, may be likened to foreign countries. Writing at roughly the same time as Edmund Burke, Jefferson's understanding of the relationship between past, present, and future stands in sharp contrast to

Burke's famous passage that "Society is . . . a partnership not only between those who are living, but between those who are living, those who are dead, and those who are to be born."[35] Eschewing an organic understanding of the unity of the collectivity, either in the present or through time, Jefferson's vision of the political collectivity mirrored his depiction of the autonomous individuals who comprised it. Individuals were self-made, and the collectivities they created were their own creations. As noted earlier, freedom and equality were possible only if one were born into the same circumstances as the very first generation. The past, then, to merge the two categories around which Jefferson organizes his thinking about time, natality and space, should be considered dead and left behind. When the past persists (through institutions, habits or memories), and is not left behind, the present is neither free nor equal to prior generations.

Jefferson and his peers who participated in the American Revolution, however, were not only sons rebelling against patriarchal authority, but parents, both personally and politically, themselves. After the Revolution, those who had championed the eradication of everything old had to turn their attention to the creation of new political and legal institutions. Hyperconscious that they were leaving a legacy, they struggled with the paradox of establishing lasting institutions for a revolutionary government. How could the revolutionary generation reject the past, reject traditions and the need for them, and at the same time, construct lasting institutions? Jefferson came back time and time again to ponder this question.[36] Jefferson's repeated attempts to resolve this dilemma signals the importance he assigned to it, as well as the larger question of how to maintain the autonomy of the present amidst the remains of the past.[37] Nowhere is this struggle more apparent than in Jefferson's troubled and troubling responses to the institution of slavery.

Jefferson's writings on slavery display an acute understanding of how human institutions grow and flourish. In *Notes on the State of Virginia*, written in 1781, he describes how slave ownership is passed on from parent to child:

> There must doubtless be an unhappy influence on the manners of our people produced by the existence of slavery among us. The whole commerce between master and slave is a perpetual exercise of the most boisterous passions, the most unremitting despotism on the one part, and degrading submissions on the other. Our children see this, and learn to imitate it; for man is an imitative animal. This quality is the germ of all education in him. From his cradle to his grave he is learning to do what he sees others do. . . . The parent storms, the child looks on, catches the lineaments of wrath, puts on the same airs in the circle of smaller slaves, gives loose to his worst of passions, and thus nursed, educated, and daily exercised in tyranny, cannot but be stamped by it with odious peculiarities.[38]

Jefferson had hoped to unearth this "odious" institution, and early in his political career he took steps in the direction of emancipation. As a member of the Virginia House of Burgesses, he supported an effort at emancipation. In his working draft of the Declaration of Independence, Jefferson condemned George III for waging "cruel war against human nature itself, violating its most sacred rights of life and liberty in the persons of a distant people who never offended him."[39] Jefferson clearly criticizes slavery in *Notes on the State of Virginia*, although he delayed publishing the work (and initially published it anonymously), evidently fearing the consequences of his stated objections to the "great political and moral evil."[40] In letters to friends and acquaintances written throughout his life, Jefferson proclaims himself a proponent of emancipation. In 1788 he wrote to Brissot de Warville, "You know that nobody wishes more ardently to see an abolition not only of the [African slave] trade but of the condition of slavery: and certainly nobody will be more willing to encounter every sacrifice for that object."[41] In 1820, Jefferson still proclaimed "that there is not a man on earth who would sacrifice more than I would to relieve us from this heavy reproach, in any practicable way."[42]

Yet, as is well known and roundly criticized, Jefferson could not see his way to publicly championing emancipation, nor even taking the necessary steps to emancipate the slaves he owned; throughout his life his slave holdings actually grew (by 1822 Jefferson owned 267 slaves).[43] Jefferson portrayed himself, as he did others in his position of slave master, as paralyzed: "We have the wolf by the ears, and we can neither hold him, nor safely let him go. Justice is in one scale, and self-preservation in the other."[44] Reports of slave uprisings inspired Jefferson to make dire predictions. In a 1797 letter to a fellow critic of slavery, William and Mary College Professor St. George Tucker, Jefferson fearfully exclaims, "If something is not done, and soon done, we shall be the murderers of our own children."[45] For the ardent believer in each generation's right to create the world anew, what could induce more guilt and misery than the prospect of passing along an institution that would cause the death of one's children? Yet the self-interest of the fathers yielded neither to justice, nor to the possibility of infanticide.

Jefferson's paralysis and inability to construct a "practicable way" to emancipate his slaves was based upon his conviction that emancipation had to be accompanied by deportation. In *Notes on the State of Virginia*, Jefferson poses the question, "Why not retain and incorporate the blacks into the State?" Jefferson's reply to his own query is fascinating: "Deep-rooted prejudices entertained by the whites; ten thousand recollections, by the blacks, of the injuries they have sustained; new provocations; the real distinctions which nature has made; and many other circumstances, will divide us into parties, and produce convulsions, which will probably never end but in the extermination of the one or the other race."[46] If emancipated ex-slaves were to remain within the State, the haunting presence of the past made race war inevitable. Deep-rooted prejudices among the whites, analyzed earlier by Jefferson to be the result of the young imitating the old, and the ex-slaves' memories of the injuries they sustained at the hands and whips of the whites, would erase any chance for peaceful coexistence between the races.

In characteristic fashion, Jefferson turned to space to solve the problems of time. If prejudices lingered, and memories refused to respect the careful boundaries that Jefferson drew between the past and present, then the logical answer for Jefferson was to look to spatial distance to compensate for the anarchic nature of time. Surely, Jefferson's writings exhibit fears of miscegenation that contributed to his calls for black colonization not only to the margins of the country, but off the continent completely.[47] In *Notes on the State of Virginia*, Jefferson wrote that the slave, "when freed . . . is to be removed beyond the reach of mixture."[48] Anywhere on the American continent was too close for Jefferson's comfort; he suggested colonization to the West Indies and later supported a proposal for African colonization which would result in "drawing off this part of our population, most advantageously for themselves as well as for us."[49] Removing blacks from the American continent would protect the alleged purity of the white race. It would also solve the nation's race problem, a problem that had buried itself in the minds and hearts of both blacks and whites, by putting distance between those whose memories would inevitably lead to bloody conflict. Where forgetting was impossible, space remained the only response.

Abraham Lincoln: The Death of the Nation over Time

Whereas Jefferson sought to resolve the dilemmas time poses for a political body through a careful delineation of past and present, Lincoln proceeded from a markedly different understanding of the dilemmas and posited very different avenues of resolution. Surely, there are moments in Lincoln's writings when one can detect the resonance of Jefferson's fears that the past would suffocate the present. But on the whole, Lincoln is much more concerned by the gradual evisceration of the past than he is by its presence. Lincoln's thinking on time and politics, like Jefferson's, is organized around the metaphors of birth and death. Contrary to Jefferson's emphasis on natality, however, Lincoln's writings display a near obsession with personal mortality and with the demise of nations. For Lincoln, death defines the personal and political meaning of life: how to wrest remembrance and redemption from the near inevitability of oblivion.

Remembrance, for Lincoln, rather than posing a threat to either the freedom or equality of the present generation, ensures the preservation of the Union, and through it, the freedom and equality of its members.[50] In one of Lincoln's earliest speeches, given in 1837, the much (psycho-) analyzed "Address to the Young Men's Lyceum of Springfield, Illinois," Lincoln takes as his subject the perpetuation of our political institutions. Much of the speech is an impassioned defense of the rule of law, delivered amidst increasing incidents of mob violence directed against gamblers, blacks, and abolitionists. In addition to the threat posed by mob rule, Lincoln acutely analyzes the dangers posed to the Union by individuals of "towering genius" who see "no distinction in adding story to story, upon the monuments of fame, erected to the memory of others." Whether Lincoln is warning the Union about someone like himself, or projecting his self-censored fantasies upon others, he keenly describes the feelings of ambitious individuals who live in the shadows of their predecessors.[51] These people, warns Lincoln, scorn "to tread in the footsteps of any predecessor, however illustrious." The nation, already founded, can offer no distinction to the ambitious "in the way of building up . . . [so] he would set boldly to the task of pulling down."[52]

In these passages, Lincoln attempts to reconcile the aspiring to the historical situation into which they are born. Unable to choose the moment or place in which one enters the world, one's life is necessarily influenced by the deeds of predecessors. In Lincoln's eyes, his predecessors have succeeded in their battle with time: Their success in demonstrating "the capability of a people to govern themselves" has resulted in their being immortalized. "Their names have been transferred to counties and cities, and rivers and mountains."[53] They have cheated the oblivion that usually accompanies death—"They have won their deathless names" in making the democratic experiment successful. However, their victory has made the attempts of future generations to wrest a similar victory nearly impossible: "This field of glory is harvested, and the crop is already appropriated."[54]

Although the founding fathers had monopolized the fame connected to winning the American Revolution and erecting the political institutions of the nation, Lincoln suggests that the content of the stories, the specifics of the scenes of the revolution, will fade from the minds of citizens. Time is a relentless foe in Lincoln's political imagination—death overtakes all, and in its path, sweeps away the living history through which the nation learns of its past glories and its identity. In the Young Men's Lyceum speech, Lincoln likens time to "silent artillery" that levels the walls of history and to "an all-resistless hurricane" that sweeps over the forest of history.[55] The living history that Lincoln sees receding from view is written on the bodies of male citizens, of husbands, fathers, sons and brothers—"the limbs mangled, in the scars of wounds received."[56]

The political institutions of the nation were created out of sacrifice, and, as those who made the sacrifices faded into the past, Lincoln feared that other pillars to uphold "the temple of liberty" would not be hewn to take their place. Needed, above all, is, "a reverence for the constitution and laws." Reverence is instilled primarily by associating the law with the sacrifices of the fathers—"Let every man remember that to violate the law is to trample on the blood of his father."[57] But why is such reverence needed? It is required to engender further blood sacrifice: "Let the old and the young, the rich and the poor, the grave and the gay, of all sexes and tongues, and colors and conditions, sacrifice unceasingly upon its [law's] altars."[58] For Lincoln, political and legal institutions are born in violence, and the violence should shine through the bloodless veneer of the law, reminding citizens of the sacrificial acts performed to create the institutions and instilling in citizens a readiness to sacrifice similarly.[59] Twenty-three years after addressing The Young Men's Lyceum Club, Lincoln, would, of course, preside over the war that extracted the greatest outpouring of blood sacrifice in our history.

Lincoln invokes the memory of Washington in his final appeal for reverence for the Constitution and laws in the 1837 Young

Men's Lyceum Speech. He begs that it may be said of his generation "that during his [Washington's] long sleep, we permitted no
hostile foot to pass over or desecrate his resting place."[60] Invoking
the name of Washington to bind citizens to the law and the Union
became an increasingly common strategy in the United States as
sectional rivalries threatened to tear the Union apart. The belief, or
the hope, was that "despite the bitter dissensions of the day . . . this
one great sentiment—veneration for the name of Washington—is
planted down in the very depths of the American heart." All
Americans were alike in this respect, and even though citizens
may "have their sectional loves and hatreds . . . before the dear
name of Washington, they are absorbed and forgotten."[61] Sharing
in the memory of Washington would allow a unity to emerge
that would precipitate forgetting sectional interests and identities.

When Lincoln assumed the presidency on March 4, 1861 with
the nation on the brink of disunity, the theme of common memories reuniting diverse interests and groups was familiar both to
him and the nation. Rarely, however, had the concept's practical
application been so severely tested. Lincoln's First Inaugural Address now reads like a rhetorical attempt to forestall the inevitable.
Lincoln attempts to reassure the Southern States that the federal
government would not start a civil war, while simultaneously asserting that secession is illegal, and that he was sworn by a solemn
oath to uphold the federal law throughout the Union. The speech
reads as if Lincoln vainly hopes that his words alone would cast
a spell holding the Union together. He opens the last paragraph
with the revealing utterance, "I am loathe to close," as if he knows
that the ritual of the inaugural is only temporarily forestalling
the dismembering of the Union. He closes with a final appeal to
affection and memory:

> We are not enemies, but friends. We must not be enemies. Though
> passion may have strained, it must not break our bonds of affection.
> The mystic chords of memory, stretching from every battlefield
> and patriot grave to every living heart and hearthstone all over
> this broad land, will yet swell the chorus of the Union when again
> touched, as surely they will be, by the better angels of our nature.[62]

Memory, as Lincoln describes it above, is mystical, binding, and yet passive. It is mystical in that it transcends the boundary between life and death, "stretching from every battlefield, and patriot grave, to every living heart and hearthstone." It is binding in that it links the dead to the living, and "every living heart . . . all over this broad land," together, as friends, and as citizens of the Union. Yet, the chords of memory lie silent if not "touched by the better angels of our nature." As a string on a musical instrument, memory must be played if it is to be heard.[63] Lincoln remains certain that the chorus of the Union will be heard again, but he also fears the chorus may be drowned out by the cacophony of sectional hatreds and conflicting interests.

If the chorus of the Union results from the better angels of our nature touching the mystic chords of memory, then the Union is a fragile, yet ever-present, possibility. Our natures may be corrupted by passions and interests; however memory, a repository of common sacrifices, remains to remind us of the meaning of our membership in the Union. During the Civil War, Lincoln defined the meaning of the Union, and membership in it, prompted by the need to legitimate the sacrifice of hundreds of thousands of lives.[64]

In the First Inaugural, Lincoln underscores the perpetuity of the Union, and following from it, the illegality of secession. Lincoln reaches back before the Constitution to date the creation of the Union, stating that it was formed by the Articles of Association in 1774, matured and continued by the Declaration of Independence in 1776, and further developed by the Articles of Confederation in 1778. Finally, in 1787, the Constitution was established "to form a more perfect Union." Two years later at Gettysburg, Lincoln would amend his dating of the birth of the Union; it was "four score and seven years ago" that "our fathers brought forth . . . a new nation," rather than four score and nine years. Seventeen seventy-six became the founding moment of the nation as Lincoln redrew the temporal boundaries of the Union, and redefined membership in it.[65] Lincoln's famous, succinct opening paragraph of the Gettysburg Address—"Four score and seven years ago our fathers brought forth on this continent, a new nation, conceived in Liberty and dedicated to the proposition that all men are created equal"—defines the Union by situating it in time and place and stating its core principle. Lincoln defines the Union as a glorious experiment, a test of whether a nation whose central meaning is a belief in equality "can long endure." To be a member of the Union, then, is not only to live within its temporal and spatial borders, but also to share a belief in the proposition that "all men are created equal." The proposition binds the members together, and legitimates their blood sacrifice. Lincoln began to apply the proposition to slaves in Confederate-held territory in the Emancipation Proclamation of January 1, 1863.

It seems fitting that a cemetery should be the site of Lincoln's most memorable speech, the Gettysburg Address. The meaning of death, and the possibility of wresting redemption from it, preoccupied Lincoln throughout his life. At Gettysburg, where the North and the South had left fifty thousand dead, wounded, or missing behind in a battle whose strategic senselessness prompted both Generals Meade and Lee to offer their resignations to their respective leaders, Lincoln attempted to endow the seemingly meaningless slaughter with historical significance[66]—contrary, of course, to Lincoln's statement that "The world will little note nor long remember what we say here, but it can never forget what they did here." To signify the meaning of the multitude of deaths, Lincoln places them in historical context, situating them between the birth of the nation in 1776 and the posterity of the nation. The speech moves the listeners through time, from the past (four score and seven years ago) to the present (now we are engaged in a great civil war) to the future (that this nation, under God, shall have a new birth of freedom).[67] The dead at Gettysburg join those who gave their lives in the Revolution, and they will be joined by others in the future, for the "work" for which the dead gave their "last full measure of devotion" is unfinished, and will require further sacrifice.

While redrawing the temporal boundaries of the Union to place Jefferson's Declaration at its center, Lincoln simultaneously repudiates the Jeffersonian principle that the dead shall not rule over the living. Standing in an enormous graveyard, Lincoln appeals to the authority of the dead to ask for continued sacrifice: "[T]hat from these honored dead we take increased devotion to that cause for which they gave the last full measure of devotion."[68] The cause of the sacrifice, and the justification of it, is the perpetuation of the Union. As Lincoln defines it, the Union's mission is stated in the proposition that "all men are created equal." Nine months later, in August 1864, in an address to the soldiers of an Ohio regiment, Lincoln explained once again why the war had to continue:

> It is in order that each one of you may have, through this free government which we have enjoyed, an open field and a fair chance for your industry, enterprise, and intelligence; that you may all have equal privileges in the race of life, with all its desirable human aspirations. It is for this the struggle should be maintained, that we may not lose our birthright—not only for one, but for two or three years. The nation is worth fighting for, to secure such an inestimable jewel.[69]

For Lincoln, membership in the Union is a birthright, an inheritance that one receives from the past, and that one is indebted to pass on to the future. In contrast to Jefferson, who feared that the past threatened the equality and freedom of the present, and therefore was to be rejected, for Lincoln, the past bequeathed to the present the right that "all have equal privileges in the race of life," and thus it was essential to American citizenship.

Lincoln's understanding of political membership as a birthright dates back at least as early as 1837; in the opening paragraph of his address to the Young Men's Lyceum he tells his listeners that "when mounting the stage of existence [we] found ourselves the legal inheritors" of the fundamental blessings of liberty and equal rights. In the language of legacy and birthright, we can detect the inherent connections between Lincoln's search for meaning in death, and one's identity at birth. If death is to be endowed with meaning, then as Lincoln reminds his listeners at Gettysburg, it is incumbent upon the living to ensure that the dead are remembered, and their legacy transmitted to posterity. For Lincoln, one is born and dies in time, and the meaning of one's birth and death can only be understood in time. Jefferson's understanding of birth as starting the world anew and receiving the world "clear of debts and incumbrances" would be unbearable for Lincoln. Such a birth would be meaningless, for the meaning of one's life, and death, can only be found within the historical narrative into which one is born, and that one leaves behind.

Lincoln drew on the concept of inheritance to think through the political dilemmas of negotiating the relation between past, present, and future both before and during the Civil War.[70] The very occurrence of the war, however, exhibits some of the difficulties of using the concept of inheritance as a means of reconciling past and present. As the name of the war implies, at least at one level, the Civil War was a fratricidal battle waged over the patrimony of Washington. Both North and South claimed they were the true heirs of Washington. Their common adulation for the memory of Washington, however, could not veil the present economic, political, and ideological differences that separated them. Nor could the North and South agree on the precise content of the inheritance they received from Washington and the founders, for the legacy, as any historical legacy, was open to differing interpretations.

How did Lincoln understand the war? Through the war years, Lincoln explained the inevitability of the war in religious as well as historical terms. The Civil War not only was a test of whether a nation dedicated to equality could long endure (as he stated in the opening of the Gettysburg Address), but also revealed God's supreme power in the affairs of individuals and nations. Eight months prior to Gettysburg, Lincoln set aside a day for "national humiliation, fasting, and prayer," in the hope that "the united cry of the nation will be heard on high, and answered with blessings no less than the pardon of our national sins, and the restoration of our now divided and suffering country to its former happy condition of unity and peace."[71] What were the national sins for which the nation was now justly plunged into a Civil War? As Lincoln reveals, it was the old sin of pride:

> And insomuch as we know that by his divine law nations, like in-
> dividuals, are subjected to punishments and chastisements in this
> world, may we not justly fear that the awful calamity of civil war
> which now desolates the land may be but a punishment inflicted
> upon us for our presumptuous sins, to the needful end of our na-
> tional reformation as a whole people? We have been the recipients
> of the choicest bounties of Heaven. We have been preserved, these
> many years, in peace and prosperity. We have grown in numbers,
> wealth, and power as no other nation has ever grown; but we have
> forgotten God. We have forgotten the gracious hand which pre-
> served us in peace, and multiplied and enriched and strengthened
> us; and we have vainly imagined, in the deceitfulness of our hearts,
> that all these blessings were produced by some superior wisdom
> and virtue of our own. Intoxicated with unbroken success, we have
> become too self-sufficient to feel the necessity of redeeming and
> preserving grace, too proud to pray to the God that made us.[72]

In the midst of the war that threatened to divide the nation
forever, Lincoln continued to speak for the whole nation, and to
emphasize what was common to both the North and the South.
Both sides were suffering through the awful calamity of the war,
and both deserved this fate for they shared in the national sin of
pride.

Two years later, in 1865 as Lincoln addressed the nation in
the Second Inaugural, with the war about to end, Lincoln once
again interpreted the war as God's just punishment for national
sins. The sin, however, was no longer pride, but slavery. In the
Gettysburg Address, Lincoln redefined the meaning of the Union;
in the Second Inaugural he redefined the meaning of the war that
threatened the Union.[73] The war, Lincoln stated for the first time,
was caused by slavery: "All know that this interest was, somehow, the cause of the war."[74] If slavery was the cause of the war,
what conclusions follow? Does it follow that those who would
"strengthen, perpetuate, and extend this interest" caused the war?
Does it follow that the North's imminent victory reveals God's
judgment that the South was sinful and the North righteous? And
does it follow that slavery was the sin of the South, and not of the

nation, and thus the nation need not answer for it? What would such conclusions suggest for the future of the post-war nation?

Lincoln's delicate, sometimes uncertain, and somewhat contradictory treatment of these questions lies at the heart of the Second Inaugural. Lincoln traces the events leading up to the war, but rather than blaming the South for attempting to dissolve the Union, Lincoln simply states: "Both parties deprecated war; but one of them would make war rather than let the nation survive; and the other would accept war rather than let it perish. And the war came."[75] Seemingly an act of nature, beyond the control of human agency, the war came, as a storm comes. But what of the institution of slavery? Could it be said of slavery that it too was beyond the control of human agency? Here, Lincoln acknowledges human agency, circumspectly strips divine sanction from slavery, but then ultimately backs away and refrains from human judgment: "It may seem strange that any man should dare to ask a just god's assistance in wringing their bread from the sweat of other men's faces; but let us judge not, that we be not judged."[76] It must be remembered that Lincoln's political purpose in the speech is "to do all which may achieve and cherish a just and lasting peace among ourselves." Lincoln suggests that if one side claims the ability or the right to judge the other, then the future unity of the nation will be imperiled.

Yet, as Anne Norton argues, the Second Inaugural is "a speech of judgment."[77] The paragraph following Lincoln's admonishment "let us judge not, that we be not judged," the penultimate paragraph of the address reads as follows:

> The Almighty has his own purposes. "Woe unto the world because of offenses! for it must needs be that offenses come; but woe to that man by whom the offense cometh." If we shall suppose that American Slavery is one of those offenses which, in the providence of God, must needs come, but which, having continued through His appointed time, He now wills to remove, and that He gives to both North and South, this terrible war, as the woe due to those by whom the offense came, shall we discern therein any departure from those divine attributes which the believers in a Living God always ascribe to Him? Fondly do we hope—fervently

do we pray—that this mighty scourge of war may speedily pass away. Yet, if God wills that it continue, until all the wealth piled by the bond-man's two hundred and fifty years of unrequited toil shall be sunk, and until every drop of blood drawn with the lash, shall be paid by another drawn with the sword, as was said three thousand years ago, so still it must be said, "the judgments of the Lord are true and righteous altogether."[78]

The paragraph exudes judgment, yet the judgment is not meant to further divide the nation, but to unite it. First, Lincoln asserts the role of God in human affairs. Earlier in the speech, Lincoln has established God and the Bible as commonalities between the two sides: "Both read the same Bible, and pray to the same God." Lincoln quotes verbatim from Matthew 18:7 and trusts that both sides will understand the meaning of the passage: God's punishment is strict. In the next lengthy sentence Lincoln reinterprets the meaning of the Civil War. He does so in the form of a question, challenging his listeners to find fault with his supposition that the Civil War is God's rightful punishment meted out for the offense of slavery. The South, though, is not alone responsible for slavery. Lincoln makes the point twice in this sentence so as not to be misunderstood, prefixing American to slavery and explaining the war as God's just punishment to both the North and the South.[79] Having joined the nation in wrongdoing, Lincoln then posits a "We," hoping and praying for the war's end, united in their reliance on God's will. Lincoln concludes the paragraph in an assertive voice. Rather than asking his listeners whether they would question God's divine justice if the war continued, Lincoln describes the precision of the justice being exacted for the unrequited toil and the drops of blood drawn with the lash. Quoting from Psalms, Lincoln joins his authority to that of God and the Bible: "So still it must be said, the judgments of the Lord are true and righteous altogether." Whereas the course of history ultimately is in God's hands, humans are still rightly held responsible for history, and Lincoln claims his authority to interpret the will of God.[80] Yet, in the final famous paragraph of the speech, Lincoln retreats from an omniscient stance with respect to God's will: We are to proceed "with firmness in the right, as God gives us to see the right."[81] The Second Inaugural exemplifies the knottiness entailed in uniting the nation when it has been separated by a Civil War, and when the past is seen through vastly different lenses. Lincoln's speech attempts to establish an authoritative interpretation of the nation's history that does not further divide the nation, but unites it.

Lincoln's understanding of the nation's present responsibilities for the "bond-man's two hundred and fifty years of unrequited toil" and the blood "drawn with the lash" contrasts markedly with Jefferson's perspective of the right of each generation to be freed from the past, as well as the injunction that the sins of the parents shall not be visited on the children. Lincoln could cite numerous verses in the Bible supporting his reading that obligations are passed down from one generation to the next.[82] The central point here, however, is not that Lincoln's is the better interpretation of the Bible, but rather that invoking the past, just like invoking the Bible to support one's point, requires interpretation, upon which there can be no unanimity.[83] Lincoln, while invoking religious language and sources, did so in a political manner; his primary concern here was the worldly, rather than the after-worldly, consequences of his words. Within the political realm, conflict is not only or strictly of an interpretive nature. Lincoln's aim in the Second Inaugural was not to offer the most compelling interpretation of the Bible. He was voicing the most compelling interpretation of American history to perform the political function of uniting the nation over a divisive history—remembering the past to reunite the present and orient the nation toward the future in a united manner.

America's Fragmented Birthright

Contemporary calls for national apologies, with or without material compensation, and the heated debates within the United States provoked by these calls, demonstrate that the past can not unproblematically serve to unify a divided present. No longer is it

feasible, if it ever was, for the past to serve "as a screen on which desires for unity and continuity, that is, identity, [can] be projected."[84]
The past, refracted through the prism of the contemporary diversity of the United States, appears fragmented and divisive rather
than unifying. From the vantage point of present-day America,
every American victory in the past is also necessarily an American
defeat.[85] The landing of the Pilgrims continued the process by
which American Indians were dispossessed; the Alamo not only
symbolizes American true grit, but American imperialism and
racism triumphant over Mexico and Indians; and Pearl Harbor led
to the incarceration of American citizens of Japanese descent.[86]
How can contemporary Americans conceptualize their relationship to the past to unify a fragmented present?

Echoes of Jefferson and Lincoln may be heard as Americans
think through this question. Time, and particularly the past's relation to the present, posed theoretical and practical problems for
these two central American political thinkers. Jefferson organized
his thought regarding time using two primary categories, biology
and space. In the first mode of thinking, the past is dead, a burden
or dead weight the living must escape from if they are to be truly
free.[87] Jefferson's nightmarish vision was that the dead weight
would suffocate the present. Writing as a revolutionary, Jefferson
feared that the past would stand in the way of the present bringing to life new political creations. He resisted any suggestion that
those who lived prior had the authority to determine the nature
of the contemporary generation's political life or allegiances. And
Jefferson, writing as the slaveholder, haunted by the specter of slavery, feared that the memories of past wrongs, the "ten thousand
recollections, by the blacks, of the injuries they have sustained,"
would profoundly and destructively affect present politics. Hoping to protect the "innocence" of the future generation, Jefferson
vainly tried to wish away the stain of slavery. Thinking within
his second category, space, Jefferson likened the past to a foreign
country. In this analogy, the past and present generations of Americans occupy different nations, sharing neither the benefits nor the
burdens of a collective existence.

Lincoln conceives of time and the past markedly differently. Whereas Jefferson attempts to free the present from the grip of the past, Lincoln does not set the present in opposition to the past. Rather, he conceives that the present polity must find meaning within time by reflecting on what the nation has been, what it is currently, and what it should will itself to be in the future. Jefferson's and Lincoln's use of the word *birthright* highlights the major differences in their thinking. For Jefferson, birth (for white males, that is) grants one the same rights as all preceding generations; one's birthright is to approach the world as if it were new. From this perspective, each generation, just like each individual, should be conceived of as born innocent: The sins of the parents should not be visited upon the children. For Lincoln, on the other hand, an American birthright provides the privilege to inherit the freedom and equality established in the past, along with the responsibilities entailed by that legacy. Within Lincoln's understanding, birth places one in a moment in time tinged both with the possibility of redemption and the fear of apocalypse. Whereas Jefferson's birthright frees one from the past, Lincoln's bears meaning and gravity; all of history has led up to one's birth, and the future hinges on one's responsible action in the present.

In thinking through the present predicament of how Americans should respond to past political wrongs, the Jeffersonian emphasis on birth and innocence, achieved either through forgetting past conflicts or putting distance between those groups whose memories could lead to conflict, would seem to suggest that we turn away from the past and face the future almost as a blank slate. Jefferson, wary of memories of past offenses and drawn to the allure of forgetting, remained uncertain, however, of individuals' abilities to forget. Although Jefferson attempted to demarcate the boundaries between past and present, he still rested much of his hope for the continuing re-creation of a political society without inherited traditions and resentments on the availability of "virgin land" where individuals could move and free themselves from the past. Even when land was available, however, memories were not necessarily erased as people traveled west. And even if space were

a viable solution to the problem of memories and historical resentments, today we no longer have the luxury of inhabiting a
"New World." Jefferson's understanding of the relationship between past and present does capture the potential inventiveness
of each individual and each political generation. The present need
not replicate nor remain in the shadows of the past. However,
the Jeffersonian emphasis on birth, virginity, and innocence mini-
mizes the givenness of the world and the extent to which we are
the historical products of acts we did not choose. The personal and
political situations into which we are born comprise an essential
part of who we are. Denying the past's presence cannot will it away.
Jefferson's likening political collectivities to simple amalgams of
individuals also resounds in contemporary American responses to
calls for national apologies. For Jefferson, if individuals are born
innocent, then so too should each "political generation." Contemporary protestations of the innocence of the present fail to
consider that while individuals may be innocent, they may still, in
their identity as members of a political collectivity, be "burdened
by the sins of the fathers" just as they are "blessed with the deeds
of the ancestors."[88]

Lincoln's voice provides an important corrective to the
Jeffersonian attempt to escape the past by fixedly focusing solely on
the present and future. Lincoln not only acknowledged the past,
but also explicitly recognized its "sins." Lincoln's Second Inaugural is extraordinary in that by referring to "the bond-man's two
hundred and fifty years of unrequited toil" he places the nation's
"sins" at the center of its history rather than the great deeds of the
founders. Rather than relegating past political wrongs to the margins of the nation's history, or actively forgetting them, Lincoln
acknowledged the historical crime of slavery and rightly stressed
the national responsibilities stemming from the national offense.
Lincoln, like Jefferson, attempted to orient the nation toward the
future, but he did so while acknowledging that the historical situation into which we are born must be consciously recognized for
it imposes obligations upon us and limits our realm of choices.[89]
Although the past may restrict the choices open to the present

generation, it does not enslave the present. It is the present generation that chooses whether and how to continue or discontinue the traditions into which they are born. Hannah Arendt defines tradition, for instance, as that "which selects and names," emphasizing the selective and critical process entailed in creating and maintaining a tradition.[90] The past, as tradition, does not speak in one voice; it must be interpreted and judged. Nor, of course, does the past speak to one person alone. Lincoln surely was aware of the multivocal quality of the past, as well as the diverse sites from which the past was being remembered. The history of slavery and the Civil War obviously provoked conflicting memories for Northerners, Southerners, and ex-slaves. Lincoln could neither assume the presence of common memories nor a common present. Nor can we. By recognizing the conflicting meanings the past holds for diverse groups of citizens, Lincoln could also remember the commonalities that tie Americans together as well as respond to the differences that divide them. That is our task as well as we confront the thorny issue of what responsibilities present-day Americans have for past political wrongs.

4

The Political Responsibilities
of Citizens

THE PRECEDING chapters have shown that, contrary to
most accounts of the relation between memory and politics, memories may divide as well as unite members of political collectivities.
Further, Chapter 3 suggests that it may be both just and politically
pragmatic for the American political body to respond to the memories that drive members apart. We now turn to explore in greater
depth the obstacles to a political response to the past wrongs that
underlie divisive memories. The chapter examines the concept of
political responsibility for past political wrongs and the primary
arguments raised in the United States against such responsibility.
This chapter's argument is premised on the belief that politics
unmoored from responsibility is dangerous if not incoherent. In
the chapter, I begin to sketch a vision of politics that accepts the
present polity's responsibility to address the burdens of the past.

Sins of the Parents is concerned with the concepts we use to understand our political life and the way that conceptual understanding defines the political questions we ask. I have noted throughout
that within the United States, theological, therapeutic, and juridical frameworks have shaped our understanding of the political
world. This chapter, in examining the obstacles to recognizing
political responsibility for past wrongs, contends that arguments

against responding to past political wrongs have been shaped by the theological language of sin and innocence, the juridical meanings of guilt and innocence, and a liberal conception of the relationship between the individual and the political collectivity. In advocating a concept of political responsibility, I examine three arguments frequently leveled against assuming that responsibility. The first is that political responsibility is intrinsically connected to guilt; many of the criticisms leveled against claims based upon past wrongs question the existence of a *political* form of responsibility, as distinct from a *moral* or *legal* responsibility.

A second, and related argument raised in the debates concerning past treatment of American Indians and Japanese Americans, is that all responsibilities should be based upon individual action—a view reflecting both the religious doctrine of individual sin,[1] and the legal doctrine that responsibility for wrongdoing flows only from individual guilt. In this view, the only responsibilities that attach to members of a political collectivity are those arising either from deeds they have done themselves or from deeds to which they have explicitly consented. While this argument accepts the existence of political responsibilities, it regards as legitimate only those to which individuals have consented. Consent, however, typically drains the political collective of its energy to engage in collective pursuits of many sorts; when members are asked to acknowledge past wrongs and possibly sacrifice to redress misdeeds, they have even less incentive to take on the identity as a member of that political collectivity and assume the responsibilities that may flow from it.[2]

A third argument raised against acknowledging political responsibility for past wrongs recognizes the desirability of nurturing a sense of political identity amongst individuals in a collectivity. Yet, this argument contends that the sorts of claims raised by American Indians, Japanese Americans, and African Americans impair precisely the sort of attachment or identification required to cultivate such an identity. This third argument further suggests that when presented by claims based on historical wrongs, many Americans will seek refuge in their membership in other groups (racial and ethnic, primarily, but not exclusively) to proclaim their innocence and disclaim responsibility. In arguing for political responsibility for past wrongs, then, three assumptions must be laid to rest: the first, that political responsibility is synonymous with collective guilt; the second, that responsibility attaches only to individual wrongdoing; and the third, that recognizing past political wrongs necessarily obstructs individuals' acknowledging their identities as members of a political collectivity that exists over time. Examining these criticisms also requires some explanation of the kind of identification between individuals and the political collective that is necessary for accepting political responsibility for past wrongs. Ultimately, the chapter aims to explain why present-day Americans, who, for the most part are not directly implicated in the wrongs perpetrated against American Indians, African Americans, and Japanese Americans, for instance, should however accept political responsibility for them.

The Meaning of Responsibility

Responsibility, as its etymology suggests, contains the root idea that people should *respond*—answer or talk back in an appropriate way.[3] To be responsible for an act is to be obliged to answer the question, "Why did you do it?"[4] In answering this question, one gives an account of one's action. As the philosopher J. R. Lucas points out, the core question can be rebutted in three ways: by objecting to whom the question is addressed (the "you"), by challenging whether the agent actually performed the action (the "do"), and by calling into question the description of the action (the "it").

Ascriptions of political responsibility are commonly rejected by individuals who proclaim their individual innocence—and from this stance of innocence, disclaim responsibility. That is, the rejection takes the form of, "I am not the one who did the deed." To provide an example drawn from political discourse, Patrick Buchanan insists that, "We have no sense of guilt about Wounded Knee because we weren't *at* Wounded Knee."[5] It is not surprising that such statements may be found in mainstream politics; the appeal to our moral and religious intuitions makes for powerful political rhetoric. What is surprising, however, is the persistence of confusion over the meaning of responsibility and guilt in theoretical treatments of collective responsibility. Peter Laslett quotes Edmund Burke's famous passage that, "Society is indeed a contract.... As the ends of such a partnership cannot be obtained in many generations, it becomes a partnership not only between those who are living, but between those who are living, those who are dead, and those who are to be born."[6] Laslett adds: "It is worth noting that Burke speaks of the ends and advantages of this intergenerational partnership (conceived in a combined temporal and procreational way) but never refers to responsibilities. The transfer of guilt seems not to be in mind. Yet the transfer of guilt between generations is perhaps the commonest form of the conversation we are examining as it goes forward with those in past time, in the historic sense."[7]

Laslett uses guilt and responsibility as synonyms, equating the transfer of responsibility with the transfer of guilt. Yet, one could argue the present government should respond to—or answer for—deeds performed in the past without presuming that contemporary citizens are guilty of past misdeeds. The philosopher Joel Feinberg defines the central components of guilt as "flawed intention, transgression, and needed atonement."[8] To claim the present government intended to enslave African Americans in the seventeenth, eighteenth, or nineteenth centuries, or inflict violence and maltreatment upon American Indians, or incarcerate Japanese Americans in 1942, or that the present government actually performed these misdeeds, would be stretching any notion of a continuous identity to the breaking point. However, to argue that the present government should *respond* to these misdeeds does not entangle us in contradiction. As Feinberg makes clear, "for guilt to transfer literally, action and intention too must transfer literally."[9] That is not the argument presented here. Rather, I argue that political responsibility—not guilt—may transfer from past to present embodiments of the U.S. government. This distinction lies at the core of the "political framework" as opposed to the theological, therapeutic, and juridical frameworks outlined in the Introduction, in that a political framework locates us in political space and time—that is, reminds us that in our identity as political beings we are engaged with others in the present, as well as with those who have proceeded us and those who will follow.

Hannah Arendt: From the German Question to the American Question

Contemporary thinking on the relationship between political responsibility and guilt is rooted in the German question.[10] Hannah Arendt stood at the center of the debate over the responsibility and/or guilt of the German people in the aftermath of World War II. From her earliest writings on the German question, Arendt warned against the traps of collective guilt. In a 1945 essay, "Organized Guilt and Universal Responsibility," Arendt identifies a central component of Nazi political strategy as convincing the Allies that there was no difference between Nazis and Germans.[11] Among the consequences of such a strategy was the impossibility of punishing war criminals, for the Allies would "find no one to whom the title of war criminal could not be applied."[12] Arendt describes how the Nazis sought to consciously destroy "the neutral zone in which the daily life of human beings is ordinarily lived," the result being to make the existence of "each individual in Germany depend either upon committing crimes or on complicity in crimes."[13] Arendt despairs of the possibility of conducting politics or satisfying the human need for justice under conditions in which "the boundaries dividing criminals from normal persons, the guilty from the innocent, have been so completely effaced."[14] She concludes that, "Where all are guilty, nobody in the last analysis can be judged."[15] Arendt locates arguments for collective guilt as part of the Nazi arsenal and criticizes the concept to defeat the Nazi strategy of obfuscating personal responsibility and individual guilt.

When Arendt attended the trial of Adolf Eichmann, she was confronted with the argument that even the potentiality of equal guilt among almost all Germans could relieve one of individual guilt. Her series of essays on the trial for *The New Yorker*, subsequently collected in a 1963 book, elicited a furious attack on her and her work; the criticism centered on her depiction of Eichmann as an exemplar of her concept of the banality of evil, on her criticisms of Jewish leaders, and on her refusal to find all Germans guilty of Nazism. In a Postscript to *Eichmann in Jerusalem*, Arendt responds to the controversy that followed the original publication of the book. She defends the human need "to make judgments in terms of individual moral responsibility" and vehemently criticizes charges of collective guilt.[16] Such charges, for Arendt, serve to obscure individual guilt and encourage people to avoid the difficult yet essential task of judging the guilt of individuals, including, possibly, themselves. In a later essay, Arendt reiterates her criticism of charges of collective guilt, writing that the cry, "'We are all guilty' . . . has actually only served to exculpate to a considerable degree those who actually were guilty. Where all are guilty, nobody is. Guilt, unlike responsibility, always singles out; it is strictly personal."[17]

Arendt criticizes not only those who charge whole nations or peoples with collective guilt, or those who use the concept of collective guilt to argue for individual mercy, but also those who wrongly admit to sharing in collective guilt. In the concluding paragraphs to *Eichmann in Jerusalem*, Arendt writes that: "Morally speaking, it is hardly less wrong to feel guilty without having done something specific than it is to feel free of all guilt if one is actually guilty of something."[18] Arendt finds nothing noble in those who feel guilty for the sins of their fathers or of their people. She fears, she later writes, that "such metaphorical statements . . . when taken literally, can only lead into a phony sentimentality in which all real issues are obscured."[19] Arendt later applied these insights to events in the United States. Observing the unrest of African Americans in the 1960s, Arendt criticized both white liberals and members of the Black Power movement for falling prey to the seductive language of collective guilt and innocence:

> We all know . . . that it has become rather fashionable among white liberals to react to Negro grievances with the cry, "We are all guilty," and Black Power has proved only too happy to take advantage of this "confession" to instigate an irrational "black rage." Where all are guilty, no one is; confessions of collective guilt are the best possible safeguard against the discovery of culprits, and the very magnitude of the crime the best excuse for doing nothing. In this particular instance, it is, in addition, a dangerous and obfuscating escalation of racism into some higher, less tangible regions. The real rift between black and white is not healed by being translated into an even less reconcilable conflict between collective innocence and collective guilt.[20]

Phony sentimentality is dangerous, in Arendt's analysis, because historically it is hypocrisy that has transformed politics into violence.[21] Arendt's objections to proclamations of collective guilt are based both on the importance she attaches to individual guilt and individual moral responsibility and on the importance of thinking and acting *politically* in response to political predicaments. Arendt witnessed how declarations of collective guilt served to obscure the existence of actual wrongdoing, and how such lofty-sounding proclamations also served to avoid confronting vexing political issues.

Although the bulk of Arendt's writings on the German question, and racism in America, are devoted to denying the existence of collective guilt, implicit—and, at times, explicit—in her argument against collective guilt lies an argument *for* political responsibility. For instance, in the quotation above from "On Violence," Arendt voices her concern that framing the political quandaries of what to do about racial problems in the United States in the language of collective guilt allows one to appear noble while freeing one from the difficult work of imagining and implementing real political solutions. If one believes the political collectivity should respond to the wrong (does have political responsibility), then confessions of collective guilt are not only unproductive but also counterproductive. In the closing paragraphs to *Eichmann in Jerusalem,*

Arendt explicitly defines political responsibility in the following manner:

> There is such a thing as *political* responsibility which, however, exists quite apart from what the individual member of the group has done and therefore can neither be judged in moral terms nor be brought before a criminal court. Every government assumes political responsibility for the deeds and misdeeds of the past.... It means hardly more, generally speaking, than that every generation, by virtue of being born into a historical continuum, is burdened by the sins of the fathers as it is blessed with the deeds of the ancestors. (emphasis in original)[22]

Arguments about political responsibility, Arendt suggests, are different sorts of arguments than those about individual sin or legal guilt. Much depends on the context in which arguments are raised. In a moral or legal context, responsibility, blameworthiness, and guilt typically are linked. Under civil law, for example, an individual is held responsible to redress a wrong if he or she is guilty of the wrongdoing. Within the framework of compensatory justice, the guilty party should return the harmed party to as good a position as they would have held had they not been wronged. The wrongdoer is best able to return the wronged to their former position—and most blameworthy. Under criminal law, a wrongdoer is guilty of a crime when it can be proven that they are responsible for the crime, and thus deserving of punishment. But the political realm is distinct from the moral and the legal realm, and part of Arendt's argument is that questions of *political* responsibility are just those—political questions, as opposed to moral or legal ones. In deciding what to do about past political wrongs, then, neither questions of intent nor punishment are strictly relevant. There are, however, supremely political issues entailed in what to do about "the sins of the fathers," including which sins, or claims, should be recognized and which ignored, and who should bear the costs of past political wrongs. To translate these questions into moral or legal language—or I would add, theological or therapeutic—is to obscure their political import.

Constituting Political Identity

To frame debates regarding if and how a political collectivity like the United States government should respond to past political wrongs in the moral or legal terms of guilt and innocence misrepresents (possibly purposefully) the nature of the political claim for responsibility. The political claim exists apart from what individual members of the group have done. In comments delivered at a 1968 meeting of the American Philosophical Society, Arendt stipulated that two conditions must be present for political responsibility to exist: "I must be held responsible for something I have not done, and the reason for my responsibility must be my membership in a group (a collective) which no voluntary act of mine can dissolve, that is, a membership utterly unlike a business partnership which I can dissolve at will."[23] To judge whether such a responsibility exists to redress past wrongs, different sorts of questions must be posed than the moral or legal questions of guilt and innocence.

As the chapters on the Oneida land claims and reparations for Japanese Americans documented, debates within the United States regarding the responsibility of present-day citizens for past wrongs tend to remain squarely within the moral or legal discourse of guilt or innocence, or the discourse of individual consent. Within the discourse of consent, for instance, as we saw in Chapter 2, in analyzing whether citizens of the United States were responsible for the internment of Japanese Americans, claimants located individuals who, in their capacity as agents for the United States, acted wrongly. Here, responsibility was assigned to individuals in the executive, legislative, and judicial branches of government and to military personnel who initiated, enforced, and legitimated the detention and forced relocation of civilians. To make the case that the U.S. government was responsible, the further point that these individuals were acting in their capacity as responsible agents for the government, rather than as lone individuals, had to be proven. Finally, the last issue examined in this approach is, did the citizens of the United States consent to the actions that led to the wrongs under question?

As we have seen, from within this perspective focusing on individual consent, in matters of intergenerational responsibility, claims for compensation for past wrongs are typically met by the response that the present and future generation neither performed nor consented to the wrongful acts and should therefore not be held responsible for them. Underlying these sentiments and echoed in the debates over Indian land claims, reparations for Japanese Americans interned, as well as reparations for African Americans, is the Jeffersonian emphasis on birth and innocence. Within this vision, individuals are born innocent, and their entrance into political society maintains if not reaffirms that innocence. Secure in the knowledge that we were not present in the eighteenth, nineteenth, or earlier twentieth century when the U.S. government committed wrongful acts against American Indians, African Americans, and Japanese Americans, many Americans have tended to resentfully deny the imposition of either guilt or responsibility for wrongful deeds. When legal or political claims are made based upon these historic misdeeds, consent theory has served as a frequently employed paradigm from which to oppose responsibility for remedying past political wrongs.[24]

Consent theory, and political liberalism generally, provides the governing American theory of how individuals are constituted politically. The most influential discussion of the process whereby an individual becomes a political being occurs in the early modern social contract theories of Hobbes, Locke, and Rousseau, theories that the eighteenth century American revolutionaries were well steeped in.[25] Rather than exploring these theories in any depth, I want here to follow Sheldon Wolin in emphasizing the centrality that *forgetting* plays in them.[26] It is especially apparent in the theory of Hobbes. The three social contract theorists mentioned above portray two states of affairs: one before, and the second after, individuals have agreed to live together in a civil society. The agreement takes the form of a contract, in which individuals agree to abide by political authority if that authority will protect them and their possessions. As Wolin points out, Hobbes's theory is particularly attuned to the importance of forgetting. Simply agreeing to the contract is not sufficient. A number of "laws of nature," also must be respected, three of which are especially noteworthy in this context. The sixth law of nature stipulates, "That upon caution of the Future time, a man ought to pardon the offences past of them that repenting, desire it."[27] The seventh, "That in Revenges, Men look not at the greatnesse of the evil past, but the greatnesse of the good to follow."[28] These two laws follow from Hobbes's fifth law of nature, "Compleasance," which stipulates "That every man strive to accomodate himselfe to the rest."[29] The accommodation may necessitate expelling individuals who "for the stubbornness of Passions, cannot be corrected."[30] Like the "stones which by the asperity, and irregularity of Figure, take more room from others," and must be cast away in building an edifice, so too must these "stubborn, insociable, froward, intractable," individuals be cast away.[31]

What makes these individuals unsuitable for entrance into the edifice of society is their refusal to forget past offenses. Wolin contends that although Hobbes's language may lead one to think that these are personal grievances that individuals refuse to pardon, actually Hobbes is thinking here of the collective actions that created the social chaos he sought to quell. If individuals could forget past political wrongs, then society could be reborn without remembered resentments.[32] The individual, in Wolin's interpretation of Hobbes's theory, was to be constituted as a political amnesiac, forgetting the past offenses that may accompany the different parts of their identity (whether it be based on categories of religion, culture, or particularly in the contemporary context, race, ethnicity, or gender). Hobbes's vision of a dehistoricized political society would find adherents in more auspicious surroundings. As examined in Chapter 3, revolutionary America provided fertile ground for the notion that the past should be left behind. Alexis de Tocqueville, observing the world that Jefferson's generation created, generalized that "in a democracy each generation is a new people."[33]

The brief depiction above of the constitution of the individual within political society informs a great deal of the American debate about the responsibility of present-day citizens for past political wrongs. The individual stands apart from political society; the relationship between the individual and the polity is established by consent. The political collectivity is the creation of individuals, a convenient fiction which always can be pierced, disclosing individuals acting in the name of the group. As noted above, within the framework of consent, questions of political responsibility are answered by determining whether an individual, acting as a responsible agent for the political collectivity, acted wrongly. If so, and if the collectivity may be said to have consented to the misdeeds, then an argument may be made that the political collectivity is responsible for them. However, where the wrongs in question predated the present members of the political collectivity, then the consent framework leads to the conclusion that political responsibility does not exist.

Although the consent framework has been the dominant paradigm employed for considering claims of political responsibility for past wrongs, it is, as we saw in our analysis of Lincoln in Chapter 3, and as Arendt and others following her have argued more recently, not the only way to think politically about the issue. Note that the stipulations Arendt establishes regarding political responsibility distinguish political responsibility from individual action in two ways. The first is that the deeds in question are not ones that the individuals held responsible, or accepting responsibility, have performed. The second is that no action on the part of the individual can dissolve the collective from which the responsibility flows. As Arendt remarks, the political collective she has in mind is "utterly unlike a business partnership which I can dissolve at will."[34] Political responsibility, in this understanding, rests not only upon a particular understanding of responsibility (that is, one that is distinct from moral or legal guilt), but also upon a particular understanding of the political collective and the individual's relationship to it.

The contention that the present generation has a responsibility for "the sins of our fathers or our people or mankind, in short, for deeds we have not done,"[35] entails an understanding of the political collective and the individual's political identity at odds with a liberal contractual understanding. The individual is not detached from political society, but becomes an autonomous self within it. Neither one's political identity nor one's political responsibility is a matter of choice alone; one can not begin the world over again. The individual's political responsibility, in this vision, is the "price we pay for the fact that we live our lives not by ourselves but among our fellow men, and that the faculty of action, which, after all, is the political faculty par excellence, can be actualized only in one of the many and manifold forms of human community."[36] Questions of present-day citizens' responsibility for past political wrongs are best not cast as moral or legal questions of guilt or innocence, but as political questions of recognition and responsibility; of whether individuals are willing and able to recognize themselves as members of a political collectivity that by existing through time has accrued an ambiguous history of proud deeds as well as shameful misdeeds.

Location in Political Time

Hannah Arendt's writings help us move toward a concept of political responsibility for past deeds because she recognized the possibility of individual *responsibility* apart from individual *guilt* and articulated the nature of a political body within which responsibility could attach to individual members. A primary characteristic of such a political body is that it exists through time; an individual's political identity, then, entails relationships both with present others who are situated within shared geographic and legal boundaries, as well as with others who preceded and those who will follow within those boundaries. Further, Arendt recognized the past as a force that shapes present political realities. Arendt was fond of the Faulkner quotation, cited earlier, that "the past is never dead, it is not even past."[37] In the Preface to *Between Past and Future*, Arendt refers to a parable written by Kafka. The parable begins: "He has two antagonists: the first presses him from behind, from the origin. The second blocks the road ahead."[38]

Arendt interprets this parable as a "thought-event" in which "the forces of the past and the future clash with each other; between them we find the man whom Kafka calls "he," who, if he wants to stand his ground at all, must give battle to both forces."[39] Arendt underscores the point that Kafka describes the past as a force that must be contended with.[40]

But precisely how is the past a force? In what ways may it be said the past penetrates the present? Those who argue for the responsibility of present-day Americans to address past wrongs point especially to the ways in which the present culture and economy are intrinsically linked to America's ambivalent history. America's history of racism, in particular, exerts a powerful force in contemporary politics. As Donald Kinder and Lynn Sanders report in *Divided by Color*, race is still "our nation's most difficult subject."[41] Kinder and Sanders' empirical analysis of the role of race in American politics uncovers a wide range of issues for which the racial attitudes of whites—in particular, the degree of resentment whites feel toward blacks—is the determining factor. They report that "On equal opportunity in employment, school desegregation, federal assistance, affirmative action at work, and quotas in college admissions, racially resentful whites line up on one side of the issue, and racially sympathetic whites line up on the other. Racial resentment is not the only thing that matters, but by a fair margin racial resentment is the most important."[42] As Jefferson feared, the racial attitudes of parents are passed on to children. As George M. Frederickson has written, "the black image in the white mind" is a cultural legacy from which contemporary Americans have not freed themselves.[43]

A second line of argument concerning the ways past injustices continue to haunt the present focuses on the significant material disadvantages experienced by African Americans relative to European Americans. As David Lyons lists, "Income and wealth gaps, more limited job opportunities, inferior housing, inferior education, inferior public services, and inferior medical care— substantially worse life prospects generally" are suffered by African Americans.[44] These present disadvantages may be, at least partly, traced back to slavery, and less distantly, to Jim Crow and the federal government's role in hindering African Americans' economic prospects. Possibly the most glaring example of the continuing presence of past wrongs is the enormous disparity in wealth between white and black households. As Thomas McCarthy reports, much of the approximately ten to one wealth gap "is due to differences in the respective rates of home ownership, which is the major form of savings in the working middle class, and . . . government housing programs from the 1930s to the 1950s overtly and almost totally excluded blacks from participation."[45] Recent scholarship has uncovered the invidious role played by federal agencies to severely limit black home ownership. "Redlining," whereby black neighborhoods were identified and within which loans for home purchases and home improvements were denied or interest rates were inflated, was practiced by the Home Owners Loan Corporation, the Federal Housing Administration, and the Veterans Administration.[46] And until 1948, the Underwriting Manual of the Federal Housing Administration included a model racial covenant, a contractual clause preventing resale to blacks.[47] The federal government was not alone in discriminating during this time. Real estate agencies systematically steered black clients away from white neighborhoods; private mortgage loan companies "redlined," and neighborhood associations encouraged the widespread use of racially restrictive covenants and the boycotting of real estate agents who represented blacks.[48] The cumulative effect of these practices, along with white flight to suburbs, resulted in black Americans becoming the most residentially segregated minority in the United States, which in turn has impacted the educational, employment, and business opportunities, as well as the electoral power, of black Americans.[49]

Solidarity and Political Responsibility

Arendt recognizes the presence of the past in her conception of political action, the presence of others in the political world, and the multiple identities that exist within each individual. Political action necessarily occurs with others amidst difference and conflict. Political actors must contend with, or respond to, the presence of the past, and they must do so with others. In acting with others, individuals must move beyond solipsism to create a "We," or a unity amidst diversity. The creation of the "We," as noted earlier, is especially important in arguments concerning political responsibility for past deeds, for individuals may assume such responsibility if they are willing and able to recognize themselves as members of the political collectivity that has inherited responsibility for misdeeds. If political responsibility rests upon the willingness and ability of individuals to think of themselves, at least partly, as members of a political collectivity, and to accept responsibility for deeds they have neither performed nor consented to, then it seems crucial to inspire individuals to embrace their identity as members of the political collectivity.

Two related criticisms, albeit from different directions, have been raised suggesting there is an intrinsic tension between the type of identification required for people to embrace this identity and the acknowledgment of past political misdeeds. One criticism is based upon a fear of the centrifugal forces dissolving the nation-state and its attendant concept of national citizenship, whereas the second is grounded upon a fear that the nation-state remains today's most dangerous agent to excluded groups of all sorts.[50] That is, one criticism raised is that in order to nurture identification with the political collective, an attachment to its customs, traditions, historical practices, as well as its historical myths is required.[51] Shared traditions, practices, and myths provide a political body with a collective self-awareness necessary for political action. However, will not the claims of American Indians, African Americans, and Japanese Americans described in earlier chapters that make clear the conflictual nature of American history deter the very sort of identification required to persuade individuals to accept the consequences for deeds of which they are innocent? This criticism contends that a critical history, and the political claims arising from one, will dissolve a collective political identity. The second criticism contends that the nation-state historically has promoted an overzealous identification with the state and an untarnished version of its history. The concern voiced here is that by encouraging a deep attachment of the individual to the political collective, the nation-state constructs a political body resistant to change, self-criticism, and the inclusion of formerly excluded groups, the very characteristics required for the state to acknowledge and respond to past political wrongs.

Steven Knapp, in an essay entitled, "Collective Memory and the Actual Past," exemplifies the first criticism noted above:

> Suppose ... that a modern American accepts a responsibility to promote egalitarianism because she believes that she has inherited this obligation from her colonial ancestors. Presumably she does so in part because of an assumption derived from certain collective narratives: the assumption that these ancestors understood egalitarianism in roughly the way she understands it. She now learns, by reading Edmund S. Morgan's account, that a crucial component of what they meant by egalitarianism was slaveholding. Nothing in principle prevents her from simply embracing this information as a discovery about the true content of her inherited obligation, and thus from taking up the banner of slavery. But a more likely outcome would seem to be uncertainty that a transhistorical American identity—and thus a body of inherited American obligations—really existed in quite the way she used to think.[52]

Knapp, in tracing the consequences of critical historical revisionism, argues that by undermining the common narratives that undergird collective identity, revisionism will "inevitably tend to qualify, even if it does not destroy, one's sense of belonging to the collectivity whose past has been revised."[53]

Knapp's argument assumes the perspective of one who formerly identified unproblematically with colonial ancestors and now has been thrown into doubt by critical scholarship linking egalitarianism to slaveholding in colonial America. Yet, isn't it just as likely, or more likely, that the individual's attachment to the collectivity would be diminished by underlying resentment of others who feel unrecognized and demeaned by a history that failed to note the racism of the colonial worldview?[54] If possible, would it not be preferable to collectively engage in a self-critical attempt to contend with the ambiguous legacy left by colonial ancestors, rather than castigating critics of American consensus history for disrupting an alleged harmony that existed prior to criticism? And what does Knapp's argument look like from the perspective of one who never could identify unproblematically with the colonial ancestors? What sort of approach to American history would best attach such a person to the collective? Philosopher Susan Wolf, in her criticism of Arthur Schlesinger's position in his *The Disuniting of America* that what is needed to ensure a greater sense of collective identity is a greater emphasis on American history and culture, wrote: "There is nothing wrong with allotting a special place in the curriculum for the study of our history, our literature, our culture. But if we are to study our culture, we had better recognize who we, as a community, are."[55] Arendt's emphasis on difference and plurality reminds us that no political collectivity is homogeneous; political identity, rather than being presupposed, must be continually recreated.

The contemporary American collectivity, more diverse than most, is comprised of various sorts of groups (religious, cultural, racial and ethnic, class, language, sexual orientation) each with their own particular identities.[56] If political responsibility may rest upon an acknowledgment of one's membership in the larger American political collectivity, then what bearing does membership in these other groups have? Knapp observes that the plethora of collectivities provides a basis upon which to deny the ascription of responsibility for the past political wrongs of the American nation-state. "Citizens born into a nation that has committed crimes can always claim innocence based on their membership in additional collectivities: not just an American but a black American, or a recent immigrant; not just a German but a socialist, a European, a Christian, an intellectual."[57] Antonin Scalia, for example, prior to becoming Justice Scalia, asserted that he had no responsibility to make restoration to African Americans for the evils of slavery for his father was a latecomer to this country from Italy and neither took part in nor derived profit from racial discrimination.[58] This understanding suggests that membership in various groups is solely a matter of choice, and the decision of which memberships trump others is also a matter of individual choice. This understanding of membership is opposed to Arendt's contention that political membership is "utterly unlike a business partnership which I can dissolve at will."[59]

Oftentimes, those arguing against political responsibility to redress past political wrongs have pointed to the "dual status" of many individuals due to their group affiliations to refute the coherence of the concept of political responsibility. Peter Laslett, who, as noted earlier, fails to distinguish between political responsibility and collective guilt, writes that if one is by American citizenship answerable for the original enslavement of black people and their subsequent exploitation, then:

> Guilt is not confined to those who are descendants of slaveowners, or to the inheritors of their possessions, or to that much larger company who themselves now profit from racial subjugation or have ancestors or relatives in that position. Indeed, unless some juggling with citizenship, its degrees and extent for different classes of people is undertaken, black American citizens would themselves seem to be guilty of their own moral degradation and that of their forebears.[60]

Laslett's reasoning, once again, does underscore the incoherence of collective guilt as applied to matters of intergenerational political responsibility. Contemporary African Americans certainly are not "guilty of their own moral degradation and that of their forebears." However, could it be that as American citizens, they too are burdened with responsibility to contend with the presence of past wrongs? Does the distinction between guilt and responsibility save the argument for political responsibility? Logically, it does, in that the argument for political responsibility claims not that contemporary African Americans were slavemasters, but that as American citizens they must accept responsibility for deeds they did not perform. However, even in this logically coherent version of the argument, a conflict still seems to endure—

that (following Laslett's example) African Americans are situated as members of the United States (and are thus responsible for its history, including slavery) and yet, as *African* Americans, may also uniquely bear the historical scars of African American slavery.[61] As Laslett's argument suggests, this conflict has been taken as proof that the concept of political responsibility is incoherent and that individuals in their roles as members of a collectivity do not bear responsibility for its past political wrongs.

However, acknowledging that an individual, by virtue of the diverse identities they may embody, may be faced with competing responsibilities, certainly need not be taken to deny the existence of responsibilities distinct to each identity. One need only consider the situation, for instance, of a parent employed outside the home who juggles responsibilities attendant to their identities as both parent and employee. If an employee works late it is not taken to mean that he or she has no responsibilities as a parent.

Rather than regarding the seeming paradox of the "dual position" of African Americans as an argument against political responsibility, I am more inclined to see the paradox as reflecting the past and present ambiguous position of some groups within the United States, which suggests why it may be politically practical for the American political collectivity to respond to past political wrongs. It certainly is not a new insight that some groups in our collectivity do feel split from their identity as members of the American political collectivity. To inherit the history of both the victimized and victimizers is to embody a dual status.[62] People are situated differently within the American political collectivity, and those differences must be acknowledged. It may be that membership in a particular group—for example, being a Japanese American ex-internee—should count as sufficiently important to outweigh one's competing membership within the American collectivity and the responsibilities attendant to it with regard to the incarceration of Japanese Americans during World War II. Or, it may be that membership in an American Indian tribe relieves one of certain responsibilities attached to American citizenship. But neither case suggests that there are no distinct responsibilities associated with being a member of the American political collective. It remains an open question, however, whether the contemporary American nation-state provides the necessary context within which those responsibilities may be recognized, or deserve to be.

Some contemporary thinkers have voiced the second concern noted earlier, warning against the nation-state's historic tendency to advance an overzealous identification with the state. Rather than focusing attention on centrifugal forces in contemporary American politics, some scholars have raised concerns about the state's promotion of an uncritical identification with an idealized vision of the state. William Connolly, in *Identity/Difference*, alerts us to what he calls the "honorable and dangerous bond of identification between the individual and the state." At its best, this bond results in "patriotism chastened by skepticism of state authority." However, the relation between the individual and the state may also degenerate "into disaffection with the state or a nationalism in which the tribulations of the time are attributed to an evil 'other' who must be neutralized."[63] Is it possible to conceive of an understanding of American political identity that integrates, rather than suffocates, self-criticism, openness to change, and inclusion of formerly excluded others?

Certainly, one real fear with regard to political identity is that it will be equated with a mythical vision of the collective's history, and any subsequent attempt to revise the interpretation of the history, or criticize traditional practices, will be perceived, and responded to, as an attack on the collective itself. Collective identity then becomes conflated with collective myth, and citizenship is understood to require unqualified loyalty to an untarnished image of the collective's past. Such a vision of political identity fosters resentment against those who criticize the collective's past actions or bring forth claims based upon those actions.

As the first chapters of the book detail, the debates that arose in the United States in the 1980s concerning the claims of American Indians, African Americans, and Japanese Americans pitted differing interpretations of United States history and the relevance of that history to present politics. Coincidentally, a similar debate raged in Germany, provoked by a clique of German historians who attempted to revise interpretations of Nazism in order to provide Germans with a positive identity freed from the burdens of Nazism.[64] Jurgen Habermas participated in the debate, arguing in an Arendtian manner both that the specific past of Nazism is intrinsically connected to the present political reality in Germany and that contemporary Germans need not, indeed must not, passively perpetuate past practices and traditions. Habermas argued that German identity of the 1980s is "linked to the life context in which Auschwitz was possible." Contemporary German life "is connected with that of our parents and grandparents through a web of familial, local, political, and intellectual traditions that is difficult to disentangle—that is, through a historical milieu that made us what and who we are today." Thus, for Habermas, "We have to stand by our traditions if we do not want to disavow ourselves." Standing by one's traditions, however, does not imply defensively defending them from criticism. Rather, Habermas contends that "a suspicious gaze" is the appropriate stance one should take in light of the moral catastrophe of Nazism.[65] In Habermas's understanding, each individual faces an existential choice to consciously and responsibly transform their personal and political identity: "Every individual first encounters himself as the historical product of contingent life circumstances, but in 'choosing' himself as this product he constitutes a self to which the rich concreteness of the life history in which he merely found himself is attributed as something for which he will account retrospectively."[66]

Each person, in Habermas's understanding, becomes an editor of their life, deciding what should be considered essential and worth transmitting. The individual, however, cannot change the practices or traditions of the political collectivity on their own. They must engage with others in a "publicly conducted debate," on which shared traditions should be continued and which should not.[67]

Arendt's, as well as Habermas's recognition of the relevance of the past to present politics, should not be misread as encouragement to turn away from the present. Neither Arendt nor Habermas would suggest contemporary Americans substitute battles over the meaning of United States history for engaging with present political realities. Any argument for political responsibility for past misdeeds that may resonate with individual members of the American political collectivity must be based on a conception of politics that recognizes that political action must "occur in real time, with real, other people."[68] It also must concern real, concrete issues—that is, present issues. I read Arendt's criticism of collective guilt as a criticism against the temptation to turn real political problems over to "some higher, less tangible regions," that is, to turn away from real problems currently besetting the political collectivity.

Political Identity and Political Responsibility

Political responsibility, then, this chapter suggests, ultimately rests upon the willingness and ability of individuals to identify with the American political collectivity and to see themselves, at least partly, as political beings capable of engaging in political action. A final question that must be posed is whether the contemporary American nation-state provides the context within which individuals can do so, apart from the legacy of past wrongs. What are the conditions under which individual members can recognize themselves as political beings and accept responsibilities based upon that identity?

Philosopher Joel Feinberg argues that three conditions must be satisfied in some degree in order for a collectivity to possess the requisite solidarity to recognize and assume political responsibility: a large community of interest among all the members, reciprocal affection between them, and sharing a common lot.[69] Let us briefly consider the three conditions. First, regarding the "large community of interest"—as Arendt reminds us, conflict is endemic to politics, though it does not necessarily foreclose the possibility of an emerging "community of interest." It is essential for members to recognize their interdependence, but this does not mean that they cease to be individuals whose interests, needs, outlooks, and desires may conflict with those of others. If members continue to recognize their interdependence, then conflicts may be fought out and resolved in a manner that does not threaten the continuing existence of the collectivity.[70] Whether there is sufficient interdependence within the American political collectivity is certainly a matter of some dispute today.

Second, although Feinberg suggests that there must be "reciprocal affection" among members, here his definition may overextend what is truly required. "Reciprocal affection" seems to best apply to a family and politics, especially as it is practiced today within the large impersonal political collectivity of the United States, bears little resemblance to family life. A definition of requisite solidarity modeled after the family may set the bar too high. Whereas relations among members of a political collectivity must be respectful, they could not, nor need not, be affectionate. Politics occurs not between two intimates, but among individuals for whom, although they must share some commonality; "there is room for much difference and conflict; . . . and the mutuality politics requires is a recognition of similarity within difference," as Hanna Pitkin writes.[71]

Finally, the third condition that Feinberg stipulates, sharing a common lot, does seem critical to engendering a sense of collective identity—and there are substantial reasons to be skeptical of how much Americans really do share in common, particularly across racial, ethnic, and class divides.[72] Once again, though, Arendt's understanding of politics may be helpful here. For politics does not presuppose a commonality, but rather the possibility of creating one. *Sins of the Parents* suggests that even the presence of a divisive past provides an opportunity for commonality to be created. Contemporary Americans do, to a certain extent, share a world and a common fate. Lisa Disch, following Arendt, writes, "We share this world together, and we cannot evade that togetherness if we want to preserve a world with space for the exercise of distinctly human capacities, and perhaps the distant possibilities of a just politics."[73]

What seems most important, and most at risk today, is individuals' willingness and ability to recognize themselves as political beings connected in any meaningful sense to the American nation-state. It is not surprising, then, that arguments for *political* responsibility for past wrongs get lost, or are infrequently voiced in contemporary American debates, for where the political realm itself has been eviscerated, and where few Americans have meaningful experience of political action, arguments for political responsibility are emptied of almost all meaning. For if our responsibility as members of the political collectivity grows out of the fact "that the faculty of action . . . can be actualized only in one of the many and manifold forms of human community,"[74] then it is only when individuals value political action, and only when they experience the nation-state as a potential site for political action, that they may be willing "to pay the price" of political responsibility. I return to these concerns in the conclusion to the book.

5

The Political Promise and Limitations of National Apologies

SINS OF THE PARENTS argues that though very few, if any, present-day American citizens may be said to be directly implicated in the U.S. government's past misdeeds, they may still bear political responsibility to take action regarding historic wrongs such as the illegal appropriation of American Indian lands, the internment of Japanese Americans, or slavery and the Jim Crow system established after slavery was outlawed.[1] This chapter examines in detail the justness and political practicality of the novel contemporary phenomena of national apologies as a response to past political wrongs. First, the chapter situates the American debate over national apologies by briefly contrasting contemporary American political conditions to those of most other nations similarly engaged in debates regarding past wrongs. Then, the chapter analyzes the costs and benefits of responding to past wrongs—in any manner—and goes on to consider the goals a political collectivity could have in responding to past wrongs. Next, the chapter considers the promise of national apologies—both with and without material compensation—to realize the collectivity's goals, as well as the particular challenges entailed in employing apologies (typically thought to concern interpersonal relations) on a collective—that is, political—scale. Finally, the chapter specifically evaluates recent calls for a national apology for slavery, suggesting both its promise and its limitations.

As documented in earlier chapters, deep and bitter disputes have erupted in the United States since the late 1970s over the meaning and appropriateness of the national government apologizing for past political acts. We have seen that the federal government's apology to Japanese Americans interned during World War II initially was opposed by the Reagan administration and only was accomplished after legislators made a number of changes to the original bill.[2] One could also expect that if the bill to "acknowledge a long history of official depredations and ill-conceived policies by the United States Government regarding Indian tribes and offer an apology to all Native Peoples on behalf of the United States," introduced in May 2004 by five co-sponsors in the U.S. Senate, gains any momentum, it will be greeted by silence by many and ardent resistance by others.[3] Similarly, calls for a national apology for slavery and John Conyers' repeated proposals for a commission to study the impact of slavery and Jim Crow, modeled after the Commission on Wartime Relocation and Internment of Civilians (CWRIC), have, on the whole, been met with a less-than-enthusiastic response. What can national apologies achieve? Can national apologies, and the forgiveness that an apology may elicit, provide an alternative to the festering of old wounds that often leads to political resentment, political alienation, and, at times, violence? And can they work on a public and collective scale? Do they hold promise as a realistic alternative to individual citizens remembering past political wrongs and feeling alienated from the nation-state, other citizens, and their identity as political beings? That is, do apologizing and forgiving provide avenues for genuine political change?

Apologies within the American Polity

To evaluate the potential efficacy of a national apology, it is essential to place it within its political context. Whereas the book's introduction points to the worldwide phenomenon of individuals and groups raising claims based on historic governmental wrongs, and some governments responding with national apologies, the cases examined in Chapters 1 and 2 disclose significant differences about the recent claims raised and the U.S. government's responses. In many cases around the globe, where claims based on past governmental wrongs have arisen, they have done so in nations in the midst of transforming from repressive regimes toward more democratic ones (e.g., South Africa, former despotisms in South America, and Communist dictatorships in Eastern and Central Europe). As the burgeoning literature on "transitional justice" makes clear, where nations are in the midst of such transformations, they may be bedeviled by a number of factors that are not present in the United States.[4] First, in many of these nations, the wrongs are much more recent, and thus raise the question of how best can victims, some of whom have been traumatized by abuses, live alongside past perpetrators. Second, the new governmental regimes must grapple with how best to respond to those who have committed wrongs, some of whom remain prominent members of society. And third, the new regimes tend to be understandably concerned with establishing and maintaining stability and worry that if they push too hard to respond to the claims of victims of governmental abuse, then individuals and groups loyal to the prior regime will attempt to destabilize the new government.

The United States, on the other hand, for the most part, faces none of these challenges. In neither the Oneida land claims nor the claims arising over the internment of Japanese Americans do the deeds under debate date from the very recent past. This is not to say that the misdeeds are "ancient history," nor that consequences of the historic deeds do not reach into the present, but it is significant that all of those directly responsible for the violation of treaties with the Oneidas, and almost all of those responsible for the internment of Japanese Americans, have died. While many Oneidas and Japanese American ex-internees clearly felt aggrieved, and have demanded apologies and some form of compensation, the personal animus against perpetrators, or fear of them, has not been a primary feature of the American debate over past wrongs and present responsibilities.

The United States also has been spared contending with the complex set of questions surrounding how to deal with past governmental perpetrators, for, as noted above, on the whole enough time has passed since the wrongs were committed that those directly responsible have died. Recent debates within the United States regarding past governmental wrongs have not had to take up whether to prosecute wrongdoers or grant them amnesty, or whether to ban past governmental officials from holding political positions or allow them to participate in politics freed of any taint of past wrongdoing. It is noteworthy in this respect that two of the most outspoken opponents of reparations for Japanese Americans, John J. McCloy and Karl R. Bendetsen, were among the few surviving individuals who had participated in conceiving and implementing the U.S. government's unjust policy toward Japanese Americans. Where wrongdoers are still alive, and fear criminal or civil sanctions, or a loss of power, respect, or reputation, they are likely to object to the government admitting wrongdoing based on their actions.

Although the absence, for the most part, of living perpetrators has allowed the political and legal debates regarding past wrongs to proceed without the complications related to criminal or civil sanctions, that absence has also meant that some, if not all, of the functions typically performed by punishing individual wrongdoers may need to be addressed in other ways. The punishment of perpetrators may accomplish a number of significant political functions: It may distinguish the new regime from the old, restore to victims a sense of dignity, individualize guilt and thus may preempt cycles of group recrimination, and deter future wrongdoing.[5] But without punishment, what can then perform these needed political goals? This chapter explores whether, and to what extent, national apologies and the forgiveness they may elicit may realize some of these political objectives.

Finally, in terms of concerns regarding regime stability, the United States by all accounts may be considered a stable regime;

its governmental leaders do not have to take into account the possibly destabilizing effects of acknowledging past wrongs. Enabling victims, or heirs of victims, to express their grievances, and documenting and responding to past misdeeds, is highly unlikely to provoke a regime crisis, as certainly could have occurred in Argentina, South Africa, or Bulgaria, for instance.

As the book has thus far documented, however, there have been, and remain, significant obstacles to the U.S. government acknowledging and responding to past wrongs. In fact, as the case study of the Oneida land claims reveals, if the amount of time that has transpired between the original wrong and contemporary calls for a response is perceived to be too great, then legal doctrines (in particular, statutes of limitations) may stand in the way of claimants receiving compensation and an apology, even if an implicit one. Political realities as well may pose an obstacle if too great an amount of time has passed between the original wrong and appeals for a response from the government. If much time has passed, then immediate victims, who may speak movingly and persuasively of the need for the government to act, may have died. Chapter 2 noted the persuasiveness of Japanese Americans who could speak firsthand of the indignities they endured under the United States' policies; without the presence of individuals who are unquestionably recognized as direct victims of a wrong, the need for an apology and possible compensation appears more ambiguous.

And whereas the U.S. government will not be dangerously destabilized by acknowledging past political wrongs, as noted in earlier chapters, such acknowledgments do entail costs and may foster resentment by some. A conservative estimate of the financial cost of acknowledging historic wrongs, particularly the expropriation of American Indian lands and enslavement of African Americans, would certainly run into the billions of dollars. And, while resentment would not be driven by fear of criminal sanctions—as is the case in many transitional regimes—in the United States, as we have seen, when individual citizens are asked to take on responsibility for deeds over which they had no control, many will resent such an imposition.

One final characteristic to consider that distinguishes the United States from most other nation-states engaged in debates over national apologies is what may be considered the repressed or hidden nature of the political fractures that may be in need of reconciliation. In South Africa after the apartheid regime fell, or in Argentina after the military regime fell, or in (Eastern) Germany, Hungary, Albania, or Lithuania after 1989, few people doubted the need for political reconciliation. The recentness of the crimes and atrocities committed, the scars written on people's bodies, and the family members killed and missing were vivid reminders of the presence of past political wrongs that continued to fracture the political body. In the United States, however, as in Australia and Canada, the need for political reconciliation is itself an unsettled question. Those pressing claims for a response to past wrongs must first make the argument that there are political wounds that need healing, or wrongs that stand in the way of "a more perfect union," before a serious discussion can take place regarding how to respond.

It appears, then, that each political context presents its own set of difficulties in constructing a just and feasible response to past governmental wrongs. If political wrongs are very recent and new governments are fragile, then, though the need for reconciliation is apparent, the trauma of victims, defensiveness of those associated with the prior regime, and possible reluctance of the new regime to "rock the boat" all may conspire against an open airing of grievances and thorough acknowledgment of past political wrongs. On the other hand, as seen in the two cases studied here, even when the political wrongs date back prior to the present generation and the government is stable, obstacles still remain to achieving national apologies and real political costs may be entailed. Why should the U.S. government acknowledge historic wrongs and invite such costs? What are the potential benefits of doing so, compared with the financial costs shared by all, were there to be material compensation in conjunction with an apology (assuming that the costs of any compensation scheme would be paid through general taxation), and electoral costs for the politicians who support apologies and possible compensation in the face of a potential political backlash?

The literature on "transitional justice" exhibits that although new regimes face significant obstacles in responding to past crimes and atrocities, many have been willing to expend political and financial resources to do so.[6] New regimes seek to distinguish themselves from the practices and culture of prior regimes and may bring to light past transgressions to further delegitimate the prior regime and to instill in citizens the belief that life under the new government will be different. Some new regimes have spoken of the simple need for truth and publicly and authoritatively acknowledge past wrongs as a step toward creating a political world in which factual truths are not hidden. And justice seems to require a response to those who have been wronged as well as to those who have committed wrongs. Here, as noted above, criminal trials with the possibility of punishment may enable the new government to perform a number of those functions: to make clear the differences between the new regime and the old, restore to victims a sense of dignity, individualize guilt, and thus preempt cycles of group recrimination and deter future wrongdoing. Truth commissions, in addition to—or in some nations, instead of—criminal trials also have played a novel role throughout the world since the 1980s. More than twenty nations have established truth commissions during the past twenty years, hoping, as the names of many of the commissions announce, both to establish the truth about past political deeds and to foster reconciliation within the nation.[7] Whether both of these goals may be achieved through establishing truth commissions remains an open question. Among other doubts, some scholars have argued that within deeply divided political environments, "shared truths" may not exist; others have expressed skepticism regarding truth's power to heal victimized individuals.[8]

As shown in the cases examined in Chapters 1 and 2, in the United States, as the government has lurched toward responses to the appropriation of American Indian lands and the internment of Japanese Americans, the government's responses have, in some ways, more closely resembled truth commissions than

criminal trials. The government has not attempted to individualize guilt. Rather, the government has responded (to the extent
that it has) to past political wrongs in reaction to demands by
aggrieved parties, or their representatives, to resolve grievances,
provide partial compensation, and express new understandings
of the political body's history and of itself. Much of the effort in
the United States has been devoted to what legal scholar Marc
Galanter calls "historical vindication": formal acknowledgment
of the wrong and apology for it.[9] In passing the Civil Liberties Act
of 1988, Congress stated its first intent was to "acknowledge the
fundamental injustice of the evacuation, relocation, and internment." Its second was to "apologize on behalf of the people of the
United States."[10] And much of the legal record in the Oneida cases
is devoted to presenting a revised interpretation of the critical role
played by the Oneidas in the Revolutionary War and, in return, of
the American government's inglorious history of broken treaties
and ineffectual protection of Oneida lands in response to the lands'
unlawful acquisition by states and private parties.

In the United States, the national government's public and formally expressed revised understanding of its history—one which
acknowledges specific historic wrongs and "redistributes blame
and honor"[11]—may both reflect its transformed collective identity as well as transform individual citizens' political identity. That
is, by owning up to the federal government's failures of both commission and omission in regards to the Oneidas, or its unjust and
what we now consider to be unconstitutional acts related to the
evacuation, relocation, and internment of Japanese Americans,
the government is able to declare that it now judges these historic
acts to be wrong and that it has become the type of government
that attempts to extend justice to those whom it victimized in
the past. By doing so, the U.S. government aims for truth and
reconciliation: establishing a public record documenting the historic wrongs and encouraging victims, specifically (or those who
identify with them) to perceive the government differently, as well
as perceiving their role in the political collectivity differently.[12]
The acknowledgment of past wrongs and the offering of national

apologies aims to make the relationship between individuals and the national government more meaningful and the relationship within individuals amongst their various identities (in particular, among their racial, ethnic, and political identities) less problematic. If the government is able to do so, then the act of apologizing, and the possibility of eliciting forgiveness, is central to the accomplishment of these aims.

Apologizing and Forgiving: Personal and Political?

Typically, apologies and forgiving are most at home in relations between individuals. Can a faculty so seemingly anchored in the realm of interpersonal relations be relevant to the political realm? Must one be an innocent to suppose that apologies and forgiveness could have any efficacy in the political realm? To determine whether and under what conditions apologies and forgiveness may be meaningful in the political realm, we must first analyze the dynamics of apologies and forgiveness and examine the power, as well as the limitations, of forgiveness. In order to consider whether they can they work on a collective scale, it may be helpful to first examine how apologies and forgiveness perform between individuals.

In the personal realm, when and under what conditions are apologies and forgiveness practiced? Apologies and forgiveness become issues when a relationship—typically between two people—is ruptured due to a wrong.[13] Apologies and forgiveness assume importance when one party commits an act against another that recasts the individuals' identities—one as the wrongdoer and the other as the wronged party. The wrong intrudes into the relationship and defines the relationship in terms of the wrong. If the relationship is to continue or is to be renewed, is ever to be experienced apart from the wrong, then the wrong calls for a response.

All wrongs, of course, do not always call forth apologies. The wrongdoer may offer excuses or try to justify the act in question.[14] And all apologies do not always call forth forgiveness. The wronged party may not forgive, judging the wrong too enormous to do so or the apology insincere or inadequate. Or the wronged may simply forget, rather than forgive.[15] For forgiveness to occur, there must be an initial agreement between the parties that there is something to be forgiven. Without a preliminary agreement that a wrong was performed, an apology will not be forthcoming, and forgiveness cannot occur.[16]

Forgiving, actually, may be the least likely outcome when a wrong has been done and has intruded into a relationship. Aristotle, in Book Four of *The Ethics*, in his discussion of the right disposition toward anger, notes that "revenge is more natural to man than forgiveness."[17] Hannah Arendt, in her discussion of forgiveness, highlights as well its extraordinariness, noting that in the New Testament Jesus likens the power to forgive to the more general power of performing miracles.[18]

A number of more likely responses to a wrong come immediately to mind. The wronged party does not completely let go of the wrong, the offense having so damaged the wronged person that the relationship is permanently spoiled because the resentment will not subside. Aristotle, in defining the right disposition toward anger, distinguishes between grades of irascibility. Bitter people, he writes, "are hard to reconcile, and keep up their anger for a long time, because they suppress their animosity. Relief comes only with retaliation; for revenge provides release from anger by substituting pleasure for pain."[19] Here, the relationship may never be righted; only by inflicting vengeance will the wronged party be pacified and let go of the hurt.[20] If a first step along the road to forgiveness is an agreement between the parties that a wrong has been done, then a next step is for the wronged party to abandon thoughts of vengeance. Forgiveness does not necessarily require an abandonment of the desire for punishment, but it does require that the relationship be free from vengeance.[21] Not all thinkers entertain the possibility of purging oneself of the desire for vengeance. Most notably, for Nietzsche, forgiveness is only weakness disguised as strength. In the "dark workshop where ideals are made . . . the inability for revenge (of the weak man) is called unwillingness to revenge, perhaps even forgiveness."[22]

Why would some relationships be permanently damaged by a wrong? As Nietzsche suggests, we should consider the psychological state of the wronged person. In doing so, two explanations may account for permanent damage. The first is that the wronged person may be unable to regain the confidence needed to renew the relationship; the wronged person may be unable to see himself or herself as anything but a victim within the confines of the relationship.[23] On the other hand, rather than feeling permanently inferior in relationship to the wrongdoer, the wronged party may feel superior, thinking that he or she could never have done such a thing to another. Besides feeling neither inferior nor superior to the other party, another prerequisite for forgiving seems to be recognition of and acknowledgment of shared humanity, or the possibility of doing wrong to another.

Forgiving may be dangerous. To borrow Aristotle's language, rather than getting angry "at the wrong things, and too much, and for too long a time,"[24] one may also forgive too easily or too lightly. Aristotle warns that it is possible to forgive "with the wrong people, for the wrong reasons, more than is right, too quickly, and for too long a time."[25] One who forgives too easily may be demonstrating that he or she cares not enough for themselves; part of forgiving is opening up oneself again to the possibility of hurt, and one who does this "with the wrong people, for the wrong reasons, more than is right, too quickly, and for too long a time" may be displaying a lack of self-regard, or a lack of judgment. Forgiving requires judgment that the other party has adequately apologized by fully recognizing the wrong and is taking the necessary steps to rectifying it.

Forgiving, then, is not without its risks. The peril described above of forgiveness slipping into condonation serves to remind us that all acts do not necessarily deserve forgiveness. Hannah Arendt contended in *The Human Condition* that forgiveness "does not apply to the extremity of crime and willed evil."[26] Her argument is based upon her interpretation of the New Testament, especially the Book of Luke, where it is written "And if he trespass against thee seven times a day, and seven times in a day turn again to thee, saying, I repent; thou shalt forgive him."[27] Arendt emphasizes the ordinariness of trespassing; it is "in the very nature of action's constant establishment of new relationships within a web of relations, and it needs forgiving, dismissing, in order to make it possible for life to go on by constantly releasing men from what they have done unknowingly."[28]

But extraordinary acts of crime and willed evil surpass the limits of the power to forgive. Certain offenses can neither be forgiven nor should they be. Arendt calls these acts, following Kant, "radical evil . . . about whose nature so little is known."[29] Arendt later traveled to Jerusalem to confront Adolf Eichmann and to explore the nature of evil. There she discovered that monstrous deeds are not necessarily the work of monsters. "Eichmann was not Iago and not Macbeth, and nothing would have been farther from his mind than to determine with Richard III 'to prove a villain.'"[30] That Eichmann did not prove to be a monster did not mean, though, that he deserved forgiveness. Examining why she could not forgive him forced Arendt to reconsider her understanding of forgiveness. In *The Human Condition,* Arendt had written that "what was done is forgiven for the sake of who did it."[31] Arendt's encounter with Eichmann compelled her to think through the potential chasm between acts and actors. Arendt admitted to her friend the poet W. H. Auden that she was wrong when she wrote that "we forgive what was done for the sake of who did it. . . . I can forgive somebody without forgiving anything."[32] Eichmann's deeds (what was done) could never be forgiven, although Arendt conceivably could have forgiven Eichmann (somebody). She later explained that whereas it may be possible to forgive somebody without forgiving their deeds, it was neither possible to forgive nor to show mercy to Eichmann:

> Mercy was out of the question, not on juridical grounds—pardon is anyhow not a prerogative of the juridical system—but because mercy is applicable to the person rather than to the deed; the act of mercy does not forgive murder but pardons the murderer insofar

> as he, as a person, may be more than anything he ever did. This
> was not true of Eichmann. And to spare his life without pardoning
> him was impossible on juridical grounds.[33]

Although Arendt believed in new beginnings, in people's potential to change their minds and start again, not all people are greater than their offenses. Some misdeeds so accurately capture who someone is that the disassociation between deeds and doer becomes impossible, thus rendering forgiveness impossible.

Forgiving, then, is not always an appropriate response to a wrong. No simple rules, though, seem capable of specifying when it is appropriate. The danger of forgiving sliding into condonation demonstrates that forgiving not only occurs within a relationship between a wronged party and a perpetrator, but also concerns the relationship between the perpetrator and the offense, and the understanding of the deed in light of the ethical rules or laws that the forgiver takes seriously. To forgive more than is right or too quickly (and here one can think of the controversy sparked by revelations concerning Arendt's seemingly too easy forgiving of Heidegger for his Nazism)[34] may display a lack of self-respect on the part of the forgiver, a lack of respect for others as moral agents, and a lack of respect for ethical or legal rules. Forgiveness, like punishment, is expressive and speaks not only to the forgiven but also speaks to other witnesses about the forgiver's regard for ethical action.

Forgiving, though, even if rare, is possibly the most liberating of potential responses to a wrong; it aims to liberate both parties from the effects of the wrongful deed and reestablish a relationship freed from them. That is not to say that an apology can actually undo what was done, nor that it, accepted by the forgiving party, can or should allow the deed to be forgotten.[35] The wrong is not erased nor are all its effects erased. However, the relationship may be renewed without the wrong at its center. Let us examine how this last step of the process of forgiving works.

Forgiving provides the possibility of "righting the scales," although in a peculiar manner. In civil law, righting the scales usually entails taking from one who has more due to their wrongful act and giving to the wronged person. In the case of forgiveness, though, it is the *wronged* person who is in the position of righting the scales.[36] Through the commission of a wrong, the wronged party is cast in the role of a victim; the perpetrator, on the other hand, somehow gains by the wrong.[37] It is essential to the process of forgiving, though, that the wronged person holds the power to forgive or not to forgive once an apology has been offered. Forgiving thus transforms the person wronged from a victim to an agent. On the other hand, the perpetrator of the wrongful deed who formerly had asserted power over the wronged person now is in the less-powerful position. Having been cast by his or her deed into the role of the morally tainted, the victimizer is now dependent upon the wronged person to free him or her from the wrongful deed. The Hebrew words used in the Old Testament to refer to forgiveness provide helpful clues in this regard. The three words typically used to refer to forgiveness are *kipper,* meaning "to cover," *nasa,* meaning "to lift up, or carry away," and *salach,* meaning "to let go."[38] All three words point to the forgiver's power to remove the sin from the wrongdoer so that each party can resume the relationship. The ritual of apology also points to the role reversal involved in forgiving: It is the former perpetrator who frequently "begs for forgiveness."[39]

Of course, if the wrongdoer has no desire to renew the ruptured relationship, or if the wrongdoer has acted from a secure position of power and is immune to the cares or power of the wronged person, then apologies will not issue and forgiving is incapable of righting the scales. Equality cannot be reestablished where it had not already been established or where there is not a desire for it to be.[40] It is essential to forgiveness that the victim holds the power to forgive. Without that act and without this power, the wronged party remains always a victim within the confines of the relationship. Just as importantly, the wronged party must completely let go of the resentment and not assume a position of superiority. What we can learn from examining the process of apologies and forgiving in the personal realm is that it is a means of reestablishing a relationship not between victim and perpetrator but between two equal parties. Forgiving falls somewhere between vengeance and condonation. And, the process of apologizing and forgiving entails a number of stages: the recognition by both parties that a deed was wrong; a call for an apology; a judgment made as to what response (including possible restitution, compensation, or punishment) will constitute an adequate apology; recognition of shared humanity between the parties; and finally, willingness on both parties to renew the relationship.[41] Apologizing and forgiving, then, are present responses to a past wrong for the sake of a future; if the relationship is to have a future untainted by a wrong then the resentment and anger related to the wrong, and even possible masochistic attachment to victimhood, must be let go.[42]

As extraordinary as forgiveness and the apologies that may elicit that forgiveness may be, it may still be the case that their power is restricted to relations between individuals, and thus have limited usefulness in the political realm. Do apologies and forgiveness belong in the political realm? Can we conceive of an understanding of politics capacious enough to encompass the potential power of national apologies and forgiveness?

It is the case that apologies and forgiveness have received scant attention from most political theorists. However, as noted earlier, forgiveness fascinated Hannah Arendt, one of the most "political" of political thinkers, and in fact it is woven into her concept of political action.[43] In a 1953 essay, Arendt described forgiveness as "one of the greatest human capacities and perhaps the boldest of human actions."[44] Arendt returned again and again to the concept, writing of it in *The Human Condition* and *Eichmann in Jerusalem*, as well as in a number of essays in *Men in Dark Times*. By briefly examining the essential role that forgiveness played in Arendt's conception of political action, we may more fully imagine the promise of national apologies in American politics.

Arendt most fully articulated her concept of forgiveness in the concluding sections to Part V of *The Human Condition*. Entitled "Action," it is in many ways Arendt's most programmatic statement on politics. Two epigraphs begin that section: one a quotation from Dante, the second a quotation from Isak Dinesen:[45] "All sorrows can be borne if you put them into a story or tell a story about them."[46] For our purposes, it is noteworthy that the section in which Arendt theorizes political action begins with sorrows and ends with a meditation of how we live in time, armed with forgiveness to relate to the past and with promises to contend with the future.

Arendt, concerned to distinguish the public realm from both the private and the social, and contending that the public realm houses the political, argues that forgiveness and promising are the *only* moral principles intrinsic to political action. She notes that promising has long been recognized as a concept central to Western political thought. On the other hand, forgiveness "has always been deemed unrealistic and inadmissible in the public realm."[47] Arendt attempts to reclaim forgiveness from the moral and religious realm and locate it in the realm of politics. Much of Arendt's larger theoretical project is devoted to explaining why individuals must engage in the public world—must act, in order to be fully human.[48] As pointed out in Chapter 4, though sensitive to the ways we are shaped by our history, Arendt maintained that we are not determined by it, and that we are capable of free action. To recognize the past as a force, to envision one's life as a story entangled with the stories of others and connected to the much larger stories of the place and the time in which we are born, may tempt us to imagine ourselves mere pawns in a game much larger than we are, mere playthings of the God of History.

Arendt's concern to call people to act, to portray the very necessity of action for individuals to live a fully human life, is evident in her careful distinction between her understanding of action and the attitude that portrays humans as the helpless products of historical factors. Yet, in Arendt's portrayal, human action is beset with complexities due to three inherent characteristics: "its futility, boundlessness, and uncertainty of outcome."[49] The futility of action is explained by the fact that it takes place in a public realm, where, falling into "an already existing web of human relationships, with its innumerable, conflicting wills and intentions ... [it] almost never achieves its purpose."[50] And although it may almost never achieve its purpose, action is not without consequences. The consequences "are boundless, because action ... acts into a medium where every reaction becomes a chain reaction and where every process is the cause of new processes.... [O]ne deed, and sometimes one word, suffices to change every constellation."[51] The consequences of acts are both boundless and unpredictable. And finally, action is also burdened by irreversibility. One is "unable to undo what one has done though one did not, and could not, have known what he was doing."[52] Arendt's unblinking portrayal of the public realm in which political action takes place leads her to recognize two different temptations that may undermine political action: turning away from political action and retreating into the private realm, or conceiving action as domination and freedom as sovereignty.

Arendt's theory of political action is an attempt to hold on to two different insights: Action is at once frustrating and miraculous, and the public realm is one of moral haphazardness, yet still individuals must use judgment and act thoughtfully within it. Action in Arendt's hands appears as a frail miracle. She knows very well that courage is needed to act in public. It is daunting to insert oneself into the public realm partly because it is impossible to fully know ourselves, and because political action necessarily entails acting with others:

> Men have known that he who acts never quite knows what he is doing, that he always becomes "guilty" of consequences he never intended or even foresaw, that no matter how disastrous and unexpected the consequences of his deed he can never undo it, that the process he starts is never consummated unequivocally in one single deed or event, and that its very meaning never discloses itself to the actor but only to the backward glance of the historian who himself does not act.[53]

For Arendt, we know neither ourselves nor our motives fully; we too may be surprised by our actions. Rather than resolving our intentions beforehand, and entering the public realm to act in a preconceived manner (as in what Arendt calls *fabrication*), we disclose ourselves in public, and even then, not to ourselves. We depend upon others not only to complete our actions, but to give them meanings and so disclose them. In light of the hazards of acting in public, of our dependence on others, and our inability to know ourselves or our intentions fully before we act, the safety of the private realm appears more inviting.

Forgiveness redeems action from many of these predicaments. Without it, Arendt writes, "our capacity to act would, as it were, be confined to one single deed from which we could never recover; we would remain the victims of its consequences forever."[54] Forgiveness allows us to act anew. Its possibility means that one wrong step in public need not haunt us forever. If acts are unpredictable, consequences boundless and limitless, and others have the last word on one's actions, yet at the same time one will have to live with those actions (for Arendt this meant to think with the person who performed them), then Arendt seems to fear that many people will be drawn to choose private comfort over public risk, retreating from the public realm and its responsibilities. In Arendt's understanding, the retreat to the private realm may not be prompted by selfishness so much as by individuals' sense of personal responsibility in a realm of moral ambiguity.[55]

If the first danger to action is to retreat to the private realm, then a second danger is the temptation to think of action as domination. Complete control of one's actions is impossible, due primarily to the plurality of agents, meaning that the political realm is one of haphazardness and moral irresponsibility.[56] Forgiveness allows people, though, to insert themselves into the public realm and, if granted, may release them (at least partly) from the consequences of what they do.[57] Part of the allure of conceiving of action as domination is the seeming clarity of questions of responsibility. The asserted control of a single agent draws a linear relation between actor and act. But in the in-between realm that Arendt portrays, the realm of freedom but not sovereignty, the realm of action but not single domination, responsibility is ambiguous.

Arendt's discussion of action was written in the wake of her account of totalitarianism. In a 1953 essay, "Understanding and Politics," Arendt wrote that: "The originality of totalitarianism is horrible, not because some new 'idea' came into the world, but because its very actions constitute a break with all our traditions; they have clearly exploded our categories of political thought and our standards for moral judgment."[58] Arendt sought to address this vacuum; if the world had been changed irrevocably by totalitarianism, then we needed new ways to think about politics and morals.[59] How should we think about political action and responsibility in this new world where action can neither be conceived as fabrication nor domination?[60]

Arendt divorces action from its consequences, as well as from motives, purposes, and antecedent conditions.[61] It is the simultaneous presence of freedom and non-sovereignty that distinguishes Arendt's thinking about responsibility from most conventional accounts. Non-sovereignty implies that individual actors are unable to foretell or determine the consequences of an act. From the perspective of the potential actor, holding one responsible for the unpredictable and boundless consequences of a deed may inhibit action. Arendt wrote approvingly that "Kant had the courage to acquit man from the consequences of his deed, insisting solely on the purity of his motives, and this saved him from losing faith in man and his potential greatness."[62] And from the perspective of the historian or the judge, to use consequences to judge actions would give up that human role to History. The last line of one of Arendt's last completed works, *Thinking*, is a favorite quotation of hers from Cato: "Victrix causa deis placuit, sed victa Catoni" (which Arendt translated as "The victorious cause pleased the gods, but the defeated one pleases Cato.")[63]

Although Arendt wrote that she stood with Kant in having the courage to acquit man from the consequences of his deed, she had been disabused of the notion that one should insist on the purity of the actor's motives. To insist on pure motives would ring untrue to Arendt's portrayal of action, for in her understanding, rather than one knowing one's self and one's motives and then acting, it is one's actions that may lead to a greater sense of self-knowledge. Nor would pure motives, even if known, necessarily vindicate one in the realm of action. In the epilogue to *Eichmann in Jerusalem*, Arendt explains why Eichmann must hang and why even his alleged pure motives are not sufficient to warrant mercy:

> We are concerned here only with what you did, and not with the possible noncriminal nature of your inner life and of your motives. . . . Let us assume, for the sake of argument, that it was nothing more than misinformation that made you a willing instrument in the organization of mass murder; there still remains the fact that you have carried out, and therefore actively supported, a policy of mass murder. For politics is not like the nursery; in politics obedience and support are the same.[64]

Unwilling to reduce the meaning of a political act to either the motives of the actor or to the consequences of the deed, Arendt writes that "action can be judged only by the criterion of greatness," or "the specific meaning of each deed."[65] Arendt's concept of forgiveness saves her conceptualization of political action from one completely divorced from responsibility. It is central, then, not only to the very possibility of political action for Arendt, but also to the judgment of political action by political terms, rather than distinctly moral, legal, or religious ones. Forgiveness presents a picture of humans as fallible (ever needful of forgiveness), yet open to change. It was Arendt's peculiar genius to perceive the need for new political thinking, and to retreat to the Greeks, the Romans, the Jews, and the early Christians to find it. In need of a new way to think about the relationship between political action and responsibility in a morally ambiguous public realm, Arendt looked to Jesus as an example of the power of forgiving.

One of the most surprising aspects of Arendt's fascination with the political possibilities of forgiveness is that it seems to contravene her concern for maintaining sharp distinctions between the public and the private realm. She contends that Jesus of Nazareth was the discoverer of the role of forgiveness, and although he made this discovery in a religious context, she argues that forgiving should be considered a political, rather than a moral or religious, experience.[66] She points out a number of characteristics that forgiving shares with political action. Forgiving depends on human plurality; no one can forgive himself.[67] It also parallels her conception of political action in that it "is the only reaction which does not merely re-act but acts anew and unexpectedly, unconditioned by the act which provoked it and therefore freeing from its consequences both the one who forgives and the one who is forgiven."[68] In its "miraculous" and unexpected quality, it exemplifies the spontaneity of political action. Apologies and forgiving also share with political action a reliance upon speech: As one scholar has written, until apologies are "articulated in the presence of the offended other, they serve only as soliloquies with little or no consequence or meaning."[69] Forgiving also calls for judgment (which elsewhere Arendt called the most political of faculties, the "hallmark" of political thinking)[70]; the potential forgiving party, in deciding whether to grant forgiveness, neither relies upon strict moral rules, legal notions of intent, nor the consequences of actions. Lastly, in *The Human Condition*, Arendt writes that "forgiving and the relationship it establishes is always an eminently personal (though not necessarily individual or private) affair in which *what* was done is forgiven for the sake of *who* did it."[71] We have seen above that in encountering Eichmann and reflecting on his deeds she later amended her understanding of forgiveness, positing the possibility of forgiving someone without necessarily forgiving their deeds.[72] Yet, while she entertained the prospect of forgiving someone while judging their deeds unthinkable to forgive, her conception of forgiveness retained an attention to the personal qualities of the actor. Can such a conception of apologies and forgiveness be meaningful in relation to historic acts committed by political collectivities?

Arendt well understood that forgiving—a miracle of sorts— was fragile and not easily transplanted from the private to the public realm. In *The Human Condition*, Arendt wrote that forgiving could only take place in a context of personal revelation, where people are "fully receptive to *who* somebody is" rather than "what they are," the *who* being their qualities, shortcomings, achievements, failings, and transgressions.[73] Such an open receptivity to who someone is usually is thought to occur only in the rarest of settings, that of love. But Arendt answers what seem to be her own objections regarding the transplanting of forgiving to the public realm by contending that "what love is in its own, narrowly circumscribed sphere, respect is in the larger domain of human affairs." Respect, which Arendt defines as "a kind of friendship without intimacy and without closeness . . . is a regard for the person from the distance which the space of the world puts between us, . . . [a] regard independent of qualities which we may admire or of achievements which we may highly esteem."[74] Arendt fears, though, that what she regards as the modern loss of respect may restrict the power of forgiving to the private realm. The indispensability of forgiveness to Arendt's concept of political action discloses the deeply personal nature of Arendt's politics. The "increasing depersonalization of public and social life" throws into doubt for Arendt both the possibility of forgiving and of political action itself.

The Limitations and (yet) the Promise of Apologies in Contemporary American Politics

The nature of politics itself, and particularly how politics is practiced in the contemporary United States, places exceptional strains upon the power of forgiveness. The personal nature of the dynamic of apologies and forgiveness raises serious doubts regarding the potential of apologies and forgiveness to work on a public and collective scale. If only the wronged has the power to forgive, and if they forgive primarily, although not only, for the sake of who the wrongdoer is, then can apologies and forgiveness work when applied to wrongs inflicted by political collectivities upon groups of people? And what can be done if the wrongdoers or the wronged have died? Can anyone speak for either the wronged or the wrongdoers? Most basically, is the power of apologizing and forgiving limited to relations between living individuals, or might it work in relations between groups?[75]

Earlier, I alluded to the stages in which we can see apologies and forgiveness occurring. At each stage of the process, political realities may limit the potential effectiveness of national apologies.

In particular, the power and conflict endemic to politics, the representativeness built into American politics, the concerns raised by Arendt in the 1950s that have only grown more dire regarding the devitalization of political action, and the related fragmentation of the American citizenry into numerous identity groups all call into question how effective national apologies may be in the United States. Let us examine the stages from apologies to forgiveness, and consider how political realities may impair their potential.

In the first stage, a preliminary agreement is reached between the parties that there is something from the past for which to apologize. Unless some consensus is reached regarding the wrongs that have been inflicted, there is no hope for an apology or for forgiveness. When wrongs have been inflicted by groups of people against other groups, it may be most difficult to reach an agreement as to who inflicted the wrongs (who was the aggressor?) on whom. One student of apologies argues, in fact, that the primary work apologies achieve in the political realm is putting the wrong on a public record.[76] Governments may be extremely loathe to create a public record declaring that they have inflicted wrongs, fearing that an admission may lead to calls for compensation not only by the specific peoples aggrieved, but by other groups who may feel similarly aggrieved. As noted in Chapter 2, a major concern voiced during the debates over reparations for Japanese Americans interned during World War II was whether a reparations law would encourage other groups to seek compensation and whether the law would establish a precedent upon which American Indians, African Americans, and Mexican Americans could demand similar compensation. It was not until Jesse Helms's amendment was tacked onto the bill explicitly stipulating that the Civil Liberties Act of 1988 did not establish a legal precedent that the law passed the Senate.

It is in this initial stage, when political wrongs may or may not be recognized, that the significance of power may be most apparent. As noted in exploring apologies and forgiveness in the private realm, if the wrongdoer is impervious to the grievances of the wronged person, then an apology likely will not be forthcoming.

Inequalities are likely to be even more common in the public realm, where the resources of some may be consolidated to form powerful groups or interests who needn't concern themselves with the demands of less powerful others. The import of inequalities is apparent in observing the manner in which the politics of national apologies in the United States has been contested over the past thirty years. Members of minority racial, ethnic, and cultural groups have voiced grievances against the government (typically the federal government but also state governments), attempting to employ various levers of power to gain an apology and possible compensation. As noted in Chapter 1, the Oneida land claims have languished for decades, and only recently have neared a response, owing to the new-found legal and economic power of the tribe, bankrolled by casino profits. And the success of the Japanese American reparations movement, as noted in Chapter 2, may be attributed to a number of strategic factors intrinsic to the movement itself, but it also would be naïve to overlook the significance of economic power. Sheldon Wolin suggests that the success of the reparations movement, after nearly three decades of official silence on the matter, may have more to do with the growing power of Japan's economy in the 1980s than with America's deepened conscience:

> What dictated this about-face? Was it less a question of injustice remembered than of a radical change in the American perceptions of Japan rather than of the Nisei, an official recognition on the part of American policy makers, both governmental and corporate, of the extraordinary power now possessed by Japan and hence of its vital importance to global political and economic strategies? [77]

It may be that national apologies are offered to those who can most effectively wield power against the government, rather than to those most wronged or in need of an apology and compensation. If that is the case, then certainly one lesson for proponents of an apology to American Indians or African Americans is to search for potential sources of power to leverage in requesting a national apology.

If a wrong is recognized by both parties, and an apology is demanded, then the next stage in the process is for the parties to judge what would mark an adequate apology. In order for apologies to issue and the chance for forgiveness to occur, judgments must be made as to what restitution, compensation, or penalty, if any, may be needed to indicate the sincerity of the apology. This stage may present the greatest difficulties in transplanting apologies and forgiveness into the public realm. In the private realm, typically parties face each other and "the offender acknowledges full responsibility for the transgression, expresses sorrow and contrition for the harm done, seeks forgiveness from the offended party, and implicitly or explicitly promises not to repeat the offense in the future."[78] A face-to-face encounter allows the offended party to judge the sincerity of the offending party's apology and to respond directly to the request for forgiveness. National apologies, on the other hand, tend to be offered by governmental representatives of the actual wrong-doers to, at times, representatives of the wronged, rather than the immediate wronged. The apologies also tend to be presented in a written rather than oral form. A number of consequences flow from these differences. First, issues related to representation arise. Who can speak for the wrongdoers? A corollary of the argument presented in Chapter 4 is that representatives of the present federal government are the appropriate parties to apologize on behalf of the past U.S. government that, in the case of the Oneidas, failed to abide by promises made, and in the case of the internment of Japanese Americans, illegally evacuated and incarcerated individuals of Japanese ancestry. However, issues related to representation may be more complex when it comes to broad and diffuse social and political wrongs such as slavery and Jim Crow. Can the present national government speak for all those involved in the systems of slavery and Jim Crow, including slave traders (many from other countries), slaveholders, and all those who benefited from the caste system established by Jim Crow?[79]

And who can speak authoritatively for the wronged, particularly if the wrongs were committed long ago? Chapter 1 noted that one of the difficulties the federal and New York State government has encountered in attempting to resolve the Oneida land claims was determining who could speak for the Oneida tribe, as conflicts have erupted within the tribe as well as between various bands of Oneidas (some who have established reservations in other states and Canada) as to what compensation would be acceptable. In the case of reparations for Japanese Americans interned, internal divisions between the more "radical" elements of the redress movement and the more mainstream movement were eventually squelched, if not healed, and the ultimate decision by the U.S. Congress to offer reparations to individuals (those alive at the time of the passage of the law) rather than to Japanese Americans as a group eliminated some of the perplexities that would have further confounded the law. Most serious proponents of an apology to African Americans for slavery and Jim Crow that would include some sort of reparations envisage a collective rather than an individual model, though, contending that it would better enable institution building within the African American community.[80] If an apology to African Americans and group reparations ever are to become more than wishful thinking, then questions of representation will have to be solved.

The U.S. government does have experience using a group model of compensation, as it is typically employed to resolve most American Indian claims. In most cases, federal law dictates that only tribes and not separate individuals may bring claims and be compensated. The law presumes a preexisting solidarity within American Indian tribes, with institutions in place to decide how resources are to be used.[81] Dissimilarities become immediately apparent when comparing African Americans to American Indian tribes, however. Members of tribes typically live close together on a reservation; African Americans are scattered across the United States. Tribes have in place institutions to decide upon matters of public concern, such as how to allocate resources, whereas no such generally agreed-upon body exists for African Americans. These dissimilarities present real administrative difficulties when considering group compensation. What group would represent

African Americans, or descendants of slavery and Jim Crow? Who would manage the money, and who would decide how the money was to be spent? Would all African Americans be given a vote, or only those who could prove they have suffered from the lingering effects of slavery and Jim Crow? And how would it be determined if one were African American?[82] These quandaries need not prove insuperable, although they do indicate that if national apologies with some material compensation are to have any chance of promoting reconciliation, then determining who a national apology should be directed to and who could administer whatever funds may be offered must be resolved.

As noted above, another noteworthy difference between the dynamics of apologies and forgiveness in the public as opposed to the private realm is the written rather than oral form that apologies tend to take when offered by nation-states. And, as Nicholas Tavuchis notes, when governments offer apologies, "as befits its formal, official, and public character, institutionally licensed and scripted apology tends to be couched in abstract, remote, measured, and emotionally neutral terms." Part of this quality Tavuchis attributes to "the discursive and practical obstacles in addressing a collective bill of particulars that documents numerous personal injuries, deprivations, and suffering, often far removed in time from the present."[83] The Civil Liberties Act of 1988 reads in such a manner; similarly the proposed joint resolution, offering "an apology for the many instances of violence, maltreatment, and neglect inflicted on Native Peoples by citizens of the United States," while including a lengthy list of wrongs, does so in detached and dispassionate language. Whatever power a national apology could have cannot reside solely in the official words. Tavuchis also notes that such apologies "are typically expressed in a compressed and summary manner."[84] Witness Congressman Tony Hall's proposed concurrent resolution on slavery: His proposal reads, "Resolved by the House of Representatives that the Congress apologizes to African-Americans whose ancestors suffered as slaves under the Constitution and the laws of the United States until 1865."[85] Although Hall's resolution dodges a host of perplexities (Are there lingering effects of slavery? What about Jim Crow?), speaks in an extraordinarily clipped manner, and does not entail any monetary compensation, as he pointed out, it still managed to erupt "a fire storm of controversy throughout the Nation," and has not moved further in Congress since its introduction in 1997.[86] Such neutered language, if offered as an apology in the private realm, doubtless would be judged lacking. And while it may ultimately be judged inadequate as a national apology as well, it is instructive that even Hall's spare words elicited angry rebuttals.[87]

Strains are apparent when representative institutions such as the U.S. Congress attempt to convey sincerity when offering national apologies. Part of the difficulty, as Tavuchis has noted, is the bloodless language typically employed by formal and official bodies. However, the problem is not the language alone, but also the context in which apologies are expressed. In an impersonal, bureaucratic megastate where politics is ordinarily understood as the competing play of interests, an apology, which uses words to achieve reconciliation between parties, may appear to be either "an empty, meaningless gesture,"[88] or a hopelessly unrealistic one. As we saw in Chapter 2, Congress, as well as national opinion leaders, debated whether words alone were sufficient to convey the sincerity of the U.S. government in apologizing for the forced evacuation, relocation, and internment of Japanese Americans. Proponents of reparations, of course, ultimately won the day, arguing that officials' words had to be accompanied by money in order to adequately convey "how absolutely clear we want to be about what is at stake."[89] As we saw, though, the payment of money was criticized by some on both the political right and left, as it was argued that money cheapened the apology, rather than communicating its sincerity.

The Civil Liberties Act of 1988, if not a legal precedent owing to Helms's amendment, still has established the expectation with other groups seeking an apology from the United States that monetary compensation should play a part in any such apology. As supporters of the 1988 Act were quick to state, though, the reparations paid as part of the national apology did not come close to fully compensating Japanese American internees for their losses. Rather, the payments of $20,000 to each internee alive at the time of the law's passage served to symbolize the United States' willingness to penalize itself to demonstrate sincerity (although critics contended the Act would penalize the next generation, and not the present). If national apologies ever are to issue to either American Indians or African Americans, Congress certainly will have to revisit the question of how much money, and paid to whom, is sufficient to convey the government's seriousness. It is likely that words without resources, in light of the Civil Liberties Act of 1988, would be scorned.

As is evident in the Oneida claims, as well as other claims by Indian tribes, land often stands at the center of the judgments made by tribes and the federal and state governments as to what would constitute an adequate apology. And as we have seen as well, tribes' demands for the return of land often conflict with the settled expectations, if not property rights, of present land owners. These seemingly zero-sum battles, as in the case of the Oneidas, at times have proven nearly intractable, although a number of noteworthy resolutions have been negotiated, most prominently the Alaska Natives Land Settlement of 1971, as well as the various claims based on the Non-Intercourse Act that have been resolved. Though land claims tend to pit tribes against present owners, vying for a scarce resource, it also serves to "ground" claims and provides an agreed-upon starting point for negotiations between tribes and governmental representatives.

The only comparable touchstone in various calls for reparations for African Americans to accompany a national apology would be the "40 acres and a mule" promised in 1865 by General Sherman to each family of freed slaves.[90] Congressman Conyers named his proposal to study reparations for African Americans HR 40. And, in the early 1990s, a number of members of the National Coalition of Blacks for Reparations in America (N'-COBRA), filed a lawsuit seeking $380 million in reparations for themselves and for local black communities. One plaintiff explained, "We're seeking reparations for our ancestors who aren't here to bear witness.... Nobody was paid 40 acres and a mule because Lincoln was assassinated before it could go through."[91] "Forty acres and a mule" also figured in the provocative suggestion that appeared in a 1993 article in *Essence* magazine that African Americans file a "Black Tax" claim for $43,209, the estimated value of "40 acres and a mule" in 1993 dollars.[92] While the trope of "40 acres and a mule" has penetrated the African American community and has figured in African American claims for reparation,[93] claims have not yet passed "the political laugh test," as Wade Henderson, the NAACP's chief Washington, DC, lobbyist remarked.[94] A number of commentators have noted the fantastic quality of many calls for African American reparations for slavery and Jim Crow.[95] Partly, the unreal quality of some of the proposals seems driven by proponents' attempts to convince the public of the magnitude of the harms done under slavery and Jim Crow and the continuing effects of the harms. (Law professor Robert Westley, for instance, estimates that due to policies of the 1950s, "The current generation of Blacks will lose about $82 billion in equity due to institutional discrimination. All things being equal, the next generation of Black homeowners will lose $93 billion."[96]) A major obstacle to be surmounted in any national apology for slavery and Jim Crow would be for both proponents and the U.S. government (as well as the public) to arrive at a judgment as to what would serve as an adequate symbolic payment that would neither dramatically underestimate the costs of slavery and Jim Crow, nor pose such an unrealistic figure as to make such a policy politically unfeasible.

Another impediment evident at this stage in the process of national apologies and possible forgiveness, in addition to the difficulties noted above in both parties agreeing as to what would mark an adequate apology, is the reluctance by present governmental representatives to judge harshly the actions of their predecessors. Harkening back to the debates over reparations for interned Japanese Americans, the two most often-voiced criticisms of offering a national apology were that it was unfair for present politicians to judge the actions of predecessors with the great advantage of hindsight, and that it is not our place to judge—only God can do so. Here we can learn from Arendt. Her writings present a passionate plea for individuals to recognize the political capacity and need to act and judge. If the past is not even past, then it is incumbent upon us to respond to past/present wrongs. And Arendt's argument in *The Human Condition* was that it was Jesus who recognized the miracle of forgiveness—but the miracle was that it was a human, not merely a divine, capacity.

As we have also noted in considering forgiveness in the personal realm, another danger that threatens the dynamic of apologies and forgiveness is the wronged party's unwillingness or inability to accept an apology and renew the relationship with the wrongdoer. This is not to say that all apologies should be judged to be adequate or sincere; as discussed earlier, it is essential to the process of apology and forgiveness that those wronged have the power to accept or reject an apology. If an apology is offered in an attempt to reestablish a relationship of equality without the pertinent wrong at its center, the wronged party may rightly judge the apology insufficient. However, not necessarily all apologies are lacking. It is essential to the process of apology and forgiveness that the wronged party actually has the potential and, where judged fitting, the willingness to give up the desire for vengeance and the resentment that the wrong may have bred. If the wronged party is unable or unwilling to do so, then the past wrong will continue to intrude into the present. If the wronged party feels either self-righteously superior or permanently inferior to the wrongdoers, then the wrong will continue to haunt the relationship and forgiveness will prove elusive. Both of these possibilities may point to an unwillingness or inability on the part of the wronged party to see themselves as anything but victims within the relationship or failure to see their relationship with the wrongdoers as defined by anything greater than the wrong. The wronged party may wed themselves both to the wrong and to the identity of victim.

These psychological tendencies may manifest themselves politically in what some, particularly within the African American community, have criticized as the "victim politics" that they perceive as endemic to calls for national apologies and reparations. A number of prominent African American public thinkers have openly disdained calls for apologies, and in particular reparations, arguing that, as Armstrong Williams writes, "The reparations movement encourages minorities to regard themselves, collectively, as helpless victims." Williams primarily blames civil rights leaders for attempting to "capitalize on free-floating white guilt."[97] Similarly, John McWhorter scornfully criticizes Randall Robinson (author of the best-selling book, *The Debt: What America Owes to Blacks*) and other black "leaders" (his quotation marks) as "hooked on the satisfactions of victimhood."[98] Shelby Steele also casts blame on the "entire civil rights establishment" that has strategized "to keep us wards of white guilt."[99] These criticisms echo Arendt's concerns over translating knotty political issues into the "phony sentimental" terms of collective innocence and collective guilt, as well as her insistence that those who perceive themselves as wronged must overcome their desire for vengeance in order for present political action to occur.

These criticisms point to the potential problematic nature of groups organizing their identities around past wrongs. What is required for such groups to see themselves as active agents rather than as passive victims? What is required for such groups "to come to terms with the past"? Williams, McWhorter, and Steele cynically view the demands of "the civil rights establishment," and suggest this establishment has no real desire to overcome the past; that doing so would put them out of business. Without calling into question the motivation of those who have voiced grievances based on past wrongs, it is still possible to suggest that dangers reside in basing one's identity around past wrongs. Political theorist Wendy Brown applies Nietzsche's insights to what she labels "the dominant political expression of the age: identity politics," and argues that a distinctive peril of such a politics is that "it becomes invested in its own subjection." In an imaginative application of Nietzsche's *On The Genealogy of Morals*, Brown maintains that a politicized identity:

> ...becomes attached to its own exclusion both because it is premised on this exclusion for its very existence as identity and because the formation of identity at the site of exclusion, as exclusion, augments or 'alters the direction of the suffering' entailed in subordination or marginalization by finding a site of blame for it. But in so doing, it installs its pain over its unredeemed history in the very foundation of its political claim, in its demand for recognition as identity."[100]

Brown argues that identity politics then, unwittingly perhaps, "makes claims for itself, only by entrenching, restating, dramatizing, and inscribing its pain in politics."

Without contending with the psychological nuances of Brown's argument, or evaluating how well the argument fits the groups under discussion, it is instructive to note that the process of apology and forgiveness requires a willingness and ability on the part of those who perceive themselves as wronged to negotiate psychologically challenging transformations in relationship to their own identity, the wrong, the wrongdoers, and their temporal orientation. Arendt's writings hold out the possibility that through the process of forgiving, these transformations may be navigated. It provides people who have been wronged with a means of actively contending with the past and thus becoming an active agent. Forgiving, for Arendt, is how we as human actors express our freedom with regard to the past—we accept the deeds of the past, yet we do not accept them passively. In "Understanding and Politics," Arendt writes that forgiving "tries the seemingly impossible, to undo what has been done, and succeeds in making a new beginning where everything seemed to have come to an end."[101] The wrong—as Arendt later corrected herself—is not undone. Rather, it assumes a new meaning and a new fixity in the past. That is, the past wrong no longer comprises the whole of the world, nor is it relived in the present. A task for victims, or those who identify themselves as such, is to move from a world in which the perceived wrong is the center of the world, to one in which it becomes only a part, thus leaving room to see other people, their needs, and desires. Similarly, forgiveness allows individuals to "come to terms with the past" so that "a serial sense of time eventually replaces the nightmare of pure simultaneity."[102] Prior to such transformations, one could say that the world of those who identify themselves as victims appears one-dimensional—that dimension being *the wrong*—which comprises the world's focus. Through forgiving, the wrong is not undone, but it becomes one dimension of many. It also takes its rightful place in the past, making room for the present and future.[103] Forgiving also demands a transformation in how the wronged view their wrongdoers. If they insist on seeing those they hold responsible for their past suffering as unredeemable, then forgiveness stalls; ex-victims must be open to seeing past wrongdoers as fallible humans worthy of a renewed relationship. Finally, and possibly most importantly, if the process of apology and forgiveness is to succeed, both in the personal as well as the public realm, it will do so not for the sake of the painful past, but for the sake of a hopeful future. One forgives a past deed primarily for the future—for the hope that the future holds of a renewed relationship. To the degree that the relationship is one that both parties have an interest in renewing or reestablishing, national apologies and forgiveness provide the possibility of political renewal.

The final stages of the process of apologies and forgiveness—the parties recognizing a sense of shared humanity and reestablishing a relationship untainted by the wrongs of the past—brings into sharp relief the particular political promise of national apologies and forgiveness. The process is not only, or primarily, a therapeutic one. It entails not only a change in consciousness, but also a change in the relationship between those who perceive themselves as wronged and those they hold responsible. This change is brought about through speech. Nor can the process remain strictly moral if it is to have political potential. That is, though sharing qualities fundamental to morality—in that apologizing and forgiving call for people to recognize each other as ends and not as objects to be exploited for one's own purposes and to use dialogue in treating each other as peers—the process, for it to be political, can be neither intimate nor strictly dialogical. National apologies typically are not offered in intimate settings nor are they offered on a one-to-one basis. The debate, deliberation, and negotiation that transpire while political bodies decide whether to offer national apologies, and what, if any, compensation is to accompany the apologies, is "not dialogical but multivocal and impersonal."[104] Finally, for the process ultimately to aim for political reconciliation and renewal, it must not remain strictly bound to the legal concerns of fixing blame for past wrongs, but must turn to the more imaginative concerns of how peoples with different identities, interests, and understandings of their shared past can continue to live and act with each other. If Americans are to do so, it may be that national apologies, and the possibility of forgiveness, in encouraging an active engagement with the nation's past prompted by the present claims of American citizens, will enable Americans to use their conflictual past as a site upon which to build a new or reinvigorated vision of the future. Such a process holds out the possibility of reconnecting citizens to their political past, present, and future, as well as reconnecting individuals and groups to the larger political collectivity.

I do not mean to be "Pollyanna-ish" and imply that national apologies and forgiving, like other political activities, may not easily be perverted. National apologies may serve as an inexpensive alternative to more far-reaching structural changes that may be needed to create a more comprehensively just society. And, while national apologies that offer only symbolic compensation for past wrongs may appear to entail only token costs, they are still limited by a moral economy: As apologies proliferate, they lose their value. For national apologies to maintain the possibility of communicating meaning and promoting change, they must not be offered too often or too easily. Difficult political choices must be made among a cacophony of claimants. And, as noted earlier, apologies—and the reparations that may be offered along with them—are sure to foster political resentment among some other Americans. Any responsible political analysis of the costs and benefits of national apologies would have to account for the resentment that would certainly be nurtured. Finally, as suggested earlier, national apologies may condone, or promote, a politics of victimization in which individuals and groups are encouraged to belittle their own capacities and blame others for conditions which they could collectively change.

Yet, national apologies and forgiveness present intriguing and promising political possibilities as means of contending with the reality and presence of past wrongs. At its most basic level, this process recognizes our common fallibility and reveals us to be continually in need of forgiveness. Although apologizing and forgiving do fall outside many of our typical ways of thinking about politics, the process may engage us in the political at its most meaningful—where issues of membership, political identity, and responsibility are central. To apologize and to forgive opens up the central political question of identity. Forgiveness involves thinking through the relationship that exists between *agent* and *act*, and implies the possibility of seeing the agent as more than— better than—the deed. The question that necessarily follows is: Who is the agent, if not only the doer of the deed? Debates in the United States prompted by the possibility of national apologies have raised searching questions concerning the American political identity: Was the expropriation of Indian lands an aberration? Was slavery an aberration? Or Jim Crow? Or the evacuation and internment of Japanese Americans? Or should these troubling episodes be viewed as defining and illuminating of our political identity? Finally, the process of deciding whether to offer national apologies and the process groups may go through in deciding whether to accept the apologies and forgive may be transforming—through it we become a people responding to our past to create a more just future, rather than simply forgetting and repressing disquieting moments that may haunt the hearts and minds of many of our fellow citizens.

Conclusion

Citizenship in the Shadows of Misdeeds

MUCH OF *Sins of the Parents* has been devoted to an examination of the concepts underlying the question of how the U.S. government should respond to calls for it to apologize and provide compensation for past governmental misdeeds. Chapter 3 of the book argued for a conception of the American polity in which the ambiguous history of the United States cannot be simply forgotten, but rather must be interpreted and responded to as it necessarily informs present political identity. Chapter 4 argued for a conception of political responsibility intrinsically linked to political identity; some political responsibilities derive from one's identity as a member of the national polity. Finally, Chapter 5 made the case that the practice of national apologies may create new political identities that may dissipate resentments that stand between individual citizens, diminish the alienation that divides citizens from the nation-state, and allow individuals to better integrate their political identities with their racial, ethnic or cultural identities.

The arguments above presume that individuals are willing and able to identify to some extent with the U.S. nation-state; that at least part of an individual's identity is connected to his or her position within the national polity. However, a sense of national identity, or national citizenship, cannot be presumed. Both the nation-state and the concept of citizenship have been scrutinized a great deal lately, as contemporary political forces have compelled political thinkers to rethink these ideas. National citizenship seems endangered by at least two countervailing trends. What has been termed "globalization" and the concurrent movement of peoples has rendered problematic any concept of citizenship based on territory alone. A concept of citizenship suitable for our times can no longer be based solely upon a relationship to any particular location. That being said, however, geographical considerations are not completely irrelevant, either. As the status of refugees in World War II made apparent, and as the contemporary status of refugees continues to remind us, within an international regime of national states, those without a state's protection are often defenseless. One strand, then, that must remain in an understanding of citizenship is that citizens are those who, based upon their birth within a particular territory, or a legal process individuals may go through, are due protection from the nation-state that they recognize and that recognizes them.

While globalization has eroded national identities from without, the nation-state also has been hollowed out from within. Theories of national citizenship that presume national unity based upon a common race, ethnicity, language, religion, or shared history or set of recollections have been problematized by what Benjamin Barber has termed tribalism, or the claims of subnational communities.[1] The fragmentation and pluralization of national unity has expressed itself in numerous ways: as ethnic politics, multiculturalism, or identity politics. National citizenship has been besieged from without and within. However, a countervailing trend may be detected as well. Similar to the dynamic noted in the Introduction, in which the contemporary erosion of the past has created a hunger for nostalgic renditions of it, the pluralization of the American nation has brought forth a drive toward what Sheldon Wolin has coined "political fundamentalism," which "aspires to a restoration of a mythical past," and includes "not only virtually unqualified loyalty to the nation, especially in times of national danger and war, but also . . . loyalty to an idealized earlier America."[2] In response to these various forces, some political thinkers have argued that the nation-state is an anachronistic construct that will (and should) melt away to allow global citizenship to become individuals' primary political identity. Others have argued that global citizenship, even more so than national citizenship, is too large and impersonal a construct around which individuals can shape their political identity. These thinkers contend that individuals have retreated into more parochial communities of race, ethnicity, language, culture, gender, or sexual orientation because the scale of these smaller communities are more prone to enlist individuals' energies and allegiances. Finally, others have looked upon the "fundamentalization" of the nation with suspicion and fear. National citizenship, and the related claim that individuals may have political responsibilities based upon their identity as citizens of the United States, is suspect.

As noted, thinkers all along the political spectrum have acknowledged the extent to which contemporary political forces have made outmoded notions of citizenship based on territory alone, or a common race, ethnicity, language, religion, shared history, or set of recollections. As some have cheered the impending death of the nation-state, while others have bemoaned its decline, many political thinkers have turned to retheorizing the relationships among the nation-state, democracy, and individual citizenship. Some of the United States' most prominent political thinkers have turned their attention to these concerns, attempting to craft concepts that attend to the contemporary state of the political world. While Sheldon Wolin,[3] Richard Rorty,[4] Michael Sandel,[5] and William Connolly,[6] for instance, may not agree on their diagnoses on what is wrong with the American political body, nor how the political body became ill, they all do seem to agree that a dose of democratic citizenship is called for (although, of course, they disagree, often quite vociferously, as to how they define this term). Outside the academy as well, as two scholars recently have noted, there is agreement that "the promotion of responsible citizenship is an urgent aim of public policy."[7]

But just what is responsible citizenship in the contemporary American political context? And what sort of political relationship should individuals have with each other and with the American nation-state? Certainly, with no shortage of recent reminders of the horrors that may be committed in the name of national solidarity, proponents of national citizenship must take pains to distinguish their aims from those who use the language of patriotism and citizenship to inspire violence and hatred of others. Within the contemporary context, if a theory of responsible citizenship is to be truly responsible, it must differentiate itself from nationalism, chauvinism, and the political fundamentalism earlier noted. On the other hand, while a real danger exists in driving the nation-state to demand excessive unity, this book's argument presumes that insufficient identification between individual citizens and a certain vision of the American nation-state is a concern as well. Citizenship in the American nation-state still performs needed work. In particular, for the concerns raised in this book, the nation-state has the potential to perform two essential tasks. The first is that its representatives are the only possible ones who can speak for the collectivity and authoritatively apologize for the misdeeds of the past. If national apologies are to mean anything, then they must issue from representatives who have the authority to speak in the name of the United States. Second, if compensation is to be provided to victims, or heirs of victims, then the nation-state remains "the main mechanism for social transfers, that is to say for collecting an appropriate fraction of the economy's total income and redistributing it among the population according to some criterion of public interest, common welfare, and social needs."[8] A central premise of *Sins of the Parents*, then, hinges on the argument that we have not yet entered a post-national political world, but rather that the American nation-state still performs required tasks.

This concluding chapter aims not to be an exhaustive account of a theory of national citizenship in the contemporary political world. Rather, its aims are more modest, seeking instead to examine the relationship between the acknowledgment of past political wrongs and the possibility for the creation of a distinct vision of national citizenship. The chapter aims to build on the book's arguments thus far to consider whether the presence of the nation's past wrongs may serve as a site upon which to create new political identities, and whether we can construct a theory of citizenship in the shadows of misdeeds. The chapter examines the particular possibilities, as well as difficulties, that past political wrongs raise for recent theories of citizenship. The primary question that remains is whether it is possible to imagine a theory of citizenship that would be sufficiently critical of the nation-state to allow citizens to acknowledge the presence of past wrongs and at the same time allow citizens to feel devoted enough to the project of the nation-state and fellow citizens to call forth a sense of political responsibility to respond to past political wrongs.

As Chapter 3 discussed, citizenship and patriotism are concepts we use to situate ourselves in political space and time.[9] These concepts encapsulate our understandings of what we owe (and what is owed us) to those with whom we share the present, as well as to those who came before us and those who will follow. One focus of *Sins of the Parents* is to search for a political language that would better enable us to see ourselves in relation to others and in time, a language with which it is possible to better understand the political value of acknowledging responsibility for past wrongs and offering national apologies.

The book has claimed that national apologies, with or without material redress, are extraordinary in that they may turn our attention to fundamental political issues ordinarily ignored. Specifically, the book has argued that to judge whether national apologies are appropriate engages the polity in questions of individual identity, political identity, and political responsibility. To judge whether the polity should apologize for a past deed, its members must reflect on their own identities, their relations with their contemporaries, as well as deliberate about the polity's past, present, and future. Discussions in the United States regarding the responsibilities that present-day Americans may have for past wrongs have been framed by our ordinary ways of understanding politics. In the Introduction, I observed that the theological, therapeutic, and juridical frameworks have predominated in most debates over national apologies and reparations. Whereas most public debates have "lurched among" these frameworks (to borrow Martha Minow's language)[10] three perspectives have been most evident in scholarly debates on the issues raised for current understandings of citizenship by present demands for justice for past political wrongs. These perspectives draw our attention to specific concerns, but simultaneously may obscure our vision of others. Below, I very briefly examine how these perspectives frame the issues of political identity and responsibility raised by contemporary calls for national apologies and reparations, and begin to sketch an alternative account.

* * *

As the cases of demands by the Oneidas and Japanese Americans document, when contemporary American legal and political bodies have deliberated over whether to apologize and offer compensation for past political wrongs, they have had to answer three primary questions: What is the nature of the alleged wrong and who or what has been wronged? Who should be held responsible for the wrong? And how far back in history should the present generation go to respond to wrongs? Answers to these questions take on a distinctive note depending upon from which theoretical political framework one works.

One primary distinction amongst theoretical frameworks is how individual political subjects are conceived. Carla Hesse and Robert Post, in the Introduction to *Human Rights in Political Transitions: Gettysburg to Bosnia*, note that contemporary discussions of how nation-states can best navigate through political transitions and respect human rights are marked by a tension between two contrasting conceptions of subjects. They label these conceptions "thin" and "thick." In the thin conception, "persons are seen as abstract bearers of universal rights, liberated from the contingencies of particular histories." In the thick conception, "they are figured as historically embedded in particular cultures and the bearers of specific collective memories."[11] These two conceptions echo points made earlier in the book in that the "thin" conception, as argued in Chapter 4, may also be conceptualized as an "amnesiac" political subject that appears in much liberal political discourse. This discourse, as argued in Chapter 4, aims to reduce political conflict by conceiving of the political subject as without a particular history. Within this "thin" and "amnesiac" vision, personhood rather than citizenship is the key marker of individual political identity. Individuals are conceived of as abstract bearers of human rights rather than as historically and culturally defined beings.[12] The political being in the liberal vision is "thinly" constituted in that the particular identities of race, ethnicity, and culture are diluted. As Sheldon Wolin makes clear in his reading of Hobbes, and as Jefferson, Paine and de Tocqueville witness in the United States, this thinning works to liberate individuals from the past and may allow peoples to break free from harmful cycles of wrongs, resentment, and vengeance. Hesse and Post similarly note that "a thinning out of particular group identities may thus be critical in transitional moments, especially where conflicts have hardened along ethnic or racial lines."[13] While this framework may perform needed work at transitional moments, *Sins of the Parents* argues that it may limit our collective abilities (as well as willingness) to respond to historic wrongs.

As we have seen, the claims by the Oneidas and Japanese Americans (as well as claims by African Americans) do not fit neatly into a liberal (or legal compensatory) model. U.S. courts and Congress were asked to determine if a political entity that exists through time, rather than solely in the present, has a responsibility to make amends for historic (if not "ancient") acts. As developed in Chapters 3 and 4, liberal theory, in its promise that "we can begin the world again," and in its constitution of the political subject as shorn of the particularities of race, ethnicity, and culture (not to mention gender and sexual orientation), inspires us to forget that our individual identity, as well as that of the political world, has a history not of our own making. The liberal concept of justice, epitomized by a blindfolded woman with scales, evinces that blindness to those historically suffused differences, as well as forgetfulness, is inherent in much of our political and legal thinking.[14] Within the primary liberal approach to collective responsibility, an extended passage of time between the commission of a political wrong and claims for justice foreclose the need for an apology or compensation on the part of the present members of the polity, as their "late birth" grants them innocence and absolution. Yet, as argued in Chapters 3 and 4, it may be that within the contemporary United States, we should neither turn our backs nor close our eyes to the ambivalent history of the polity, for that history may be not so much behind us and our fellow citizens as within us.

* * *

As Hesse and Post note, those who argue for "thick" subjects contend that thinning political identities runs the danger of diminishing the solidarity required to unify a nation-state. They summarize the argument in this manner: "Civil peace and lasting political stability do not ultimately depend on the cohabitation of abstract individuals, but rather on the development of relatively thick national cultures created from shared ideals and shared historical experiences. It is through dense and particular cultural narratives that nations are forged."[15] "Thick" political selves enhance not only political stability, but also a sense of political responsibility based upon one's identity as a member of a particular political society. Within this vision, the individual strives to act responsibly and justly not because of an abstract notion of justice, but because they "view the goodness of their own lives as bound up with the justice of their society and world."[16]

The argument that a "thin" or "amnesiac" vision neither adequately cultivates the solidarity needed to hold the nation-state together nor provides sufficient justification for sacrifices that may be needed for the sake of the collective has figured prominently as well in debates over the claims raised by the Oneidas and Japanese Americans. This argument, voiced by some in the contemporary United States (particularly those who have been labeled

as "neo-conservatives,") contends that solidarity, or a commitment
to the nation-state, must rest on more than a common allegiance to
abstract rights. In this vision, a sense of pride about the nation-state
and its history holds the collective together. The claims for present
justice for past wrongs examined in this book pose two dangers,
in particular, to neo-conservative visions of a "thick" national culture upon which, in this vision, national citizenship relies. The
first, as discussed in Chapter 4, is that the sort of critical history
upon which the Oneida land claims or the arguments for reparations for Japanese Americans rest, by undermining the common
narratives that undergird collective identity and by puncturing
pride in the nation's history, will "inevitably tend to qualify, even
if it does not destroy, one's sense of belonging to the collectivity
whose past has been revised."[17] The second and related danger
is that "multiculturalism" or "identity politics" will so fragment
the nation that solidarity will be impossible to achieve. These
concerns coalesce into the argument for "political fundamentalism" noted earlier, a central component of which is loyalty to an
idealized common history (or myth) unsullied by past wrongs.
This argument was made most conspicuously by political theorist
Allan Bloom, who bemoaned the fact that "the unity, grandeur
and attendant folklore of the founding heritage" has been attacked
in the last half century.[18] Bloom castigated a long list of debunkers,
from Carl Becker to John Dewey to Charles Beard, Southern historians, and the radicals in the civil rights movement, all of whom
contributed to "killing off the local deities" and "weakening our
convictions of the truth or superiority of American principles and
our heroes."[19] In the early 1990s, Arthur M. Schlesinger Jr.'s *The
Disuniting of America* gained a following due to the same vein of
thought. Schlesinger argued for the maintenance of the "mar-
velous inheritance that history bestows on us," lest we "invite
the fragmentation of the national community into a quarrelsome
spatter of enclaves, ghettos, tribes."[20] Although Schlesinger
acknowledged the racism that nonwhite minorities face, and the
racism written into American history, his vision remained celebratory, plotting the advances of the American Creed through the

Second World War, which, "If it did not end American racism, at least it drove much racial bigotry underground."[21] The evacuation, relocation, and incarceration of Americans of Japanese descent contravenes rather dramatically, however, Schlesinger's self-satisfied portrayal of American history and identity.

The contention that a common and proud history may unify a fragmented present presupposes that history should serve a political function. Schlesinger seemed anxious for *The Disuniting of America* to be read as an impassioned defense of "honest history" against what he regarded as the functionalization of history. Yet, for all of Schlesinger's passion for "honest history," his argument vacillated between locating the enemy in those who turn history into a weapon, and those who turn history into a weapon for the wrong purposes. The brunt of his attack is focused on multiculturalism, referred to as "the cult of ethnicity" and its proponents "the militants of ethnicity."[22] Although Schlesinger does not explicitly justify "exculpatory history," which he defines as history that "vindicates the status quo and the methods by which power is achieved and maintained," his book is a paean to the American Creed, and a warning against straining the fragile bonds of cohesion in our society.[23] The quotations chosen for the book jacket and first page that prompted consumers to make it a national bestseller, hailed the book as a "devastating attack on multiculturalism," and an accusation against radical multiculturalists "of dividing our population and distorting our past."[24]

As Chapter 3 made clear, a central question of *Sins of the Parents*, though, is what are we to do if our history, rather than serving as glue to hold together a divisive and disintegrating present, is a source of discord because history itself was discordant? While the United States is not extraordinary in its struggles, neither is it exceptional in lacking struggles, as contemporary historians (and political activists) have called our attention to. As past struggles and past wrongs increasingly come to light and complicate our sense of history and national identity, the attempt to constitute the United States as a cultural and political community through mythic remembrances of the nation's heroic past intended to instill pride in "thick" political selves seems an increasingly un-likely and misguided strategy. The "imagined community" of the United States no longer seems able to generate a portrayal of harmony nor offer much respite from present divisiveness and fragmentation.[25] As once-marginalized voices emerge within the nation, and bring to the fore memories of the wronged, the de-piction of a harmonious, conflict-free, and unsullied tradition has become impossible to maintain. As much as Allan Bloom or Arthur Schlesinger, Jr. mourn that our history is no longer common nor is able to fill us with unequivocal pride, there is no going back. As Cornel West writes, "The United States has become the land of hybridity, heterogeneity, and ambiguity."[26]

* * *

The recognition of past political wrongs, apologies for them, and possibly compensation, become problematic, then, within Bloom's or Schlesinger's neo-conservative vision. For such an ac-knowledgment may detract from the national pride that a neo-conservative framework takes to be essential for national solidarity. Within this vision, past political wrongs tend to be denied, excused, or marginalized. Notice, though, that unlike the liberal "thin" or "amnesiac" vision, where the history of the polity does not inform the present, here it is the investment in the polity's historical narra-tive and an anxious concern to maintain it as a source of pride that poses the primary obstacle to the recognition and response to past political wrongs. In a liberal amnesiac vision, past wrongs, on the whole, tend to be portrayed as "ancient history," whereas in the neo-conservative vision, past wrongs cannot be allowed to pierce the idealized history thought essential to inspiring the attachment to the nation-state that constitutes loyal citizenship.

A third framework, exemplified by the thinking of William Connolly discussed in Chapter 4, also is present in scholarly treat-ments of the concerns of this book. Connolly's vision, as well as that of other postmodern thinkers, counters the neo-conservative common narrative with a multi-perspectival and multicultural portrayal of America's past and present. Likewise, where the neo-conservative vision strives to firmly attach the individual to the nation-state, the wary postmodern such as Connolly sees the "bond of identification between the individual and the state" as both "honorable and dangerous."[27] As noted earlier, Connolly fears the relation between the individual and the state may degenerate "into disaffection with the state or a nationalism in which the tribulations of the time are attributed to an evil 'other' who must be neutralized."[28] And in a later essay, Connolly implores his readers not to fall "right into the black hole of the nation."[29]

The differentiated aspect of the postmodern vision provides a corrective to the anxious neo-conservative defense of a single national narrative. And its wariness of the power of the nation-state and of fostering an overzealous identification between individual citizens and the nation-state is a helpful reminder that theories of citizenship or patriotism, particularly in our post-September 11, 2001 reality, can too easily become variants of intolerant nationalism. However, while the differentiated aspect of the vision creates an opening to criticize a polity's past and to voice grievances against the nation-state, it is not apparent that the wariness of the theory enables a sufficient sense of political responsibility to be created in the polity to call forth an apology and possible compensation for past political wrongs done in the name of the nation-state.[30] While this vision may provide us the perspective from which to criticize the nation's past, unlike the neo-conservative one, it may also leave us, similar to the "thin" and "amnesiac" liberal vision, insufficiently attached to the nation-state to feel responsible for its deeds, and exceedingly wary of enhancing such an attachment. Thus, while past wrongs may be recognized within this vision, there may not be adequate motivation to address the wrongs by the current polity. We are left, then, with the question of whether it is possible to imagine a theory of citizenship "thin" and differentiated enough to allow the critical distance to recognize the misdeeds of the polity's past, and yet "thick" enough to inspire the requisite sense of responsibility in present-day citizens to respond to them.

Citizenship in the Shadows of Misdeeds

While past wrongs raise vexing difficulties for theories of citizenship, I conclude by suggesting that debates over present responsibilities for past wrongs may provide an opportunity to create a distinct sense of citizenship in the shadows of misdeeds.

As noted above, I contend only the nation-state could offer apologies and possible reparations for past political wrongs. Having said that, however, not just any conception of a nation-state will do, but rather a certain image of the nation-state, and of the individual's relationship to it, is required to enable present-day citizens to acknowledge and respond to past wrongs. First, as argued in Chapter 3 with reference to Lincoln's image of the American polity, the nation-state must be conceived as existing over time rather than existing in an ever-present present. That is, the nation-state must be considered a "collective historical enterprise,"[31] or an "ongoing historical project" in which individual citizens both look back to the founding of the nation as well as look forward to the continuation of the project for future generations.[32] Only by fostering an appreciation of where citizens stand in time will they be willing to recognize the responsibilities that may derive from their membership in the historical polity. The "thin" or "amnesiac" vision is fatally flawed in this regard.

Second, the nation-state must exist as more than a geographic entity, and individual citizens must be encouraged to see each other as sharing more than jurisdiction under a common legal sovereign.[33] An emotional involvement is required between the individual citizen and the nation-state, as well as amongst citizens. However, underlying this conception of the nation-state, it is not race, or ethnicity, or religion that provides the social and political glue to hold it together, nor is it a common culture. Rather, the attachment must be created and recreated based upon a consciousness that individuals are collectively engaged in a significant project that "transcends their individual lives in time and space."[34] That consciousness, however, dependent as it is upon experiences of collective engagement, is most at doubt in the contemporary

American polity where few people perceive the nation-state as a site for meaningful political action.

However, the moments of extraordinary politics provoked by debates over past wrongs and present responsibilities stand as reminders of what political action can achieve and toward what the American nation-state could aspire. The recognition of past wrongs, and the collective attempt to respond to them justly, may encourage the development of political virtues particularly needed today, and may foster an image of the nation-state within which those virtues may be nurtured. First, the recognition of past wrongs provides a helpful reminder of our imperfections. By acknowledging past injustices, such recognition may chasten the present polity and educate present citizens of the need to critically, and at times, suspiciously, view the activities of the nation-state. Second, the calls for national apologies make apparent that citizens need not be passive, either in response to historical wrongs, or in response to present inequities. National apologies, and in response to them, forgiveness, may enable individuals to see themselves as democratic citizens: worthy of equal respect, capable of action, and responsive to the calls for justice by those with whom they share the political world.

Sins of the Parents has sought to explore the ways in which we imagine our relationship to others who have considered themselves "Americans" in the past, to others with whom we share the present, and to future Americans. In particular, the book has focused on the question of whether those of us who consider ourselves "Americans" today have a responsibility to make amends for the wrongs perpetrated by our political predecessors. Rather than offering a general answer to this question, the book has argued that present claims for justice arising out of past wrongs should be interrogated to ascertain what the past may say about present political identity, and whether the past has really passed. In doing so, the book has argued that underlying the thorny issue of past wrongs and present responsibilities lie two central relationships— that between past, present, and future; and that between individual citizens and the political collective (the "I" and the "We"). The book suggests that thinking carefully about the issues raised by present claims for justice for past wrongs calls not for erasing the differences between past, present, and future, nor between "I" and "We" (nor between responsibility and guilt or sin), but neither does it call for solidifying these differences. The boundaries between past, present, and future, and those that separate individuals from the political collective, while extant, are also permeable. The past does intrude into the present and future, individuals are rooted in the collective, and present-day citizens may share in the responsibility, although not the guilt, for deeds done long ago. It is the negotiation of these boundaries, rather than falling prey to anxiously holding on to one or the other of the polarities, that the issues examined in this work call for. Going too far in the direction of the "present-oriented I" in defense of individual agency and present-oriented action may blind us to the permeability of time as well as to the needs and presence of others. On the other hand, going too far in the other direction in defense of "thick" attachments to the nation-state may collapse the distinction between past, present, and future, and between "I" and "We", and thus fail to leave room for both individual agency and present political action. Thinking carefully through the issues clarifies the space between the polarities allowing us to see the possibility that a recognition of the unjust deeds performed by our political collectivity and debate and discussion regarding what, if anything, should be done about them, could inspire a sense of citizenship that reminds us of our susceptibility to acts of hubris and human fallibility, and yet also of our collective ability to continue together in the shadows of wrongs and in the face of the future's uncertainty. Through responding to past wrongs, we may connect to fellow citizens, collectively become who we would want to be, and partially liberate ourselves from past injustices by present political action.

Notes

Introduction

1. The Oxford English Dictionary defines *rectification* as "The correction of error; a setting straight or right; amendment, improvement, correction." Three terms, in particular, have been used to refer to the ways in which governments have attempted to make rectification. *Restitution* typically refers to the return of actual property that was wrongfully taken, whereas *redress* and *reparations* typically refer to compensation, usually money, provided in lieu of that which cannot be returned, such as lost lives, destroyed communities, or violated rights.

2. Leslie T. Hatamiya, *Righting a Wrong: Japanese Americans and the Passage of the Civil Liberties Act of 1988* (Stanford: Stanford University Press, 1993).

3. See, for instance, Randall Robinson, *The Debt: What America Owes to Blacks* (New York: Dutton Press, 2000); Congress, House, Representative Tony Hall speaking for *The Apology for Slavery Resolution of 2000,* HR Res. 356, 106th Cong., 2nd sess., *Congressional Record* (19 June 2000): H4596–4597.

4. Judith N. Shklar, *Legalism: Laws, Morals, and Political Trials* (Cambridge: Harvard University Press, 1964), 5. Michael Sandel defines *public philosophy* as "the political theory implicit in our practice, the assumptions about citizenship and freedom that inform our public life" in *Democracy's Discontent: America In Search of a Public Philosophy* (Cambridge: Harvard University Press, Belknap Press, 1996), 4.

5. Ezekiel 18:20, and see Jeremiah 31:28–40 as well. However, the idea that sins *will* be visited upon children is also found in the Hebrew Bible. See Exodus 20: 5; Exodus 34: 7; Numbers 14: 14–18; and Deuteronomy 5: 9.

6. Elazar Barkan, *The Guilt of Nations: Restitution and Negotiating Historical Injustices* (New York: W.W. Norton & Company, 2000), xxiv.

7. Ibid., xxiii.

8. Ibid.

9. Karl Jaspers, *The Question of German Guilt*, trans. E. B. Ashton (New York: The Dial Press, 1947) and Hannah Arendt, *The Origins of Totalitarianism* (New York: Harcourt Brace Jovanovich, 1973). And see John Torpey, "Making Whole What Has Been Smashed: Reflections on Reparations," *The Journal of Modern History* 73 (June 2001): 333–358 for an insightful analysis of the roots of what he calls "reparations politics."

10. Congress, House, *Committee on Indian Affairs, Creation of Indian Claims Commission*: Hearing before the Committee on Indian Affairs, 79th Cong., 1st sess., 1945, 108 (statement of Ernest L. Wilkinson, Esq.), quoted in Nell Jessup Newton, "Indian Claims for Reparations, Compensation, and Restitution in the United States Legal System," in *When Sorry Isn't Enough*, ed. Roy L. Brooks, 262 (New York: New York University Press, 1999).

11. Newton, "Indian Claims," in *When Sorry Isn't Enough*, 262.

12. National Committee for Redress, *Redress* (1978); on file at The Bancroft Library, University of California, Berkeley.

13. This was the case despite the best efforts of Jesse Helms, who appended an amendment to the law "to preclude . . . this legislation from being used as a precedent in the courts or elsewhere to give standing to any precedent or future claims on the part of Mexico or Mexicans or any other citizen or group claiming to have been dealt an injustice by the American Government at some time in the past." Congress, Senate, Senator Helms of North Carolina speaking for Amendment 1969 to S. 1009, 100th Cong., 2nd sess., *Congressional Record* 134 (April 20, 1988): S 4394.

14. Sue Davis, *American Political Thought: Four Hundred Years of Ideas and Ideologies* (Englewood Cliffs, NJ: Prentice Hall, 1996), 375–403.

15. "In the beginning All the world was America," wrote John Locke in *The Second Treatise of Government*, ed. Peter Laslett (New York: New American Library, 1965).

16. See, for instance, Louis Hartz, *The Liberal Tradition in America* (New York: Harcourt Brace Jovanovich, 1955); Daniel Bell, *The End of Ideology: On the Exhaustion of Political Ideas in the Fifties* (Cambridge: Harvard University Press, 1988); Daniel Boorstin, *The Genius of American Politics* (Chicago: The University of Chicago Press, 1953); and Robert Dahl, *Who Governs? Democracy and Power in an American City* (New Haven, CT: Yale University Press, 1961). And for the revising of portrayals of

American history, see Frances Fitzgerald, *America Revised: History Schoolbooks in the Twentieth Century* (Boston: Little, Brown, 1979).

17. Richard Slotkin, *Regeneration Through Violence: The Mythology of the American Frontier, 1600–1860* (Middletown, CT: Wesleyan University Press, 1973); *The Fatal Environment: The Myth of the Frontier in the Age of Industrialization 1800–1890* (New York: Atheneum Press, 1985); and *Gunfighter Nation: The Myth of the Frontier in Twentieth Century America* (New York: Atheneum Press, 1992).

18. Torpey, "Making Whole What Has Been Smashed," 351–355 also makes this point.

19. Charles Taylor, "The Politics of Recognition," *Multiculturalism and "The Politics of Recognition,"* ed. Amy Gutmann (Princeton: Princeton University Press, 1992), 64.

20. Ibid., 36.

21. Ibid.

22. Fitzgerald, *America Revised.*

23. Ibid.

24. Donald L. Horowitz, *The Courts and Social Policy* (Washington, DC: The Brookings Institution, 1977).

25. See Horowitz, *The Courts and Social Policy,* for the role of courts in social policy.

26. George C. Shattuck, *The Oneida Land Claims: A Legal History* (Syracuse: Syracuse University Press, 1991), 3–12.

27. Roger Daniels, "The Redress Movement," in *Japanese Americans: From Relocation to Redress,* ed. Roger Daniels, Sandra C. Taylor, and Harry H. L. Kitano, 188 (Seattle: University of Washington Press, 1991).

28. Boris Bittker, *The Case For Black Reparations* (New York: Random House, 1973).

29. Martha Minow, *Between Vengeance and Forgiveness* (Boston: Beacon Press, 1998), 147.

30. Donald W. Shriver Jr., *An Ethic For Enemies: Forgiveness in Politics* (New York: Oxford University Press, 1995), 7–8. And see Hannah Arendt, *The Human Condition* (Chicago: University of Chicago Press, 1974), 247.

31. Arendt, *The Human Condition,* 241.

32. Ibid. And see Jeffrie G. Murphy and Jean Hampton, *Forgiveness and Mercy* (Cambridge: Cambridge University Press, 1988), 38.

33. Murphy and Hampton, *Forgiveness and Mercy,* 83.

34. Alexis de Tocqueville, was, of course, the first in a long line of political and legal observers to note this tendency. See *Democracy in America,* ed. J. P. Mayer, trans. George Lawrence (Garden City, NY: Doubleday, 1969).

35. The most recent efforts to achieve reparations for slavery are being led by Charles Ogletree Jr. of Harvard Law School and other noted law professors.

36. See Carrie Menkel-Meadow, "The Transformation of Disputes by Lawyers: What the Dispute Paradigm Does and Does Not Tell Us," *Missouri Journal of Dispute Resolution* (1985): 25–44, for an account of how attorneys frame legal arguments.

37. Mary Ann Glendon, *Rights Talk: The Impoverishment of Political Discourse* (New York: Free Press, 1991).

38. Barkan, *The Guilt of Nations*, xix.

39. Ibid.

40. Kathleen Sullivan, "The Sins of Discrimination: Last Year's Affirmative Action Cases," *Harvard Law Review* 100 (November 1986): 78–98. See also Jeremy Waldron, "Superseding Historic Injustice," *Ethics* 103 (October 1992): 4–28.

41. This "counterfactual" dilemma has been oft-noted as well. See Andrew Koppelman, *Antidiscrimination Law and Social Equality* (New Haven, CT: Yale University Press, 1996), 90. And see Waldron, "Superseding Historic Injustice."

42. Randall Robinson's best-selling book arguing for reparations for slavery is entitled *The Debt: What America Owes to Blacks* (New York: Dutton Press, 2000).

43. The history of American colonialism reaches up to at least the end of the nineteenth century and across the Pacific to the United States' assistance in illegally overthrowing the sovereign Kingdom of Hawaii in 1893. One hundred years later, the U.S. government did issue an apology. See Brooks, *When Sorry Isn't Enough*, 511, and Barkan, *Guilt of Nations*, 216–231.

44. The United States shares with Canada, Australia, and New Zealand its past of a British settler society colonizing land inhabited by others and similar claims have arisen in these ex-British colonies as well. See Barkan, *Guilt of Nations*, 159–261, and Duncan Ivison, Paul Patton, and Will Sanders, *Political Theory and the Rights of Indigenous Peoples* (Cambridge: Cambridge University Press, 2000).

45. In 1619, John Rolfe recorded that the first African slaves arrived in Jamestown, Virginia on board a Dutch ship. And it was not until 1954 that legal segregation was deemed unconstitutional by the Supreme Court in *Brown v. Board of Education*.

46. However, as this book documents, discussion has become more serious regarding an apology and some sort of reparations.

47. Commission on Wartime Relocation and Internment of Civilians, *Personal Justice Denied* (Washington, DC: United States Government Printing Office, 1983), 73–74.

48. Alexis de Tocqueville, *Democracy in America*, notes how the Americans have used the law to effect a "legal transfer" of land.

49. Edward Lazarus, *Black Hills/White Justice: The Sioux Nation versus the United States, 1775 to the Present* (New York: Harper Collins, 1991), 413.

50. See James Clifford, *The Predicament of Culture: Twentieth Century Ethnography, Literature, and Art* (Cambridge: Harvard University Press, 1988), for a discussion of tribal recognition issues.

51. Camille Paglia, "Ask Camille: Camille Paglia's Online Advice for the Culturally Disgruntled," in Brooks, *When Sorry Isn't Enough*, 353.

52. See Michelle Malkin, "Reparations Calculations," *San Francisco Chronicle*, 15 August 2002, A21. In it, she writes that by virtue of her Filipino descent, "Anyone . . . whose family members ingested Filipino-harvested asparagus, peas, cauliflower, onions, tomatoes, grapes or fish, or who burned Filipino-cut firewood, or who lived in homes built of Filipino-sawed lumber from 1923–1947, can settle their debt by sending me a check for $999.99."

53. Ronald Dworkin, *Law's Empire* (Cambridge: Harvard University Press, Belknap Press, 1986), 172–173.

54. See, for example, Stokely Carmichael and Charles V. Hamilton, *Black Power: The Politics of Liberation in America* (New York: Vintage Books, 1967).

55. Minow, *Between Vengeance and Forgiveness*, 131; Hannah Arendt, *Eichmann in Jerusalem: A Report on the Banality of Evil* (New York: Viking Press, 1963), 298.

56. Richard Rorty, *Achieving Our Country* (Cambridge: Harvard University Press, 1998), 3: "Emotional involvement with one's country—feelings of intense shame or of glowing pride aroused by various parts of its history, any by various present-day national policies—is necessary if political deliberation is to be imaginative and productive. Such deliberation will probably not occur unless pride outweighs shame."

57. Waldron, "Superseding Historic Injustice."

58. Sigmund Freud, "Remembering, Repeating and Working-Through (Further Recommendations on the Technique of Psycho-Analysis, 2," in *The Standard Edition of the Complete Psychological Works of Sigmund Freud*, trans. and ed. James Strachey, Volume 12, 147–159 (London: Hogarth Press, 1958).

59. See, for instance, Theodor W. Adorno, "What Does Coming to Terms with the Past Mean?" first published in 1959, trans. Timothy Bahti and Geoffrey Hartman, in *Bitburg In Moral and Political Perspective* (Bloomington: Indiana University Press, 1986).

60. Hannah Arendt, *Between Past and Future: Six Exercises in Political Thought* (New York: Penguin Books, 1954), 10.

61. Stanley Kubrick's *The Shining* is particularly chilling and suggestive in this matter, as the hotel where the murderous action takes place, we are told, lies atop an American Indian burial ground.

62. See Freud, "Remembering, Repeating, and Working-Through," as well as Toni Morrison's *Beloved*, where the character Sethe is given an opportunity to revisit her past deed, and act differently.

63. Exodus 20: 5.

64. This last stance of attempting to make moral sense of history is perhaps best exemplified by Lincoln's Second Inaugural, examined in Chapter 3. See, as well, James Boyd White, *Acts of Hope* (Chicago: University of Chicago Press, 1994).

65. *Black's Law Dictionary*, 5th ed., 1983, 477. And see Minow, *Between Vengeance and Forgiveness*, 134, and Waldron, "Superseding Historic Injustice." I take this issue up in Chapter 2.

66. Recently, for instance, individuals responsible for the 1963 bombing of a Birmingham church leading to the death of four children were prosecuted.

67. Minow, *Between Vengeance and Forgiveness*, 134. Consider in this regard the time it took for the United States to be able to hear the truths of Japanese Americans speaking about the wrongs committed to them during their evacuation, relocation, and internment.

68. Benedict Anderson, *Imagined Communities* (London and New York: Verso, 1991). And see Michael Shapiro, "Time, Disjuncture, and Democratic Citizenship," in *Democracy and Vision: Sheldon Wolin and the Vicissitudes of the Political*, ed. Aryeh Botwinick and William E. Connolly, 232–255 (Princeton: Princeton University Press, 2001); and William Connolly, "The Liberal Image of the Nation," in *Political Theory and Indigenous Rights*, ed. Ivison, Patton, and Sanders, 183–198.

69. Sanford Levinson, *Written in Stone: Public Monuments in Changing Societies* (Durham: Duke University Press, 1998).

70. Sheldon S. Wolin, "What Time Is It?" *Theory & Event* 1, no. 1 (January 1997); found at http://muse.jhu.edu/theory_&_event/v001/1.1wolin.html.

71. Ibid.

72. Ibid.

73. Although the United States in the beginning of the twenty-first century may come close to perfectly embodying the dynamic of the erosion and the recreation of the past, one should be circumspect in overstating its uniqueness in this regard. David Lowenthal, in *The Past Is a Foreign Country* (Cambridge: Cambridge University Press, 1985) documents the existence of this pattern in many cultures. And see Michael Kammen, *Mystic Chords of Memory: The Transformation of Tradition in*

American Culture (New York: Alfred A. Knopf, 1991), 534, for the dynamic of the rejection of the past and overcompensation through nostalgia in the United States in the 1960s.

74. For the erosion of the presence of the past, see Sheldon S. Wolin, *The Presence of the Past: Essays on the State and the Constitution* (Baltimore: The Johns Hopkins University Press, 1989), and "Postmodern Politics and the Absence of Myth," *Social Research* 52 no. 2 (Summer 1985): 217.

75. Geoffrey Hartman, ed. *Bitburg in Moral and Political Perspective* (Bloomington: Indiana University Press, 1986).

76. US News and World Report, in *When Sorry Isn't Enough*, ed. Brooks, 352.

77. Hanna Fenichel Pitkin, *Fortune Is a Woman: Gender and Politics in the Thought of Niccolo Machiavelli* (Berkeley: University of California Press, 1984), 300.

Chapter 1

1. *Statutes at Large*, 80, sec. 304 (1966). And see John Edward Barry, "Comment: *Oneida Indian Nation v. County of Oneida:* Tribal Rights of Action and the Indian Trade and Intercourse Act," *Columbia Law Review* 84: 1852–1870.

2. *Statutes at Large*, 91, sec. 268 (1977); *Statutes at Large*, 94 sec. 126 (1980); *Public Law*, 96–217 (1982).

3. Jack Campisi, "The Trade and Intercourse Acts," in *Irredeemable America: The Indians' Estate and Land Claims*, ed. Imre Sutton (Albuquerque: University of New Mexico Press, 1985), 341.

4. As of this writing, the following claims have been filed with the following results: the Passamaquoddy and Penobscots of Maine reached an $80 million settlement for 10 million acres; the Mashpees of Massachusetts were denied tribal status after claiming 13,000 acres; the Wampanoags of Massachusetts have negotiations pending for 250 acres; the Western Pequots of Connecticut arrived at a 1983 settlement for 800 acres; the Schaghticokes of Connecticut and the Mohegans have filed claims for 1300 acres and 1900 acres respectively; the Cayugas of New York have reached a tentative settlement over 64,000 acres; the Mohawks of New York have negotiations pending for a claim of 15,000 acres; the Shinnecocks of New York are in the midst of negotiations for 3200 acres; the Catawbas of South Carolina have reached a $50 million settlement for 144,000 acres; the Chitimacha of Louisiana have filed claims for 800 acres; and the Narragansetts of Rhode Island reached a 1978 settlement that calls for them to receive 3200 acres.

5. *Maine Indian Claims Settlement Act of 1980*, 25 U.S.C. 1721 (Supp. IV 1980).

6. *Catawba Indian Tribe of South Carolina Land Claims Settlement Act*, Pub. L. No. 103–116, 107 Stat. 1118 (1993)—codified at 25 U.S.C. 941 (Supp. V 1993).

7. See Glenn Coin, "Proposal Would Give Oneidas 35,000 Acres," *The Post-Standard*, December 9, 2004, A1. See also Jim Adams, "New York Offer of Tribal Casinos for Land Causes Upheaval," *Indian Country Today*, December 15, 2004; and Kirk Semple, "Catskill Casino Politics: Game of Delicate Balance," *The New York Times*, January 31, 2005, B2.

8. *County of Oneida v. Oneida Indian Nation*, 470 U.S. 226 (1985).

9. The third set of claims was initially filed in 1978 and conclusively decided by the Court of Appeals for the Second Circuit in 1988 (*Oneida Indian Nation of Wisconsin et al., plaintiffs v. The State of New York, et al., defendants; Oneida Indian Nation of New York, et al., plaintiffs v. The State of New York, et al., defendants;* 79-CV-798 and 78-CV-104). The Supreme Court announced on the opening day of the 1989 term that it refused to hear an appeal by the Oneidas. The claims concerned two treaties, concluded in 1785 and 1788 between the Oneidas and the State of New York. The Oneidas contended that these treaties were invalid under the Proclamation of 1783 and the 1784 Treaty of Fort Stanwix, agreed to by the American government and the Six Nations Iroquois Confederacy, of which the Oneidas were a member. The magnitude of the Oneidas' claim to title and the right to possess approximately 4.5 million acres of land in central New York, and the complexity of administering a case in which the defendant class is comprised of roughly 60,000 individuals, businesses, and government entities, may have encouraged the courts to remain within the relative safety of textual analysis, even if that text were the Articles of Confederation. The courts did not reach the issue of the effect of the passage of time, instead restricting their analysis to Congress' authority during the pre-Constitutional period. The conclusion that Congress had limited authority under the Articles of Confederation doomed the Oneidas's claims, for the court decided that during the period from 1783–1788, "Congress had neither the authority nor the intent to prohibit the states from purchasing Indian land located within their boundaries" and that "New York had the right to purchase the land in question" (79-CV-798 and 78-CV-104).

10. Franklin B. Hough, ed., *Proceedings of the Commissioners of Indian Affairs, Appointed by Law for the Extinguishment of Indian Titles in the State of New York*, 2 vols. (Albany, NY: Joel Munsell, 1861), 1: 225, quoted in Jack Campisi, "From Fort Stanwix to Canandaigua: National Policy, States' Rights and Indian Land," in *Iroquois Land Claims*, eds. Christopher

Vecsey and William A. Starna, 49–65, (Syracuse, NY: Syracuse University Press, 1988), 59.

11. Jack Campisi, "From Fort Stanwix to Canandaigua," 59.

12. *1 Statutes at Large*, 137 (1790).

13. Campisi, "Trade and Intercourse Acts," 337 and 470 U.S. 226 (1985).

14. *1 Statutes at Large*, 138 (1790).

15. *1 Statutes at Large*, 330 (1793). This act has been in effect continuously since 1790, and is now codified at 25 U.S.C. 177.

16. *1 American State Papers*: Indian Affairs 142 (1832).

17. 434 F. Supp. 534–535.

18. Brief for Petitioner at 103, *County of Oneida, New York v. Oneida Indian Nation of New York State,* 105 S. Ct. 1245 (1985) (citing the treaty of 1795).

19. Prior to 1966 it was unclear whether Indian tribes could bring suit in federal court and state courts tended to be hostile to tribal plaintiffs. Illiteracy, unfamiliarity with the American legal process, and sovereign immunity arguments all posed serious obstacles to Indian land claims. See John Edward Barry, "Comment, *Oneida Indian Nation v. County of Oneida:* Tribal Rights of Action and the Indian Trade and Intercourse Act," *Columbia Law Review* 84:1858–1860.

20. See Sandra C. Danforth, "Repaying Historical Debts: The Indian Claims Commission," *North Dakota Law Review* 49: 359–403; and Harvey D. Rosenthal, "Indian Claims and the American Conscience," in *Irredeemable America*, ed. Sutton, 35–70, for useful overviews of the Indian Claims Commission.

21. *Indian Claims Commission Annual Report* 1 (1969).

22. 470 U.S. 226, ft. 23.

23. 217 Court of Claims 45 (May 17, 1978).

24. 231 Court of Claims 990 (September 10, 1982).

25. 70-CV-35 and 464 F2d 916 (1972).

26. 414 U.S. 661 (1974).

27. See *Seneca Nation of Indians v. Christie,* 126 N.Y. 122 (1891) for an exposition of this view.

28. The argument that Congress, and not the courts, should resolve disputes over Indian land claims is voiced by many judges. Typically, the argument contains the following points: Congress is more likely to reflect the opinions of the people than are the courts; legislative bodies have better investigative tools than do the courts; relations with Indians are rooted in international affairs, and thus do not fall under the province of the courts; and the Constitution assigns power in these matters to the executive and legislative branches, not to the judicial branch.

See, for instance, Joshua N. Lief, "The Oneida Land Claims: Equity and Ejectment," *Syracuse Law Review* 39 no. 2 (Summer 1988): 825–844.

29. 434 F. Supp. 527 (1977).

30. 719 F. 2d 525 (1983).

31. 719 F. 2d 525 (1983).

32. 470 U.S. 226 (1985).

33. In 1984, sitting on the Supreme Court were Chief Justice Warren Burger, William Brennan, Byron White, Thurgood Marshall, Harry Blackmun, Lewis Powell, William Rehnquist, John Paul Stevens, and Sandra Day O'Connor.

34. Allan van Gestel, "Oral Argument before Supreme Court," 470 U.S. 226 (1985), 4–29.

35. Some of Van Gestel's fears have been realized. In a case directly growing out of the Oneida claims, *Sherrill, NY v. Oneida Indian Nation of New York, et al.*, the Oneida tribe has thus far successfully argued that land they bought in Sherrill county is Indian country, and thus exempt from local property taxes and the tribe is exempt from collecting and remitting sales taxes. The Supreme Court, in their 2004–2005 term, agreed to hear Sherrill's appeal of a Second Circuit Court of Appeals ruling (337 F.3d 139) siding with the Oneidas. As of February 2005, the Supreme Court has not handed down a decision.

36. This case involved a secondary question, as well, whether the counties could sue New York State in federal court to indemnify them for any losses suffered.

37. *Journal of Continental Congress*, quoted in Arlinda Locklear, "Oneida Land Claims," in *Iroquois Land Claims*, ed. Vecsey and Starna, 146.

38. Arlinda Locklear, "Oral Argument before Supreme Court," 470 U.S. 226 (1985), 39–66.

39. Ibid.

40. *Statutes of limitations* are statutes of repose, enacted by legislatures, prescribing periods within which actions may be brought (*Black's Law Dictionary*, 5th ed. [1983], 477). *Laches* is also a doctrine of repose which acts as a bar in equity where the plaintiff has unreasonably neglected to bring a claim which should have been brought (*Black's Law Dictionary*, 5th ed. [1983], 453).

41. The tapes and written records of the oral arguments before the Supreme Court do not note which justice is speaking.

42. Lief, "The Oneida Land Claims: Equity and Ejectment," 830.

43. 470 U.S. 226, 84 L.Ed. 2d at 191.

44. See Glenn Coin, "Paperwork Hampers Oneida Land Case: Government, Oneidas Share about 200 Years of Records before Trial Can Be Set," *The Post-Standard*, May 30, 2004, B1. As noted earlier,

Governor Pataki has proposed a settlement that calls for the land claims to be dropped.

45. See *Cherokee Nation v. Georgia,* 30 U.S. (5 Pet.) 1, 18 (1831).

46. See Vine Deloria, "Congress in Its Wisdom: The Course of Indian Legislation," in *The Aggressions of Civilization,* ed. Sarah L. Cadwalader and Vine Deloria, 112 (Philadelphia: Temple University Press, 1984).

47. As late as 1942, the preeminent Indian law scholar Felix Cohen wrote in *The Handbook of Federal Indian Law* that this was an unsettled question (284).

48. 434 F. Supp., at 541.

49. 470 U.S. 226, 84 L.Ed. 2d at 192.

50. 470 U.S. 226, 84 L. Ed. 2d. at 197.

51. 470 U.S. 226, 84 L.Ed. 2d. at 201.

52. 470 U.S. 226, 84 L.Ed. 2d. at 203.

53. 470 U.S. 226, 84 L.Ed. 2d at 193.

54. 470 U.S. 226, 84 L.Ed. 2d. at 203.

55. 470 U.S. 226, 84 L.Ed. 2d. at 199.

56. 470 U.S. 226, 84 L.Ed. 2d. at 203. See also Wolin, "Contract and Birthright," in *The Presence of the Past.,* 137–150.

57. A. John Simmons, "Historical Rights and Fair Shares," *Law and Philosophy* 14 (1995): 176.

58. Minow, *Between Vengeance and Forgiveness,* 108.

59. David W. Chen, "Talks to Settle Indian Land Claim Fall Apart," *New York Times,* March 11, 2000, A13.

60. See Glenn Coin, "Wisconsin Oneidas OK Deal," *The Post-Standard,* December 15, 2004, A1.

61. See James M. Odato, "Pataki's Big Bet No Sure Thing," *The Times Union* December 8, 2004, A1.

62. *County of Oneida v. Oneida Indian Nation of New York,* 84 L.Ed.2d 169, 191, n. 27.

63. See Campisi, "Trade and Intercourse Acts," 360.

64. Diane Kiesel, "Indians, Congress Spar over Land Claims Bill," *The American Bar Association Journal* 68, issue 5 (May 1982): 529.

65. Joseph William Singer, "Well Settled? The Increasing Weight of History in American Indian Land Claims," *Georgia Law Review* 28 (1994): 529–530.

66. Legal scholar Roy L. Brooks suggests a theory of redress that contains four elements: the claims must be placed in the hands of legislators rather than judges; political pressure is needed; strong internal support of the victims required; and the claims must be meritorious. Brooks argues that courts "can and have been used to interpret and enforce extant rights and laws handed down by the legislature." I argue

that courts, in addition, are almost essential in putting pressure on legislators to act to redress past wrongs. See Roy L. Brooks, "The Age of Apology," in *When Sorry Isn't Enough*, ed. Brooks, 3–11.

67. See F. Supp. 527 (1977): "It is incumbent upon great nations, like great men, to keep their word."

68. See Kiesel, "Indians, Congress Spar over Land Claims Bill," *The American Bar Association Journal*, 529.

69. See David Lyons, "The New Indian Claims and Original Rights to Land," *Social Theory and Practice* 4 (Fall 1977): 249–272, for an insightful article on the nature of Indian rights to land.

Chapter 2

1. *Wartime Relocation of Civilians, Statutes at Large* 102 (1988): 903. I restrict my attention in this chapter to those parts of the law concerned with the internment of Japanese Americans. I do not discuss Title II, added by the Senate that provides restitution to the Aleut residents of the Aleutian and Pribilof Islands.

2. Barkan, *Guilt of Nations*, 30–31.

3. Brooks, ed., *When Sorry Isn't Enough*, 159–160.

4. Shriver Jr., *An Ethic For Enemies*, 165–166.

5. Part of the letter read, "In enacting a law calling for restitution and offering a sincere apology, your fellow Americans have, in a very real sense, renewed their traditional commitment to the ideals of freedom, equality, and justice." See Roger Daniels, Sandra C. Taylor, and Harry H. L. Kitano, eds. *Japanese Americans: From Relocation to Redress* (Seattle: University of Washington Press, 1991).

6. For histories of the redress movement, see William Minoru Hohri, *Repairing America: An Account of the Movement for Japanese-American Redress* (Pullman, Washington: Washington State University Press, 1988), and Daniels, Taylor, and Kitano, eds. *Japanese Americans: From Relocation to Redress*.

7. Hatamiya, *Righting a Wrong*.

8. Ibid., 194.

9. The classic depiction of ordinary American politics is distilled in James Madison's Federalist 10, of course. See James Madison, Alexander Hamilton, and John Jay, *The Federalist Papers*, ed. Isaac Kramnick (Harmondsworth: Penguin Books, 1987). See also Boorstin, *The Genius of American Politics* and Dahl, *Who Governs?*

10. Congressman Robert Matsui, comments made at the Institute for Governmental Studies in Berkeley, California, December 1989.

11. Barkan, *Guilt of Nations*, 39–40.

12. Of course, there were exceptions to this generalization. Congressman Stratton went so far as to say that "if President Roosevelt had not done this he would have been derelict in his duty." U.S., Congress, House, HR 442, 100th Cong., 1st sess., *Congressional Record* 133 (September 21, 1987): 7567. This justification of the government's actions pursuant to Executive Order 9066 has been repeated and amplified in a recent book by conservative columnist Michelle Malkin, *In Defense of Internment: The Case for "Racial Profiling" in World War II and the War on Terror* (Washington, DC: Regnery Publishing, 2004).

13. The Supreme Court's June 2003 decisions on the constitutionality of the University of Michigan's affirmative action programs (*Gratz v. Bollinger* and *Grutter v. Bollinger*) are unlikely to put the controversy to rest.

14. See Sandra C. Taylor's essay for a comprehensive history of the internment in Daniels, Taylor, and Kitano, eds., *Japanese Americans: From Relocation to Redress*.

15. Quoted in Shriver Jr., *Ethic for Enemies*, 159.

16. Commission on Wartime Relocation, *Personal Justice Denied*, 73, 74.

17. Hatamiya, *Righting a Wrong*, 12.

18. Ibid., 16.

19. Ibid., 23.

20. *Hirabayashi v. United States,* 320 U.S. 81 (1943) and *Korematsu v. United States,* 323 U.S. 214 (1944).

21. See the dissenting opinions of Justices Roberts, Murphy, and Jackson in *Korematsu v. United States,* 323 U.S. 214 (1944).

22. Minow, *Between Vengeance and Forgiveness*, 96.

23. 323 U.S. 283 (1944).

24. See Howard Ball, "Loyalty, Treason, and the State: An Examination of Justice William O. Douglas's Style, Substance, and Anguish," in *He Shall Not Pass This Way Again,* ed. Stephen Wasby, 14 (Pittsburgh: University of Pittsburgh Press, 1990).

25. Hatamiya, *Righting a Wrong,* 24.

26. 50 U.S. C. 1981–1987 (1994).

27. Commission, *Personal Justice Denied,* cited in *Justice Delayed: The Record of the Japanese American Internment Cases,* ed. Peter Irons, 114 (Middletown, Connecticut: Wesleyan University Press, 1989).

28. McCarran-Walter Act, aka, Immigration and Nationality Act, *Statutes at Large,* 66, 163 (1952).

29. Roger Daniels, "Relocation, Redress, and the Report," in *When Sorry Isn't Enough,* ed. Brooks, 183.

30. Daniels, quoted in Barkan, *Guilt of Nations,* 34.

31. Daniels, "Relocation, Redress, and the Report," in *When Sorry Isn't Enough*, ed. Brooks, 183.

32. Hitamiya, *Righting a Wrong*, xix.

33. Ibid., 130–136; and see Daniels, Taylor, and Kitano, eds. *Japanese Americans: From Relocation to Redress,* for a history of the movement.

34. Federal Register, 41, no. 35 (February 20, 1976).

35. JACL statement, quoted in Barkan, *Guilt of Nations*, 35.

36. Hitamiya, *Righting a Wrong*, xix.

37. See Hitamiya, *Righting a Wrong,* 110–119 for biographical sketches of the four.

38. See Hitamiya, *Righting a Wrong*, 81–98 for a thorough legislative history.

39. Commission, *Personal Justice Denied*, 18.

40. See Irons, ed., *Justice at War* for a thorough history of the lawsuits.

41. See Hitamiya, *Righting a Wrong* for a legislative chronology.

42. Quoted in Hitamiya, *Righting a Wrong,* 149.

43. Ibid., 149–150.

44. Proclamation 4417, in *When Sorry Isn't Enough*, ed. Brooks, 201.

45. Commission, *Personal Justice Denied*, 18.

46. Hitamiya, "Institutions and Interest Groups: Understanding the Passage of the Japanese American Redress Bill," in *When Sorry Isn't Enough,* ed. Brooks, 195.

47. See Public Law 100-383, Section 2(a).

48. Congress, House, Congressman Lungren speaking against HR 442, 100th Cong., 1st sess., *Congressional Record*, 133 (September 21, 1987): H 7575.

49. Congress, Senate, Senator Hollings speaking against S 1009, 100th Cong., 2nd sess., *Congressional Record* 134 (April 20, 1988): S 4280.

50. Congress, Senate, Senator Chafee speaking against S 1009, 100th Cong., 2nd sess., *Congressional Record* 134 (April 20, 1988): S 4335.

51. Congress, Senate, Senator Wallop speaking against S 1009, 100th Cong., 2nd sess., *Congressional Record* 134 (April 20, 1988): S 4393.

52. Congress, Senate, Senator Inouye speaking against Senator's Hecht's amendment to S 1009, 100th Cong., 2nd sess., *Congressional Record* 134 (April 20, 1988): S 4323–4324.

53. Congress, Senate, Senator Matsunaga speaking for S 1009, 100th Cong., 2nd sess., *Congressional Record* 134 (April 20, 1988): S 4330, S 4415.

54. The House and Senate agreed that the date of passage of the law, and not the date of payment of compensation, was to serve as the demarcation between individuals who were to be compensated and those who were not. In this way, the government could not be charged with

intentionally dragging out the appropriations, which could be spread over a ten-year period, to save itself from paying elderly persons soon to die. See Title 1, Section 7 of 102 Statute 903.

55. Congress, House, *World War II Japanese-American Human Rights Violations Redress Act*, 96th Cong., 1st sess., 1979, HR 5977.

56. Congress, House, Congressman Shumway speaking against HR 442, 100th Cong., 1st sess., *Congressional Record* 133 (September 21, 1987): H 7564.

57. Public Law 100-383, Section 1 (6).

58. Congress, *Senate Report* (Governmental Affairs Committee), No. 100-202, October 20, 1987, 15.

59. I rely here on Owen Fiss' definition of a group. In his definition, a group has two characteristics: "(1) It is an entity ... the group has a distinct existence apart from its members, and also that it has an identity. ... You can talk about the group without reference to the particular individuals who happen to be its members at any one moment. (2) There is also a condition of inter-dependence. The identity and well-being of the members of the group and the identity and well-being of the group are linked." Owen M. Fiss, "Groups and the Equal Protection Clause," *Philosophy and Public Affairs* 5 (1976): 147.

60. Congress, *Senate Report* (Governmental Affairs Committee) No. 100–202, October 20, 1987, 17.

61. Congress, Senate, 100th Cong., 2nd sess., *Congressional Record* 134 (April 20, 1988): S 4396–4397.

62. Congress, *House Conference Report* No.100-785, July 26, 1988, 21.

63. Congress, House, Congressman Mineta speaking for HR 442, 100th Cong., 1st sess., *Congressional Record* 133 (September 21, 1987): H 7585.

64. See, for instance, the comments of Congressman Dymally of California: "I have lived in that area [around the University of Southern California] and I was haunted by the notion that I was living in a house which was taken away by the government from a Japanese-American and which was sold by real estate developers for very little money. And that notion always haunted me." Congress, House, 100th Cong., 1st sess., *Congressional Record* 133 (September 21, 1987): H 7589.

65. Congress, House, 100th Cong., 1st sess., *Congressional Record* 133 (September 17, 1987): H 7587.

66. Shriver Jr., *Ethic for Enemies*, 158–160.

67. Commission, *Personal Justice Denied*, 73, 74.

68. Shriver Jr., *Ethic for Enemies,* 159.

69. James Kilpatrick, "$1.2 Billion Worth of Hindsight," *The Washington Post*, March 5, 1988, A23.

70. Congress, House, Congressman Frenzel speaking for the Lungren amendment to HR 442, 100th Cong., 1st sess., *Congressional Record* 133 (September 21, 1987): H 7583.

71. Helmut Kohl, quoted in Charles S. Maier, *The Unmasterable Past: History, Holocaust, and German National Identity* (Cambridge, MA.: Harvard University Press, 1988), 50.

72. I take these issues up more thoroughly in Chapters 3 and 4.

73. Congress, House, Congressman Matsui speaking for HR 442, 100th Cong., 1st sess., *Congressional Record* 133 (September 17, 1987): H 7584.

74. One of the purposes of the Act "is to make restitution to Aleut residents of the Pribilof Islands and the Aleutian Islands west of Unimak Island," but this part of the law is beyond the scope of this chapter.

75. See Section I of Public Law 100-383.

76. Congress, Senate, Senator Helms speaking against S 1009, 100th Cong., 2nd sess., *Congressional Record* 134 (April 20, 1988): S 4410.

77. Quoted in Hohri, *Repairing America*, 146.

78. Ibid., 146, 147.

79. Ibid., chapter 9. It is also worth noting that S.I. Hayakawa was a Canadian citizen at the time, and during the internment years he taught at the University of Wisconsin. I thank Norman Jacobson for this information.

80. Commission, *Personal Justice Denied, Part 2: Recommendations*, 5.

81. Ibid., 6.

82. Congress, House, Congressman Shumway offering amendment to HR 442, 100th Cong., 1st sess., *Congressional Record* 133 (September 17, 1987): H 7589.

83. Shirley Castelnuovo, "With Liberty and Justice for Some: The Case for Compensation to Japanese-Americans Imprisoned During World War II," in *From Relocation to Redress*, ed. Daniels, Taylor, and Kitano, 203–211.

84. Congress, House, Congressman Frank speaking against the Shumway amendment, 100th Cong., 1st sess., *Congressional Record* 133 (September 21, 1987): H 7591.

85. The Civil Liberties Act of 1988 did, however, fail to include approximately 2,200 Japanese Latin American former internees. In 1996, a federal suit was filed claiming a violation of the constitutional right to equal protection. In 1998, the Justice Department settled the lawsuit, paying former Japanese Latin American internees $5000 each. See "The Case of the Japanese Peruvians," in *When Sorry Isn't Enough*, ed. Brooks, 217–221.

86. See Congressman Fish's comments, citing *Bivens v. Six Unknown Agents of the Federal Bureau of Investigation*, 403 U.S. 388 (1971), 100th Cong., 1st sess., *Congressional Record* 133 (September 21, 1987): H 7561.

87. Congress, House, Congressman Mineta speaking for HR 442, 100th Cong., 1st sess., *Congressional Record* 133 (September 21, 1987): H 7585.

88. Public Law 100-383; esp. Title 1, Section 103(a).

89. "Restitution", in *Black's Law Dictionary, 5th ed.,* 1983.

90. Congress, House, Congressman Frank speaking for HR 442, 100th Cong., 1st sess., *Congressional Record* 133 (September 17, 1987): H 7561.

91. Congress, House, Congressman Bruce A. Morrison speaking for HR 442, 100th Cong., 1st sess., *Congressional Record* 133 (September 21, 1987): H 7578.

92. Congress, Senate, Senator Kassebaum speaking for S 1009, 100th Cong., 2nd sess., *Congressional Record* 134 (April 20, 1988): S 4406.

93. Congress, Senate, Senator Helms speaking against S 1009, 100th Cong., 2nd sess., *Congressional Record* 134 (April 20, 1988): S 4411. See statements by the other senators at S 4391, S 4393, and S 4406.

94. *New York Times*, 4 August 1981, quoted in Brooks, ed., *When Sorry Isn't Enough*, 203.

95. T. Alexander Aleinikoff, *Semblances of Sovereignty: The Constitution, the State, and American Citizenship* (Cambridge: Harvard University Press, 2002), 190.

96. The first amendment would have barred appropriations for the law in any year in which there was a federal deficit. It was defeated 61–35. The second would have blocked appropriations until the government of Japan fairly compensated the families of those killed at Pearl Harbor. It garnered 4 votes.

97. Congress, Senate, Senator Helms speaking for the Amendment 1969 to S 1009, 100th Cong., 2nd sess., *Congressional Record* 134 (April 20, 1988): S 4394.

98. Public Law 100-383, Title III—Territory or Property Claims against United States. Sec 301. Exclusion of Claims. "Notwithstanding any other provision of law or of this Act, nothing in this Act shall be construed as recognition of any claim of Mexico or any other country or any Indian tribe (except as expressly provided in this Act with respect to the Aleut tribe of Alaska) to any territory or other property of the United States, nor shall this Act be construed as providing any basis for compensation in connection with any such claim."

99. Charles Ogletree Jr., "Human Rights, Accountability and the Reparations Movement," (Valerie Gordon Human Rights Lecture, University of Michigan Law School, April 2003). Reported as "Ogletree Calls for Slavery Reparations," *University of Michigan Quarterly News* (Spring 2003): 14.

Chapter 3

1. Michael Walzer, for instance, in *Spheres of Justice: A Defense of Pluralism and Equality* (Oxford: Martin Robertson, 1983), in the chapter entitled "Membership" (31–63), devotes the whole of it to spatial matters.

2. Peter Laslett and James S. Fishkin, "Introduction: Processional Justice," in *Justice between Age Groups and Generations* (New Haven: Yale University Press, 1992), 1.

3. See Peter Euben, *Tragedy of Political Theory* (Princeton: Princeton University Press, 1990), 39–43; *The Oxford English Dictionary*, "Remember"; and Regina M. Schwartz, "Joseph's Bones and the Resurrection of the Text: Remembering in the Bible," *PMLA* 103 (March 1988): 114–124.

4. Bruce James Smith, *Politics and Remembrance* (Princeton: Princeton University Press, 1985). The term *vessel of remembrance* is Hannah Arendt's, from *The Human Condition*.

5. Smith suggests that these terms may be distinguished by the fact that citizenship is a category of space, and patriotism one of time: Whereas one is a *citizen* in relation to certain contemporaries, one is a *patriot* in relationship to predecessors. *Politics and Remembrance*, 10.

6. John Schaar, "The Case for Patriotism," in *Legitimacy in the Modern State* (New Brunswick: Transaction Books, 1981), 288. This is not to say that there is only one concept of patriotism. Schaar distinguishes among three sorts of patriotism: land patriotism, patriotism of the city, and covenanted patriotism. Judith Shklar, in *American Citizenship: The Quest for Inclusion* (Cambridge: Harvard University Press, 1991) distinguishes among four basic notions of citizenship: standing, nationality, active participation, and ideal republican. For the relationship between patriotism and citizenship, see footnote 5 above.

7. Walter Lippmann, *The Public Philosophy* (New York: New American Library, 1955).

8. Anne Norton, "The Virtues of Multiculturalism," in *Multiculturalism and American Democracy*, ed. Arthur M. Melzer, Jerry Weinberger, and M. Richard Zinman, 131 (Lawrence: University Press of Kansas, 1998).

9. Milan Kundera, *The Book of Laughter and Forgetting*, trans. Michael Henry Heim, 113 (New York: Penguin, 1981).

10. See the special issue of *Representations* 26 (Spring 1989) entitled "Memory and Counter-Memory," esp. "Introduction."

11. Thomas Jefferson, "To James Madison," 6 Sept. 1789 in *The Writings of Thomas Jefferson*, ed. Albert Ellery Bergh, definitive ed. (Washington, DC: Thomas Jefferson Memorial Association, 1907) 6: 454.

12. Jefferson, "To John W. Eppes," 24 June 1813 in *Writings* 13: 269; "To John W. Eppes," 11 Sept. 1813 in *Writings* 13:360; "To Samuel Kercheval," 12 July 1816 in *Writings* 15: 42; "To Thomas Earle," 24 Sept. 1823 in *Writings* 15: 470.

13. Jay Fliegelman, *Prodigals and Pilgrims: The American Revolution against Patriarchal Authority, 1750–1800* (Cambridge: Cambridge University Press, 1982). George B. Forgie has shown that this metaphor would remain predominant through the Civil War in *Patricide in the House Divided: A Psychological Interpretation of Lincoln and His Age* (New York: W.W. Norton & Company, 1979).

14. Tom Paine, "The American Crisis, III" (1777), 203, quoted in David Lowenthal, *The Past Is a Foreign Country,* 107 (Cambridge: Cambridge University Press, 1985).

15. Nathaniel Hawthorne, *Septimis Felton*, quoted in Forgie, *Patricide in the House Divided*, 90.

16. Tom Paine, "Common Sense," 51.

17. Jefferson, "To James Madison," 6 September 1789, in *Writings* 7: 456.

18. Paine, "Common Sense," 207.

19. "The Rights of Man, Part I" in *The Writings of Thomas Paine*, ed. Moncure Daniel Conway (New York: 1894) 2: 278.

20. Shklar, *American Citizenship*, 77. Compare to Sheldon Wolin's depiction of the good citizen within the contemporary political economy, responding to factory closures and relocations: "He or she is one who is mobile, who is willing to tear up all roots and follow the promptings of the job market." In Wolin, "Injustice and Collective Memory," in *The Presence of the Past*, 45.

21. Pitkin, *Fortune Is a Woman*, 297.

22. Forgie, in *Patricide in the House Divided*, 33: "Its name notwithstanding...the concept of the self-made man did not so much assert that men made themselves without assistance or that there were no longer relevant models, as it did the much less dramatic proposition that people could now look elsewhere for those models. In other words, the self-made man theme is as parricidal as the term implies, but not in the service of autonomy. Emotions and expectations once directed to actual fathers could now be transferred to metaphorical fathers."

23. Frederick Jackson Turner, "The Frontier in American History," (1893) quoted in Lowenthal, *The Past Is a Foreign Country*, 119. It is interesting to note, however, that the original emigration was actually experienced not only as an escape from bondage but also as a sorrowful estrangement. The sorrow entailed in emigration was movingly captured by William Bradford's "Of Plymouth Plantation", and quoted at great length by de Tocqueville in the second chapter of *Democracy In America*, "Concerning Their Point of Departure And Its Importance For The Future Of The Anglo-Americans." For Bradford, and for de Tocqueville, leaving the past behind was more of a human rending than an achievement of human autonomy. "Truly doleful was the sight of that sad and mournful parting, to hear what sighs and sobs and prayers did sound amongst them; what tears did gush from every eye, and pithy speeches pierced each other's heart, that sundry of . . . strangers . . . could not refrain from tears."

24. Henry Nash Smith, *Virgin Land: The American West as Symbol and Myth* (New York: Vintage Books, 1957), esp. chapter 1, "A Highway to the Pacific: Thomas Jefferson and the Far West."

25. Sheldon S. Wolin, *Tocqueville between Two Worlds* (Princeton: Princeton University Press, 2001), 272–273.

26. Jefferson, "Autobiography," in *Writings* 1: 36.

27. Daniel J. Boorstin, *The Lost World of Thomas Jefferson* (Boston: Beacon Press, 1948), esp. 204–212.

28. Jefferson, *Writings* 7: 454–463.

29. Ibid.

30. I consider the issue of collective identity more thoroughly in Chapter 4.

31. Jefferson, *Writings* 7: 455.

32. Ibid.

33. Ibid., 455–457.

34. Ibid., 459. Jefferson later refined his calculations, and determined that the natural span of a political generation was eighteen years and eight months. See *Writings* 13: 269.

35. Edmund Burke, *Reflections on the Revolution in France* (Anchor Books: New York, 1973), 110.

36. As noted earlier, in addition to the letter that Jefferson wrote to Madison from Paris in 1789, he wrote two letters to John W. Eppes in 1813, a letter to Samuel Kercheval in 1816, and a letter to Thomas Earle in 1823, all explaining his calculations of the length of a generation and its political importance.

37. Benjamin Barber, "Liberal Democracy and the Costs of Consent," in *Liberalism and the Moral Life*, ed. Nancy L. Rosenblum, 64

(Cambridge: Harvard University Press, 1989), argues that there are two ways of reading Jefferson on this issue: one in which Jefferson is calling for complete newness, and a second in which he calls for constant remembering, deliberation, and possible reinvention to earn the legitimacy of the living.

38. Jefferson, *Notes on the State of Virginia*, *Writings* 2: 226.

39. Jefferson, "A Declaration by The Representatives of the United States of America, In General Congress Assembled," *Writings* 1:34.

40. Jefferson, *Notes on Virginia*, *Writings* 2: 124 and see Daniel Boorstin, *The Lost World of Jefferson*.

41. Jefferson, "To Brissot de Warville," 12 February 1788, *Writings* 6: 428.

42. Jefferson, "To John Holmes," 22 April 1820, *Writings* 15: 248.

43. Ronald Takaki, *Iron Cages: Race and Culture in Nineteenth Century America* (New York: Alfred Knopf, 1979), 43.

44. Jefferson, "To John Holmes," 22 April 1820, *Writings* 15: 248.

45. Jefferson, "To St. George Tucker," 28 Aug. 1797, *Writings* 9: 418.

46. Jefferson, *Notes on Virginia*, *Writings* 2: 192–194. Jefferson calls these objections political and goes on to discuss other objections, which he calls physical and moral.

47. Jefferson's relationship with Sally Hemings surely complicates further his thoughts on racial boundaries. For an article summarizing recent DNA analysis of his relationship with Hemmings, see Eric S. Lander and Joseph J. Ellis, "Founding Father," *Nature* 396, (05 November 1998): 13–14.

48. Jefferson, *Notes on Virginia*, *Writings* 2:201. For an analysis of Jefferson's fears of miscegenation, see Takaki, *Iron Cages*, 42–55.

49. Jefferson, *Writings* 13: 10.

50. See John Gillis, ed., *Commemorations: The Politics of National Identity* (Princeton: Princeton University Press, 1994) for a description of the new rituals instituted in the 1820s to mark the birth of the American nation.

51. See Forgie, *Patricide in the House Divided*; John P. Diggins, *The Lost Soul of American Politics: Virtue, Self-Interest, and the Foundations of Liberalism* (Chicago: The University of Chicago Press, 1984), 306–312.

52. Abraham Lincoln, "Address Before The Young Men's Lyceum of Springfield, Illinois," 27 Jan. 1837, *Complete Works of Abraham Lincoln*, ed. John G. Nicolay and John Hay (New York: Francis D. Tandy & Co., 1905) 1: 47. Please note that in *The Complete Works* the speech is incorrectly dated 1838.

53. Lincoln, *Complete Works* 1: 45.

54. Ibid., 46.

55. Ibid., 49.

56. Ibid. These fears are similar to those expressed by Holocaust survivors and by internment camp survivors.

57. Ibid., 43.

58. Ibid. And see Diggins, *Lost Soul of American Politics*, 320–321.

59. Robert Cover, "Violence and the Word," 95 *Yale Law Journal* 1604: "A legal world is built only to the extent that there are commitments that place bodies on the line."

60. Lincoln, *Complete Works* 1: 50.

61. Quoted in Forgie, *Patricide In The House Divided*, 186.

62. Lincoln, "First Inaugural Address," *Complete Works* 6: 169.

63. Forgie, *Patricide in the House Divided*, 194.

64. Union deaths totalled over 360,000 and Confederate deaths over 160,000 during the Civil War, more casualties than any other war in U.S. history.

65. Garry Wills, *Lincoln at Gettysburg: The Words That Remade America* (New York: Simon & Schuster, 1992).

66. Wills, *Lincoln at Gettysburg*, 19.

67. Anne Norton, *Alternative Americas* (Chicago: The University of Chicago Press, 1986), 304–309.

68. Ibid.

69. Lincoln, "Address To The 166th Ohio Regiment," 22 August 1864, *Complete Works* 10: 203.

70. Compare to Edmund Burke: "[T]he people of England well know, that the idea of inheritance furnishes a sure principle of conservation, and a sure principle of transmission; without at all excluding a principle of improvement." *Reflections on the Revolution in France*, 45. I thank Norman Jacobson for pointing out to me that Lincoln uses the same term "conservation" in his Lyceum Address.

71. Lincoln, *Complete Works* 8: 236. Lincoln was not the first U.S. president to declare a day of repentance. See Dean Hammer, *The Puritan Tradition in Revolutionary, Federalist, and Whig Political Theory: A Rhetoric of Origins* (New York: Peter Lang, 1998).

72. Lincoln, *Complete Works* 8: 236.

73. Norton, *Alternative Americas*, 310–311.

74. Lincoln, *Complete Works* 11: 45.

75. Ibid.

76. Ibid. And see Diggins, *Lost Soul of American Politics*, 328–333 for his treatment of the Second Inaugural, as well as James Boyd White, *Acts of Hope: Creating Authority in Literature, Law, and Politics* (Chicago and London: University of Chicago Press, 1994).

77. Norton, *Alternative Americas*, 311.

78. Lincoln, *Complete Works* 11: 46–47.

79. See Wills on the Second Inaugural: "In the Gettysburg Address, the people was consecrated as a whole; it could overthrow its government only as a whole. . . . Now we see that it sins in solidarity as well." In *Lincoln at Gettysburg,* 186.

80. Diggins, in *The Lost Soul of American Politics,* 330, argues contrariwise, that Lincoln does not claim authority to interpret the will of God.

81. Lincoln, *Complete Works* 11: 46–47. And see Reinhold Niebuhr, *The Irony of American History* (New York: Charles Scribner's Sons, 1952), 170–173.

82. See Exodus 20:5; Exodus 34: 7; Numbers 14: 14–18; Deuteronomy 5: 9. On the other hand, see Jeremiah 31: 28–40 and Ezekiel 18 ("The son shall not bear the iniquity of the father") for the opposing view.

83. Wolin, "Contract and Birthright," in *The Presence of the Past,* 140–142.

84. Gillis, ed., *Commemorations,* 9.

85. Slotkin, *Gunfighter Nation,* 658.

86. The battle over the Alamo is reported on in "For Defenders of the Alamo, The Assault Is Joined Anew," *The New York Times,* March 31, 1994, A1, A10.

87. Arendt, *Between Past and Future,* 10.

88. Arendt, *Eichmann in Jerusalem,* 298.

89. See Pitkin, *Fortune Is a Woman,* 296–298; and Jurgen Habermas, *The New Conservatism: Cultural Criticism and the Historians' Debate,* ed. and trans. Shierry Weber Nicolsen (Cambridge: The MIT Press, 1989), 260–263.

90. Arendt, *Between Past and Future,* 5.

Chapter 4

1. See, for instance, Patrick Buchanan's statement in *Right from the Beginning* (Boston: Little Brown, 1988), 285: "To us, sin is personal, not collective; it is a matter for personal confession, personal contrition, personal reconciliation with God. Our sense of shame and sense of guilt are about what we have done ourselves, our own transgressions against our own moral code. We have no sense of guilt about Wounded Knee; because we weren't *at* Wounded Knee."

2. Benjamin R. Barber, "Liberal Democracy and the Costs of Consent," in *Liberalism and the Moral Life,* ed. Nancy Rosenblum, 58 (Cambridge: Harvard University Press, 1989).

3. Melissa A. Orlie, "Forgiving Trespasses, Promising Futures," in *Feminist Interpretations of Hannah Arendt,* ed. Bonnie Honig, 346 (University Park: The Pennsylvania State University Press, 1995).

4. J. R. Lucas, *Responsibility* (Oxford: Clarendon Press, 1993), 5.

5. Patrick Buchanan, *Right from the Beginning*, 285.

6. Edmund Burke, *Reflections on the Revolution in France*, 110.

7. Peter Laslett, "Justice Between Generations," in *Justice Between Age Groups and Generations,* ed. Peter Laslett and James S. Fishkin, 40 (New Haven: Yale University Press, 1992).

8. Feinberg, "Collective Responsibility," in *Doing and Deserving: Essays in the Theory of Responsibility* (Princeton: Princeton University Press, 1970), 231.

9. Feinberg, "Collective Responsibility," 232.

10. Important works written at the time include, in addition to the works by Hannah Arendt cited below, Karl Jaspers, *The Question of German Guilt*, trans. E.B. Ashton (New York: The Dial Press, 1947), and Dwight MacDonald, "The Responsibility of Peoples." Recent works that are indebted to these are Habermas, *New Conservatism* (Cambridge: The MIT Press, 1989), and Larry May, *Sharing Responsibility* (Chicago: The University of Chicago Press, 1992).

11. Hannah Arendt, "Organized Guilt and Universal Responsibility," originally published in *Jewish Frontier,* Vol. 12 (1945), collected in *Guilt: Man and Society,* ed. Roger W. Smith, 255–267 (New York: Anchor Books, 1971).

12. Arendt, "Organized Guilt," 255.

13. Ibid., 258, 259.

14. Ibid., 259.

15. Ibid., 261.

16. Arendt, *Eichmann in Jerusalem*, 297.

17. Hannah Arendt, "Collective Responsibility," in *Amor Mundi: Explorations in the Faith and Thought of Hannah Arendt,* ed. James W. Bernauer, S.J., 43 (Boston: Martinus Nijhoff Publishers, 1987).

18. Arendt, *Eichmann in Jerusalem*, 298.

19. Arendt, "Collective Responsibility," 43.

20. Hannah Arendt, "On Violence," in *Crises of the Republic* (New York: Harcourt Brace Jovanovich, 1969), 161–162.

21. Ibid., 162–163.

22. Arendt, *Eichmann in Jerusalem*, 298.

23. Arendt, "Collective Responsibility," in *Responsibility and Judgment,* ed. Jerome Kohn, 149 (New York: Schocken Books, 2003).

24. Don Herzog, in *Happy Slaves* (Chicago: The University of Chicago Press, 1989), contends that consent theory "provides perhaps the single most prevalent paradigm structuring our thinking about law, society, morality and politics" (215).

25. Hartz, *Liberal Tradition in America.*

26. Wolin, "Injustice and Collective Memory," 32–46.

27. Thomas Hobbes, *Leviathan*, ed. C.B. Macpherson (Harmondsworth: Penguin Books, 1968), chap. 15, 210.

28. Ibid.

29. Ibid., 209.

30. Ibid.

31. Ibid., 210.

32. Wolin, "Injustice and Collective Memory," 38.

33. De Tocqueville, *Democracy In America*, Vol. 2, chap. 13, 473. Jefferson's writings capture the allure of the theory: the promise of liberation is held out to us as individuals each day. De Tocqueville, on the other hand, captures its pathos: "Not only does democracy make every man forget his ancestors, but it hides its descendants and separates his contemporaries from him; it throws him back forever upon himself alone and threatens in the end to confine him entirely within the solitude of his own heart." Quoted in Lowenthal, *The Past Is A Foreign Country*, 242–243.

34. Arendt, "Collective Responsibility," 149.

35. Ibid., 147.

36. Ibid., 158.

37. Arendt quotes Faulkner in the Preface to *Between Past and Future* (New York: Penguin Books, 1954), 10. The fact that Arendt was fond of quoting this statement is noted in Elisabeth Young-Bruehl, *Hannah Arendt: For Love of the World* (New Haven: Yale University Press, 1982), 385.

38. Arendt, *Between Past and Future*, 7.

39. Ibid., 10.

40. Much of Arendt's work, in fact, may be likened to this parable, Kafka's "he" standing for Arendt, and one of the battles to extract meaning from the past.

41. Donald R. Kinder and Lynn M. Sanders, *Divided by Color* (Chicago: University of Chicago Press, 1996), 11.

42. Kinder and Sanders, 124, as quoted by Thomas McCarthy, "Vergangenheitsbewaltigung in the USA: On the Politics of the Memory of Slavery," *Political Theory* 30 (5): 623–648.

43. See generally, McCarthy, "Vergangenheitsbewaltigung in the USA."

44. David Lyons, "Corrective Justice, Equal Opportunity, and the Legacy of Slavery and Jim Crow," *Boston University School of Law Working Paper Series*, Public Law and Legal Theory Working Paper No. 03-15, 8.

45. Desmond King, *Separate and Unequal: Black Americans and the U.S. Federal Government* (Oxford, England: Oxford University Press, 1995), cited by McCarthy, "Vergangenheitsbewaltigung in the USA," 640.

46. Lyons, "Corrective Justice, Equal Opportunity, and the Legacy of Slavery and Jim Crow," 29.

47. McCarthy, "Vergangenheitsbewaltigung in the USA," 640.

48. See Lyons, and McCarthy, generally, as well as Douglas Massey and Nancy A. Denton, *American Apartheid: Segregation and the Making of the Underclass* (Cambridge: Harvard University Press, 1993).

49. McCarthy, "Vergangenheitsbewaltigung in the USA," 641.

50. On the concept of "centrifugals," see Sheldon S. Wolin, *Politics and Vision*, (exp. ed.) (Princeton: Princeton University Press, 2004), 585–586.

51. Ronald Beiner, *What's the Matter with Liberalism?* (Berkeley: University of California Press, 1992), 109.

52. Knapp, "Collective Memory and Actual Past," *Representations* 26 (Spring 1989): 144–145.

53. Ibid., 144.

54. Arthur M. Schlesinger, Jr. in *The Disuniting of America* (New York: W.W. Norton & Company, 1992) refers to "the sullen and resentful minorities."

55. Susan Wolf, "Comment," in *Multiculturalism and "The Politics of Recognition,"* ed. Amy Gutmann, 85 (Princeton: Princeton University Press, 1992).

56. See Amy Gutmann, *Identity in Democracy* (Princeton: Princeton University Press, 2003), for a careful exploration of the issues raised by "identity politics."

57. Knapp, "Collective Memory and Actual Past," 143–144.

58. Antonin Scalia, "The disease as cure: In order to get beyond racism, we must first take account of race," *Washington University Law Quarterly* (1979): 147, cited by Kenneth Karst, *Belonging to America* (New Haven: Yale University Press, 1989), 166.

59. Arendt, "Collective Responsibility," 149.

60. Laslett, "Justice between Generations," 40.

61. This simple dichotomy has been problematized by recent scholarship that has pointed to the fact that some African Americans were slaveholders themselves. See Brent Staples, "Strom Thurmond Continued: The Known World of Ms. Washington-Williams," *The New York Times* National Edition, July 17, 2004, A24.

62. The key work here is W.E.B. Du Bois, *The Souls of Black Folk,* intro. Herb Boyd (New York: Modern Library, 1996).

63. William E. Connolly, *Identity/Difference: Democratic Negotiations of Political Paradox* (Ithaca: Cornell University Press, 1991), 199.

64. For accounts of the "German Historikerstreit," the "historians' controversy," see Charles Maier, *The Unmasterable Past* (Cambridge, MA and London, England: Harvard University Press, 1988) and

Richard J. Evans, *In Hitler's Shadow: West German Historians and the Attempt to Escape the Nazi Past* (New York: Pantheon Books, 1989).

65. Jurgen Habermas, "On Public Use of History," in *The New Conservatism*, 233–235.

66. Habermas, "Historical Consciousness and Post-Traditional Identity: The Federal Republic's Orientation to the West," in *The New Conservatism*, 260.

67. Ibid., 262.

68. Martha Minow, *Not Only for Myself* (New York: The New Press, 1997), 145.

69. Feinberg, "Collective Responsibility," 234.

70. Pitkin, *Fortune Is A Woman*, 299–301.

71. Ibid., 301. Arendt writes that "what love is in its own, narrowly circumscribed sphere, respect is in the larger domain of human affairs. . . . Respect, not unlike the Aristotelian *philia politike,* is a kind of 'friendship' without intimacy and without closeness." Arendt, *The Human Condition*, 243.

72. The Bureau of Census reported in 2000, for instance, that the 1998 median family income for whites was $49,023, whereas for blacks the figure was $29,404. The gap in wealth between white and black households is estimated to be approximately ten to one. See Melvin L. Oliver and Thomas M. Shapiro, *Black Wealth / White Wealth* (New York: Routledge, 1995).

73. Lisa J. Disch, "On Friendship in Dark Times," in Honig, *Feminist Interpretations of Hannah Arendt*, 307.

74. Arendt, "Collective Responsibility," 50.

Chapter 5

1. This is not intended to be an exhaustive list of the historic wrongs that may burden contemporary Americans.

2. A similar outburst occurred in response to the Smithsonian Institute's exhibition on the atomic bombing of Hiroshima and Nagasaki. Some thought the exhibition too sympathetic to the Japanese and overly critical of the actions of the United States government.

3. SJ Res. 37. A similar resolution has been proposed in the House, HJ Res. 98. Bills have been proposed offering an apology to Native Americans and establishing a commission to study the effects of slavery and Jim Crow.

4. See, for an excellent overview of issues, Neil J. Kritz, ed., *Transitional Justice: How Emerging Democracies Reckon With Former Regimes* (Washington, DC: United States Institute of Peace Press, 1995).

5. Carla Hesse and Robert Post, "Introduction," in *Human Rights in Political Transition: Gettysburg to Bosnia,* ed. Carla Hesse and Robert Post, 15–16 (New York: Zone Books, 1999).

6. In addition to Kritz, ed., *Transitional Justice,* and Hesse and Post, *Human Rights in Political Transition,* see Robert I. Rotberg and Dennis Thompson, eds., *Truth v. Justice: The Morality of Truth Commissions* (Princeton: Princeton University Press, 2000), and Priscilla B. Hayner, *Unspeakable Truths: Confronting State Terror and Atrocity* (New York: Routledge, 2001).

7. See Hayner, *Unspeakable Truths.*

8. See Hesse and Post, *Human Rights in Political Transition* and Rotberg and Thompson, eds., *Truth v. Justice,* and Hayner, *Unspeakable Truths.*

9. Marc Galanter, "Righting Old Wrongs," in *Breaking the Cycles of Hatred: Memory, Law, and Repair,* ed. Martha Minow, introduced and commentaries edited by Nancy L. Rosenblum, 107–131 (Princeton: Princeton University Press, 2002), see esp. 118.

10. See Section I of Public Law 100-383.

11. Galanter, "Righting Old Wrongs," 119.

12. Nicholas Tavuchis, in *Mea Culpa: A Sociology of Apology and Reconciliation* (Stanford: Stanford University Press, 1991), argues that the principal function of what he calls a *collective apology* is to "put things on a public record." See 116–117.

13. Jean Hampton, in "Forgiveness, Resentment and Hatred," in Jeffrie Murphy and Jean Hampton, *Forgiveness And Mercy,* argues that forgiveness involves overcoming a point of view—the point of view of the other as "the one who wronged me." See 38.

14. Jeffrie Murphy, in "Forgiveness and Resentment," in *Forgiveness and Mercy,* distinguishes "to excuse" from "to forgive" by arguing that *to excuse* is to say that what was done was morally wrong, but because of certain factors about the agent it would be unfair to hold the wrongdoer responsible or blame him for the wrong action. He writes that *to justify* is to say that what was done was *prima facie* wrong, but because of other morally relevant factors considered, the action was—all morally relevant factors considered—the right thing to do. *Forgiveness* is directed toward responsible wrongdoing—wrongdoing neither excused nor justified.

15. Murphy, "Forgiveness and Resentment," 20–23, argues that an important distinction between mercy and forgiving is that with respect to mercy, it is not necessary that the wronged person respond. For example, governors may show *mercy* to convicted murderers. With *forgiveness,* it is the wronged who must forgive. *Forgetting* is, on the whole, less active

than forgiving, even though both Nietzsche and Freud have taught us that forgetting is not simply a loss of memory.

16. Shriver Jr., *Ethic for Enemies*, 7.

17. Aristotle, *The Nicomachean Ethics*, 1126a. And a recent study described in *The New York Times* seems to confirm Aristotle's insight. See Benedict Carey, "Payback Time: Why Revenge Tastes So Sweet," *The New York Times*, July 27, 2004, National Edition, 1 (F).

18. Arendt, *The Human Condition*, 247.

19. Aristotle, *Ethics*, 1125b.

20. Ibid., 1126a.

21. Shriver Jr., *Ethic for Enemies*, 7.

22. Friedrich Nietzsche, *On The Genealogy Of Morals*, trans. Walter Kaufmann and R. J. Hollingdale (New York: Vintage Books, 1989), 47. See also B. Honig, "Arendt, Identity, and Difference," *Political Theory* 16 (1): 77–98, esp. fts. 47 and 49.

23. Hampton, in "Forgiveness, Resentment and Hatred," 85, presents a portrayal of forgiveness as involving a number of stages. The first stage is marked by psychological preparation in which one regains confidence in one's worth despite the action challenging it.

24. Aristotle, *Ethics*, 1126a.

25. Ibid., 1125b.

26. Arendt, *The Human Condition*, 239.

27. Luke 17: 3–4.

28. Arendt, *The Human Condition*, 240.

29. Ibid., 241.

30. Arendt, *Eichmann in Jerusalem*, 287.

31. Arendt, *The Human Condition*, 241.

32. Arendt to Auden, February 14, 1960, Library of Congress, quoted by Elisabeth Young-Bruehl in *Hannah Arendt: For Love of the World* (New Haven: Yale University Press, 1982) 371.

33. Arendt, *The Jew as Pariah: Jewish Identity and Politics in the Modern Age*, ed. Ron H. Feldman (New York: Grove Press, 1978), 250.

34. See, in particular, Elzbieta Ettinger, *Hannah Arendt/Martin Heidegger* (New Haven: Yale University Press, 1995).

35. Tavuchis, *Mea Culpa*, 5, and Minow, *Between Vengeance and Forgiveness*, 114.

36. I thank Jill Frank for pointing this out to me.

37. Hampton, "Forgiveness, Resentment and Hatred," 83.

38. "Forgiveness," in *A Theological Word Book of the Bible*, quoted by Hampton, *Forgiveness and Mercy*, 37.

39. Murphy, "Forgiveness and Resentment," 28.

40. Honig argues in her article "Arendt, Identity, And Difference," that the parties involved in forgiving become the one who forgives and the one who is forgiven. Thus, she argues, the former has cause to feel virtuous or generous, and the latter grateful and indebted, thus undermining relations of equality.

41. See Shriver Jr., *Ethic for Enemies*, 7–8, and Tavuchis, *Mea Culpa*, 100.

42. Hanna Fenichel Pitkin, *The Attack of the Blob: Hannah Arendt's Concept of the Social* (Chicago: The University of Chicago Press, 1998), 267.

43. The literature on Hannah Arendt is, of course, massive. For her "politicalness" see Pitkin, *The Attack of the Blob*, and Emily Hauptmann, "A Local History of 'The Political,'" *Political Theory* 32 (1): 34–60.

44. Hannah Arendt, "Understanding and Politics," *Partisan Review* 20 (1953): 377.

45. Arendt translates the Dante quotation as follows: "For in every action what is primarily intended by the doer, whether he acts from natural necessity or out of free will, is the disclosure of his own image. Hence, it comes about that every doer, in so far as he does, takes delight in doing; since everything that is desires its own being, and since in action the being of the doer is somehow intensified, delight necessarily follows. . . . Thus, nothing acts unless [by acting] it makes patent its latent self."

46. Quoted by Arendt, *The Human Condition*, 175.

47. Arendt, *The Human Condition*, 243.

48. "A life without speech and without action . . . is literally dead to the world; it has ceased to be a human life because it is no longer lived among men," Arendt writes in *The Human Condition*, 176.

49. Arendt, *The Human Condition*, 195.

50. Ibid., 184.

51. Ibid., 190.

52. Ibid., 237.

53. Ibid., 233–234.

54. Ibid., 237.

55. Stanley Cavell, in *Must We Mean What We Say?*—cited by Hanna Fenichel Pitkin in *Wittgenstein And Justice* (Berkeley: University of California Press, 1972), 333—describes this dilemma: "Such persons shun responsibilities not out of selfishness but because they no longer know where responsibilities end. . . . The newspaper tells me that everything is relevant, but I cannot really accept that because it would mean that I do not have one life, to which some things are relevant and some not. I cannot really deny it either because I do not know why things happen

as they do and why I am not responsible for any or all of it. And so to the extent that I still have feelings to contend with, it is a generalized guilt, which only confirms my paralysis."

56. Arendt, *The Human Condition*, 220.

57. Ibid., 237.

58. Arendt, "Understanding and Politics," 377.

59. Benhabib makes a similar point regarding *The Origins of Totalitarianism*. See "Redemptive Power of Narrative," 180. See also Richard J. Bernstein, *Philosophical Profiles: Essays in a Pragmatic Mode* (Cambridge, England: Polity Press, 1986), for a similar point regarding Arendt's preoccupation while she was writing *The Life of the Mind*.

60. Arendt, in the Preface to *Between Past and Future* wrote that "thought itself arises out of incidents of living experience and must remain bound to them as the only guideposts by which to take its bearings" (14).

61. Hanna Fenichel Pitkin, "Justice: On Relating Private and Public," *Political Theory* 9 (3): 341.

62. Arendt, *The Human Condition*, 235, ft. 75.

63. Arendt, *The Life of the Mind* (New York: Harcourt Brace Jovanovich, 1971), 216.

64. Arendt, *Eichmann in Jerusalem*, 278.

65. Arendt, *The Human Condition*, 205–206.

66. Ibid., 239.

67. Ibid., 237.

68. Ibid., 241.

69. Tavuchis, *Mea Culpa*, 121.

70. Arendt, *Lectures on Kant's Political Philosophy*, ed. Ronald Beiner (Chicago: The University of Chicago Press, 1982), 43; and Pitkin, *Attack of the Blob*, 270.

71. Arendt, *The Human Condition*, 241.

72. "I can forgive somebody without forgiving anything." Arendt to W.H. Auden, February 14, 1960, Library of Congress, quoted by Young-Bruehl, *For Love of the World*, 371.

73. Arendt, *The Human Condition*, 242.

74. Ibid., 243.

75. Tavuchis, *Mea Culpa*, 98–117; and see P. E. Digeser, *Political Forgiveness* (Ithaca: Cornell University Press, 2001).

76. Tavuchis, *Mea Culpa*, 108–117.

77. Sheldon S. Wolin, "Injustice and Collective Memory," 35–36.

78. Tavuchis, *Mea Culpa*, 121.

79. Galanter, "Righting Old Wrongs," 113.

80. Boris I. Bittker, *The Case for Black Reparations* (New York: Random House, 1973), 131. Also see Darrell L. Pugh, "Collective Rehabilitation," in Brooks, ed., *When Sorry Isn't Enough*, 372–373.

81. Shirley Castelnuovo, "With Liberty and Justice for Some: The Case for Compensation to Japanese-Americans Imprisoned During World War II," in Daniels, Taylor, and Kitano, eds, *Japanese Americans: From Relocation to Redress*, 203–205.

82. Ibid.; and Bittker, *Case for Black Reparations*, 73.

83. Tavuchis, *Mea Culpa*, 103.

84. Ibid., 102–103.

85. 105th Cong., 1st sess., *Congressional Record* 143 (June 18, 1997): H 3890–3891.

86. Ibid.

87. President Clinton, while not angrily, opposed a national apology for slavery. See "Clinton Opposes Slavery Apology," *US News & World Report*, April 6, 1998, 7, in Brooks, ed., *When Sorry Isn't Enough*, 352.

88. Congressman Tony Hall, in his comments, responded to the charge that a national apology would be "an empty, meaningless gesture." *Congressional Record* 143: H 3890–3891.

89. Congress, House, Representative Bruce A. Morrison speaking for HR 442, 100th Cong., 1st sess., *Congressional Record* 133 (September 21, 1987): H 7578.

90. See Special Field Order No. 15, Headquarters, Military Division of the Mississippi, in the Field, Savannah, Georgia, January 16, 1865, in Brooks, ed., *When Sorry Isn't Enough*, 365–366.

91. Stephen Magagnini, "Descendants Suing U.S. over Slavery," *Sacramento Bee,* April 14, 1994, A1, quoted in Joe R. Feagin and Eileen O'Brien, "The Growing Movement for Reparations," in Brooks, ed. *When Sorry Isn't Enough*, 342.

92. Wes Smith, "40 Acres, A Mule Plus 132 Years' Interest; Man's Crusade for Slavery Reparations Picks up Momentum," *Chicago Tribune,* July 10, 1997, 1N, quoted in Feagin and O'Brien, in Brooks, ed. *When Sorry Isn't Enough*, 342.

93. Spike Lee's movie production company is named *40 Acres and a Mule.*

94. Wade Henderson, quoted by Michael Fletcher, "Is It Time to Consider Reparations for Black Americans?" *Columbian* (October 21, 1994), cited in Barkan, *Guilt of Nations*, 286.

95. Barkan, *Guilt of Nations*, 283–293. And see Raymond A. Winbush, Ph.D., ed., *Should America Pay? Slavery and the Raging Debate on Reparations* (New York: Amistad, 2003), for a collection of articles on the issue.

96. Robert Westley, "Many Billions Gone: Is It Time to Reconsider the Case for Black Reparations?" *Boston College Law Review*, Volume 40, no. 1 (December 1998): 429–476.

97. Armstrong Williams, "Presumed Victims," in Winbush, ed., *Should America Pay?* 166, 165.

98. John McWhorter, "Against Reparations," in Winbush, ed., *Should America Pay?* 194.

99. Shelby Steele, ". . . Or a Childish Illusion of Justice? Reparations Enshrine Victimhood, Dishonoring our Ancestors," in Winbush, ed., *Should America Pay?* 198.

100. Wendy Brown, "Wounded Attachments," in *States of Injury: Power and Freedom in Late Modernity* (Princeton: Princeton University Press, 1995): 72–74.

101. Arendt, "Understanding and Politics," 377. As noted in the text, later Arendt will amend this statement and clarify that forgiveness does not actually undo what has been done.

102. Michael Ignatieff, "Articles of Faith," *Index on Censorship* 5 (1996): 110–122.

103. Ibid.

104. Pitkin, *Fortune Is a Woman*, 301. I am indebted to Pitkin for the point above on the distinction between morality and politics.

Conclusion

1. Benjamin R. Barber, *Jihad vs. McWorld* (New York: Ballantine Books, 1995).

2. Wolin, *Politics and Vision*, 561.

3. Ibid., see esp. 581–606.

4. Richard Rorty, *Achieving Our Country* (Cambridge: Harvard University Press, 1998).

5. Michael J. Sandel, *Democracy's Discontent: America in Search of a Public Philosophy* (Cambridge: Harvard University Press, 1996).

6. Connolly, *Identity/Difference*.

7. Will Kymlicka and Wayne Norman," Return of the Citizen: A Survey of Recent Work on Citizenship Theory," in *Theorizing Citizenship*, ed. Ronald Beiner, 300 (Albany, New York: State University of New York Press, 1995).

8. Eric Hobsbawn, quoted in Aleinikoff, *Semblances of Sovereignty*, 194. See also Charles Taylor's essay in Martha C. Nussbaum with respondents, *For Love of Country*, ed. Joshua Cohen (Boston: Beacon Press, 1996).

9. For a discussion of the differences between citizenship and patriotism, see Chapter 3 above, and Smith, *Politics and Remembrance*.

10. Minow, *Between Vengeance and Forgiveness*, 147.

11. Carla Hesse and Robert Post, "Introduction," in *Human Rights in Political Transitions: Gettysburg to Bosnia*, ed. Carla Hesse and Robert Post, 30 (New York: Zone Books, 1999).

12. See Frederick Schauer, "Community, Citizenship, and the Search for National Identity," *Michigan Law Review* 84 (June 1986): 1504; and Hesse and Post, "Introduction," in *Human Rights in Political Transitions*, 30–31.

13. Hesse and Post, "Introduction," 30–31.

14. See Michael Rogin, "Make My Day!: Spectacle as Amnesia in Imperial Politics," *Representations* 29 (Winter 1990): 99–123.

15. Hesse and Post, "Introduction," 31.

16. Amy Gutmann, *Identity in Democracy* (Princeton: Princeton University Press, 2003), 206.

17. Steven Knapp, "Collective Memory and the Actual Past," *Representations* 26 (Spring 1989), 144–145. And see Chapter 4 above.

18. Allan Bloom, *The Closing of the American Mind* (New York: Simon and Schuster, 1987), 55.

19. Bloom, *Closing of American Mind*, 56.

20. Schlesinger, *Disuniting of America*, 137–138.

21. Ibid., 58–59, 40.

22. Ibid., 16–17.

23. Ibid., 138.

24. The first quotation is credited to Roger Kimball in *The Wall Street Journal*, and the second to David M. Oshinsky in *The New Leader*.

25. The phrase is Benedict R. Anderson's from *Imagined Communities: Reflections on the Origins and Spread of Nationalism* (New York: Verso Books, 1991).

26. Cornel West, "Diverse New World," in *Debating P.C.*, ed. Paul Berman, 327 (New York: Dell Publishing, 1992).

27. Connolly, *Identity/Difference*, 199.

28. Ibid.

29. William E. Connolly, "The Liberal Image of the Nation," in *Political Theory and the Rights of Indigenous Peoples*, ed. Duncan Ivison, Paul Patton and Will Sanders (Cambridge: Cambridge University Press, 2000), 183–198, 195.

30. Will Kymlicka and Wayne Norman argue that "it seems clear that the left has not yet found a language of responsibility that it is comfortable with, or a set of concrete policies to promote these responsibilities," in "Return of the Citizen: A Survey of Recent Work on Citizenship Theory," in Beiner, ed. *Theorizing Citizenship*, 293.

31. Rogers M. Smith, "Transnational, Transhistorical: Identities, Interests, and the Tasks of Political Science in the 21st Century," Paper presented at the 2002 APSA Conference, August 2002.

32. Aleinikoff, *Semblances of Sovereignty*, 178.

33. Schauer, "Community, Citizenship, and the Search for National Identity," 1504.

34. Smith, "Transnational, Transhistorical."

Bibliography

Ackerman, Bruce. *We the People.* Vol. 1, *Foundations.* Cambridge: Harvard University Press, 1991.

Aleinikoff, T. Alexander. *Semblances of Sovereignty: The Constitution, the State, and American Citizenship.* Cambridge: Harvard University Press, 2002.

Anderson, Benedict R. *Imagined Communities: Reflections on the Origins and Spread of Nationalism.* New York: Verso Books, 1991.

Arendt, Hannah. *Between Past and Future.* New York: Penguin Books, 1954.

———. "Collective Responsibility." In *Amor Mundi: Explorations in the Faith and Thought of Hannah Arendt,* edited by James W. Bernauer, S.J., 43–50. Boston: Martinus Nijhoff Publishers, 1987.

———. "Collective Responsibility." In *Responsibility and Judgment,* edited and with an introduction by Jerome Kahn, 147–158. New York: Schocken Books, 2003.

———. *Crises of the Republic.* New York: Harcourt Brace Jovanovich, 1969.

———. *Eichmann in Jerusalem.* New York: Viking Press, 1963.

———. *The Human Condition.* Chicago: The University of Chicago Press, 1958.

———. *The Jew as Pariah: Jewish Identity and Politics in the Modern Age.* Edited by Ron H. Feldman. New York: Grove Press, 1978.

———. *Lectures on Kant's Political Philosophy.* Edited by Ronald Beiner. Chicago: The University of Chicago Press, 1982.

———. *The Life of the Mind.* New York: Harcourt Brace Jovanovich, 1971.

———. *Men in Dark Times.* New York: Harcourt, Brace & World, 1968.

———. *On Revolution.* New York: Penguin Books, 1963.

———. "Organized Guilt and Universal Responsibility." Originally published in *Jewish Frontier,* Vol. 12 (1945). In *Guilt: Man and Society,* edited by Roger W. Smith, 255–267. New York: Anchor Books, 1971.

———. *The Origins of Totalitarianism*. New York: Harcourt Brace Jovanovich, 1951.

———. "Understanding and Politics." *Partisan Review* 20 (1953): 377–393.

Aristotle. *The Nicomachean Ethics*. Translated by J. A. K. Thomson. London: Penguin Books, 1976.

———. "Liberal Democracy and the Costs of Consent." In *Liberalism and the Moral Life*, edited by Nancy L. Rosenblum, 54–68. Cambridge: Harvard University Press, 1989.

Barber, Benjamin R. *Jihad vs. McWorld*. New York: Ballantine Books, 1995.

Barkan, Elazar. *The Guilt of Nations: Restitution and Negotiating Historical Injustices*. New York: W.W. Norton & Company, 2000.

Barry, John Edward. "Comment: *Oneida Indian Nation v. County of Oneida:* Tribal Rights of Action and the Indian Trade and Intercourse Act." *Columbia Law Review* 84: 1852–1870.

Beiner, Ronald. *What's the Matter with Liberalism?* Berkeley: University of California Press, 1992.

Beiner, Ronald, ed. *Theorizing Citizenship*. Albany: State University of New York Press, 1995.

Bell, Daniel. *The End of Ideology: On the Exhaustion of Political Ideas in the Fifties*. Cambridge: Harvard University Press, 1988.

Benhabib, Seyla. "Hannah Arendt and the Redemptive Power of Narrative." *Social Research* 57, no. 1 (Spring 1990): 155–175.

Benjamin, Walter. *Illuminations*. Edited and with an introduction by Hannah Arendt. New York: Schocken Books, 1969.

Bernstein, Richard. *Philosophical Profiles: Essays in a Pragmatic Mode*. Cambridge, England: Polity Press, 1986.

Bittker, Boris I. *The Case for Black Reparations*. New York: Random House, 1973.

Bloom, Allan. *The Closing of the American Mind*. New York: Simon and Schuster, 1987.

Bodnar, John. *Remaking America: Public Memory, Commemoration, and Patriotism in the Twentieth Century*. Princeton: Princeton University Press, 1992.

Boorstin, Daniel J. *The Genius of American Politics*. Chicago: University of Chicago Press, 1953.

———. *The Lost World of Thomas Jefferson*. Boston: Beacon Press, 1948.

Borneman, John. *Settling Accounts: Violence, Justice, and Accountability in Postsocialist Europe*. Princeton: Princeton University Press, 1997.

Botwinick, Aryeh, and William E. Connolly, eds. *Democracy and Vision: Sheldon Wolin and the Vicissitudes of the Political*. Princeton: Princeton University Press, 2001.

Brooks, Roy L., ed. *When Sorry Isn't Enough: The Controversy over Apologies and Reparations for Human Injustice*. New York: New York University Press, 1999.

Brown, Wendy. *States of Injury: Power and Freedom in Late Modernity*. Princeton: Princeton University Press, 1995.

Buchanan, Patrick J. *Right from the Beginning*. Boston: Little, Brown, 1988.

Burke, Edmund. *Reflections on the Revolution in France*. New York: Anchor Books, 1973.

Campisi, Jack. "The Trade and Intercourse Acts." In *Irredeemable America*, edited by Imre Sutton, 337–362. Albuquerque: University of New Mexico Press, 1985.

Carmichael, Stokely, and Charles V. Hamilton. *Black Power: The Politics of Liberation in America*. New York: Vintage Books, 1967.

Castelnuovo, Shirley. "With Liberty and Justice for Some: The Case for Compensation to Japanese-Americans Imprisoned During World War II." In *Japanese Americans: From Relocation to Redress*, edited by Roger Daniels, Sandra C. Taylor, and Harry H. L. Kitano, 203–209. Seattle: University of Washington Press, 1988.

Churchill, Ward. "The Earth is our Mother: Struggles for American Indian Land and Liberation in the Contemporary United States." In *The State of Native America: Genocide, Colonization, and Resistance*, edited by M. Annette Jaimes, 139–188. Boston: South End Press, 1992.

Clifford, James. *The Predicament of Culture: Twentieth Century Ethnography, Literature, and Art*. Cambridge: Harvard University Press, 1988.

Clymer, Adam. "A Daughter of Slavery Makes The Senate Listen." *The New York Times*, 23 July 1993, A10.

———. "Helms Loses 2d Battle of Dixie." *The New York Times*, 6 August 1993, A11.

Connolly, William E. *Identity/Difference: Democratic Negotiations of Political Paradox*. Ithaca: Cornell University Press, 1991.

———. "The Liberal Image of the Nation." In *Political Theory and the Rights of Indigenous Peoples*, edited by Duncan Ivison, Paul Patton, and Will Sanders, 183–198. Cambridge: Cambridge University Press, 2000.

———. *The Terms of Political Discourse*. Lexington, MA: D.C. Heath and Company, 1974.

Cover, Robert. "Violence and the Word." *Yale Law Journal* 95 (1986): 1601–1617.

Dahl, Robert. *Who Governs? Democracy and Power in an American City*. New Haven, CT: Yale University Press, 1961.

Dale, Nina. "*County of Oneida v. Oneida Indian Nation:* The Continuing Saga of American Indian Territorial Wars." *Pace Environmental Law Review* 4 (1986): 221–251.

Danforth, Sandra C. "Repaying Historical Debts: The Indian Claims Commission." *North Dakota Law Review* 49: 359–403.

Daniels, Roger, Sandra C. Taylor, and Harry H. L. Kitano. *Japanese Americans: From Relocation to Redress*. Seattle: University of Washington Press, 1991.

Davis, Sue, ed. *American Political Thought: Four Hundred Years of Ideas and Ideologies*. Englewood Cliffs, NJ: Prentice Hall, 1996.

De Tocqueville, Alexis. *Democracy in America*. Translated and edited by J. P. Mayer. New York: Anchor Books, 1969.

Deloria, Vine. "Congress in Its Wisdom: The Course of Indian Legislation." In *The Aggressions of Civilization*, edited by Sarah L. Cadwalader and Vine Deloria, 105–130. Philadelphia: Temple University Press, 1984.

Digeser, P. E. *Political Forgiveness*. Ithaca: Cornell University Press, 2001.

Diggins, John P. *The Lost Soul of American Politics: Virtue, Self-Interest, and the Foundations of Liberalism*. Chicago: The University of Chicago Press, 1984.

Dworkin, Ronald. *Law's Empire*. Cambridge: The Belknap Press of Harvard University Press, 1986.

Euben, J. Peter. *The Tragedy of Political Theory*. Princeton: Princeton University Press, 1990.

Evans, Richard J. *In Hitler's Shadow: West German Historians and the Attempt to Escape the Nazi Past*. New York: Pantheon Books, 1989.

Feinberg, Joel. *Doing and Deserving: Essays in the Theory of Responsibility*. Princeton: Princeton University Press, 1970.

Fingarette, Herbert. *On Responsibility*. New York: Basic Books, 1967.

Fiss, Owen M. "Groups and the Equal Protection Clause." *Philosophy and Public Affairs* 5, no. 2 (Winter 1976): 107–177.

Fitzgerald, Frances. *America Revised: History Schoolbooks in the Twentieth Century*. Boston: Little, Brown, 1979.

Fliegelman, Jay. *Prodigals and Pilgrims: The American Revolution against Patriarchal Authority, 1750–1800*. Cambridge: Cambridge University Press, 1982.

Forgie, George B. *Patricide in the House Divided: A Psychological Interpretation of Lincoln and His Age*. New York: W. W. Norton & Company, 1979.

Freud, Sigmund. *The Standard Edition of the Complete Psychological Works of Sigmund Freud*. Translated and Edited by James Strachey. Volume 12, 147–159. *Remembering, Repeating and Working-Through (Further Recommendations on the Technique of Psycho-Analysis, 2)*. London: Hogarth Press, 1958.

Galanter, Marc. "Righting Old Wrongs." In *Breaking the Cycles of Hatred: Memory, Law, and Repair,* edited by Martha Minow. Introduced and commentaries edited by Nancy L. Rosenblum, 107–131. Princeton: Princeton University Press, 2002.

Gillis, John, ed. *Commemorations: The Politics of National Identity.* Princeton: Princeton University Press, 1994.

Glendon, Mary Ann. *Rights Talk: The Impoverishment of Political Discourse.* New York: Free Press, 1991.

Gordon, Robert W. "Undoing Historical Injustice." In *Justice and Injustice in Law and Legal Theory,* edited by Austin Sarat and Thomas R. Kearns, 35–75. Ann Arbor: University of Michigan Press, 1996.

Gutmann, Amy. *Identity in Democracy.* Princeton: Princeton University Press, 2003.

Habermas, Jurgen. *The New Conservatism: Cultural Criticism and the Historians' Debate.* Edited and translated by Shierry Weber Nicolsen; introduction by Richard Wolin. Cambridge: The MIT Press, 1989.

Hartman, Geoffrey, ed. *Bitburg in Moral and Political Perspective.* Bloomington: Indiana University Press, 1986.

Hartz, Louis. *The Liberal Tradition in America.* New York: Harcourt Brace Jovanovich, 1955.

Hatamiya, Leslie T. *Righting a Wrong: Japanese Americans and the Passage of the Civil Liberties Act of 1988.* Stanford: Stanford University Press, 1993.

Hauptmann, Emily. "A Local History" of "The Political." *Political Theory* 32, no. 1 (February 2004): 34–60.

Hayner, Priscilla B. *Unspeakable Truths: Confronting State Terror and Atrocity.* New York: Routledge, 2001.

Herzog, Don. *Happy Slaves.* Chicago: University of Chicago Press, 1989.

Hesse, Carla, and Robert Post, eds. *Human Rights in Political Transitions: Gettysburg to Bosnia.* New York: Zone Books, 1999.

Hobbes, Thomas. *Leviathan.* Edited by C. B. Macpherson. Harmondsworth: Penguin Books, 1968.

Hohri, William Minoru. *Repairing America: An Account of the Movement for Japanese-American Redress.* Pullman, WA: Washington State University Press, 1988.

Honig, B. "Arendt, Identity, and Difference." *Political Theory* 16, no. 1 (February 1988): 77–98.

Honig, B., ed. *Feminist Interpretations of Hannah Arendt.* University Park: The Pennsylvania State University Press, 1995.

Horowitz, Donald L. *The Courts and Social Policy.* Washington, DC: The Brookings Institute, 1977.

Hyde, Lewis. *The Gift: Imagination and the Erotic Life of Property.* New York: Vintage Books, 1979.

Ignatieff, Michael. "Articles of Faith." *Index on Censorship* 5 (1996): 110–122.

Irons, Peter, ed. *Justice Delayed: The Record of the Japanese American Internment Cases.* Middletown, CT: Wesleyan University Press, 1989.

Ivison, Duncan, Paul Patton, and Will Sanders, eds. *Political Theory and the Rights of Indigenous Peoples.* Cambridge: Cambridge University Press, 2000.

Jaspers, Karl. *The Question of German Guilt.* Translated by E. B. Ashton. New York: The Dial Press, 1947.

Jefferson, Thomas. *The Writings of Thomas Jefferson.* Edited by Albert Ellery Bergh. Definitive Edition. Washington, DC: Thomas Jefferson Memorial Association, 1907.

Kammen, Michael. *Mystic Chords of Memory: The Transformation of Tradition in American Culture.* New York: Alfred A. Knopf, 1991.

Karst, Kenneth L. *Belonging to America: Equal Citizenship and the Constitution.* New Haven: Yale University Press, 1989.

———. "Citizenship, Law, and the American Nation." *Indiana Journal of Global Legal Studies* 7 (Spring 2000): 595–601.

———. "Universal Rights and Cultural Pluralism: The Bonds of American Nationhood." *Cardozo Law Review* 21 (February 2000): 1141–1181.

Kateb, George. *Hannah Arendt: Politics, Conscience, Evil.* Oxford: Martin Robertson, 1983.

Kilpatrick, James. "1.2 Billion Worth of Hindsight," *The Washington Post,* March 5, 1988, A23.

Kinder, Donald R., and Lynn M. Sanders. *Divided by Color.* Chicago: University of Chicago Press, 1996.

Knapp, Steven. "Collective Memory and the Actual Past." *Representations* 26 (Spring 1989): 123–149.

Koppelman, Andrew. *Antidiscrimination Law and Social Equality.* New Haven, CT: Yale University Press, 1996.

Kritz, Neil J., ed. *Transitional Justice: How Emerging Democracies Reckon With Former Regimes.* Washington, DC: United States Institute of Peace Press, 1995.

Kundera, Milan. *The Book of Laughter and Forgetting.* Translated by Michael Henry Heim. New York: Penguin Books, 1981.

Kymlicka, Will. *Multicultural Citizenship.* Oxford: Oxford University Press, 1995.

Kymlicka, Will, ed. *The Rights of Minority Cultures.* Oxford: Oxford University Press, 1995.

Laslett, Peter, and James S. Fishkin, eds. *Justice between Age Groups and Generations.* New Haven, CT: Yale University Press, 1992.

Lazarus, Edward. *Black Hills/White Justice: The Sioux Nation versus The United States, 1775 to the Present*. New York: Harper Collins, 1991.

Levinson, Sanford. *Constitutional Faith*. Princeton: Princeton University Press, 1988.

———. *Written in Stone: Public Monuments in Changing Societies*. Durham: Duke University Press, 1998.

Lewis, R. W. B. *The American Adam: Innocence, Tragedy, and Tradition in the Nineteenth Century*. Chicago: The University of Chicago Press, 1955.

Lief, Joshua N. "The Oneida Land Claims: Equity and Ejectment." *Syracuse Law Review* 39 no. 2 (Summer 1988): 825–844.

Lincoln, Abraham. *Complete Works of Abraham Lincoln*. Edited by John G. Nicolay and John Hay. New York: Francis D. Tandy & Co., 1905.

Lippmann, Walter. *The Public Philosophy*. New York: The New American Library, 1955.

Locke, John. *Two Treatises of Government*. Edited by Peter Laslett. New York: New American Library, 1965.

Lowenthal, David. *The Past Is a Foreign Country*. Cambridge: Cambridge University Press, 1985.

Lucas, J. R. *Responsibility*. Oxford: Clarendon Press, 1993.

Lummis, C. Douglas. *Radical Democracy*. Ithaca: Cornell University Press, 1996.

Lyons, David. "Corrective Justice, Equal Opportunity, and the Legacy of Slavery and Jim Crow." *Boston University School of Law Working Paper Series*. Public Law and Legal Theory Working Paper No. 03-15.

———. "The New Indian Claims and Original Rights To Land." *Social Theory and Practice* 4 (Fall 1977): 249–272.

MacIntyre, Alasdair. *After Virtue*. Notre Dame: University of Notre Dame Press, 1981.

———. "Is Patriotism a Virtue?" The Lindley Lecture presented at the University of Kansas, Department of Philosophy, March 26, 1984.

Maier, Charles S. *The Unmasterable Past: History, Holocaust, and German National Identity*. Cambridge: Harvard University Press, 1988.

Massey, Douglas and Nancy A. Denton. *American Apartheid: Segregation and the Making of the Underclass*. Cambridge: Harvard University Press, 1993.

Max, Theodore C. "Conundrums along the Mohawk: Preconstitutional Land Claims of the Oneida Indian Nation." *New York University Review of Law and Social Change* 40 (Fall 1982): 473–519.

May, Larry. *Sharing Responsibility*. Chicago: University of Chicago Press, 1992.

McCarthy, Thomas. "Vergangenheitsbewaltigung in the USA: On the Politics of the Memory of Slavery." *Political Theory* 30 no. 5 (October 2002): 623–648.

Melzer, Arthur M., Jerry Weinberger, and M. Richard Zinman, eds. *Multiculturalism and American Democracy*. Lawrence: University Press of Kansas, 1998.

Menkel-Meadow, Carrie J. "The Transformation of Disputes by Lawyers: What The Dispute Paradigm Does and Does Not Tell Us." *Missouri Journal of Dispute Resolution* 1985 (1985): 25–44.

Michelman, Frank I. *Brennan and Democracy*. Princeton: Princeton University Press, 1999.

Minow, Martha. *Between Vengeance and Forgiveness: Facing History after Genocide and Mass Violence*. Boston: Beacon Press, 1998.

———. *Breaking the Cycles of Hatred: Memory, Law, and Repair*. Introduced and commentaries edited by Nancy L. Rosenblum. Princeton: Princeton University Press, 2002.

———. *Making All the Difference: Inclusion, Exclusion, and American Law*. Ithaca: Cornell University Press, 1990.

———. *Not Only for Myself*. New York: The New Press, 1997.

Mouffe, Chantal, ed. *Dimensions of Radical Democracy: Pluralism, Citizenship, Community*. London: Verso, 1992.

Murphy, Jeffrie G., and Jean Hampton. *Forgiveness and Mercy*. Cambridge: Cambridge University Press, 1988.

National Committee for Redress. *Redress*. Special Collections. The Bancroft Library, University of California, Berkeley, 1978.

Newton, Nell Jessup. "Compensation, Reparations, and Restitution: Indian Property Claims in the United States." *Georgia Law Review* 28 (1994): 453–480.

Niebuhr, Reinhold. *The Irony of American History*. New York: Charles Scribner's Sons, 1952.

Nietzsche, Friedrich. *On The Genealogy of Morals*. Translated by Walter Kaufmann and R. J. Hollingdale. New York: Vintage Books, 1989.

Norton, Anne. *Alternative Americas: A Reading of Antebellum Political Culture*. Chicago: The University of Chicago Press, 1986.

———. "The Virtues of Multiculturalism." In *Multiculturalism and American Democracy*, edited by Arthur M. Melzer, Jerry Weinberger, and M. Richard Zinman, 130–138. Lawrence: University Press of Kansas, 1998.

Nussbaum, Martha C., with Respondents. *For Love of Country*. Edited by Joshua Cohen. Boston: Beacon Press, 1996.

Osiel, Mark. *Mass Atrocity, Collective Memory, and the Law*. New Brunswick, NJ: Transaction Publishers, 1997.

Paine, Thomas. "Common Sense." In *Common Sense and Other Political Writings,* edited by Nelson F. Adkins, 3–52. Indianapolis: Bobbs-Merrill, 1953.

———. *The Writings of Thomas Paine.* Edited by Moncure Daniel Conway. New York, 1894.

Phillips, Derek L. *Looking Backward: A Critical Appraisal of Communitarian Thought.* Princeton: Princeton University Press, 1993.

Pitkin, Hanna. *The Attack of the Blob: Hannah Arendt's Concept of the Social.* Chicago: University of Chicago Press, 1998.

———. *Fortune Is a Woman: Gender and Politics in the Thought of Niccolo Machiavelli.* Berkeley: University of California Press, 1984.

———. "Justice: On Relating Private and Public." *Political Theory* 9, no. 3 (August 1981): 330–350.

———. "Obligation and Consent." *American Political Science Review* 59 (December 1965): 990–999; and 60 (March 1966): 39–52.

———. *Wittgenstein and Justice.* Berkeley: University of California Press, 1972.

Pocock, J.G.A. *The Machiavellian Moment.* Princeton: Princeton University Press, 1975.

———. *Politics, Language and Time.* New York: Antheneum, 1973

Robinson, Randall. *The Debt: What America Owes to Blacks.* New York: Dutton Press, 2000.

Rogin, Michael Paul. *Blackface, White Noise: Jewish Immigrants in the Hollywood Melting Pot.* Berkeley: University of California Press, 1996.

———. *Fathers and Children: Andrew Jackson and the Subjugation of the American Indian.* New York: Knopf, 1975.

———. "Make My Day! Spectacle as Amnesia in Imperial Politics." *Representations* 29 (Winter 1990): 99–123.

———. *Ronald Reagan, the Movie and Other Episodes in Political Demonology.* Berkeley: University of California Press, 1987.

———. *Subversive Genealogy: The Politics and Art of Herman Melville.* Berkeley: University of California Press, 1979.

Rorty, Richard. *Achieving Our Country.* Cambridge: Harvard University Press, 1998.

Rosenthal, Harvey D. "Indian Claims and the American Conscience." In *Irredeemable America,* edited by Imre Sutton, 35–70. Albuquerque: University of New Mexico Press, 1985.

Rotberg, Robert I., and Dennis Thompson, eds. *Truth v. Justice: The Morality of Truth Commissions.* Princeton: Princeton University Press, 2000.

Sandel, Michael J. *Democracy's Discontent: America in Search of a Public Philosophy.* Cambridge: Harvard University Press, Belknap Press, 1996.

―――. *Liberalism and the Limits of Liberalism.* Cambridge: Cambridge University Press, 1982.

Schaar, John H. *Legitimacy in the Modern State.* New Brunswick, NJ: Transaction Books, 1981.

Schauer, Frederick. "Community, Citizenship, and the Search for National Identity." *Michigan Law Review* 84, no. 7 (June 1986): 1504–1517.

Schlesinger, Jr., Arthur M. *The Disuniting of America: Reflections on a Multicultural Society.* New York: W. W. Norton & Company, 1992.

Schuck, Peter, and Rogers M. Smith. *Citizenship without Consent.* New Haven: Yale University Press, 1985.

Schwartz, Regina M. "Joseph's Bones and the Resurrection of the Text: Remembering in the Bible." *PMLA* 103 (March 1988): 114–124.

Seery, John Evan. "The Columbus Controversy as Confession: Personal Ramblings and Political Recommendations." Talk given at Pomona College Blue Room Lunch Series, November 1992. [copy in possession of author]

―――. *Political Theory for Mortals: Shades of Justice, Images of Death.* Ithaca: Cornell University Press, 1996.

Shattuck, George C. *The Oneida Land Claims: A Legal History.* Syracuse: Syracuse University Press, 1991.

Sheldon, Garrett Ward. *The Political Philosophy Of Thomas Jefferson.* Baltimore: The Johns Hopkins University Press, 1991.

Shklar, Judith N. *American Citizenship: The Quest for Inclusion.* Cambridge: Harvard University Press, 1991.

―――. *Legalism: Laws, Morals, and Political Trials.* Cambridge: Harvard University Press, 1964.

Shriver, Jr., Donald W. *An Ethic for Enemies: Forgiveness in Politics.* New York: Oxford University Press, 1995.

Simmons, A. John. "Historical Rights and Fair Shares." *Law and Philosophy* 14, no. 2 (May 1995): 149–184.

Singer, Joseph William. *Entitlement: The Paradoxes of Property.* New Haven: Yale University Press, 2000.

―――. "Well Settled? The Increasing Weight of History in American Indian Land Claims." *Georgia Law Review* 28, no. 2 (Winter 1994): 481–532.

Slotkin, Richard. *The Fatal Environment: The Myth of the Frontier in the Age of Industrialization, 1800–1890.* New York: Atheneum Books, 1985.

―――. *Gunfighter Nation: The Myth of the Frontier in Twentieth Century America.* New York: Atheneum Books, 1992.

―――. *Regeneration through Violence: The Mythology of the American Frontier, 1600–1860.* Middletown, CT: Wesleyan University Press, 1973.

Smith, Bruce James. *Politics & Remembrance: Republican Themes in Machiavelli, Burke, and Tocqueville.* Princeton: Princeton University Press, 1985.

Smith, Henry Nash. *Virgin Land: The American West as Symbol and Myth.* New York: Vintage Books, 1957.

Smith, Rogers M. *Civic Ideals: Conflicting Visions of Citizenship in U.S. History.* New Haven: Yale University Press, 1997.

———. "Transnational, Transhistorical: Identities, Interests, and the Tasks of Political Science in the 21st Century." Paper Presented at the 2002 APSA Conference.

Staples, Brent. "Strom Thurmond Continued: The Known World of Ms. Washington-Williams." *The New York Times,* National Edition, July 17, 2004, A24.

Strong, Tracy B. *The Idea of Political Theory: Reflections on the Self in Political Time and Space.* Notre Dame: University of Notre Dame Press, 1990.

Sullivan, Kathleen. "The Sins of Discrimination: Last Year's Affirmative Action Cases." *Harvard Law Review* 100 (November 1986): 78–98.

Sutton, Imre, ed. *Irredeemable America: The Indians' Estate and Land Claims.* Albuquerque: University of New Mexico Press, 1985.

Takaki, Ronald. *Iron Cages: Race and Culture in Nineteenth Century America.* New York: Alfred Knopf, 1979.

Tavuchis, Nicholas. *Mea Culpa: A Sociology of Apology and Reconciliation.* Stanford: Stanford University Press, 1991.

Taylor, Charles. *Multiculturalism and "The Politics of Recognition."* With commentary by Amy Gutmann, editor, and Steven C. Rockefeller, Michael Walzer, Susan Wolf. Princeton: Princeton University Press, 1992.

Thompson, Janna. *Taking Responsibility for the Past: Reparation and Historical Justice.* Cambridge, England: Polity Press, 2002.

Torpey, John. "Making Whole What Has Been Smashed: Reflections on Reparations" *The Journal of Modern History* 73 (June 2001): 333–358.

U.S. Commission on Wartime Relocation. *Personal Justice Denied.* Washington, DC: United States Government Printing Office, 1983.

U.S. Congress. House. 1987. Representatives speaking for and against HR 442. 100th Cong., 1st sess. *Congressional Record* 133 (September 21).

U.S. Congress. Senate. 1988. Senators speaking for and against S 1009. 100th Cong., 2nd sess. *Congressional Record* 134 (April 20).

U.S. Congress. Senate. 2004. Senators speaking for HJ Res. 98. 108th Cong., 2nd sess. *Congressional Record* S5002–5003 (May 6).

Vecsey, Christopher, and William A. Starna, eds. *Iroquois Land Claims.* Syracuse: Syracuse University Press, 1988.

Vidal, Gore. *United States: Essays 1952–1992*. New York: Random House, 1993.

Waldron, Jeremy. "Superseding Historic Injustice." *Ethics* 103 (October 1992): 4–28.

Wallace, Henry B. "Indian Sovereignty and Eastern Indian Land Claims." *New York Law School Review* 27, no. 3 (1982): 921–950.

Walzer, Michael. *Spheres of Justice: A Defense of Pluralism and Equality*. New York: Basic Books, 1983.

Weschler, Lawrence. "A Reporter At Large: The Great Exception." *The New Yorker*, 3 April 1989, 43–85; and 10 April 1989, 85–108.

West, Cornel. "Diverse New World." In *Debating P.C.*, edited by Paul Berman, 326–332. New York: Dell Publishing, 1992.

———. *Race Matters*. Boston: Beacon Press, 1993.

Westley, Robert. "Many Billions Gone: Is It Time to Reconsider the Case for Black Reparations?" *Boston College Law Review*, Volume 40 no. 1 (December 1998): 429–476.

White, James Boyd. *Acts of Hope*. Chicago: University of Chicago Press, 1994.

———. *When Words Lose Their Meaning: Constitutions and Reconstitutions of Language, Character, and Community*. Chicago: The University of Chicago Press, 1984.

Williams, Melissa S. *Voice, Trust, and Memory: Marginalized Groups and the Failings of Liberal Representation*. Princeton: Princeton University Press, 1998.

Wills, Garry. *Lincoln at Gettysburg: The Words That Remade America*. New York: Simon & Schuster, 1992.

Winbush, Raymond A., ed. *Should America Pay? Slavery and the Raging Debate on Reparations*. New York: Amistad, 2003.

Wolf, Susan. "Comment." In *Multiculturalism and "The Politics Of Recognition,"* Charles Taylor, edited by Amy Gutmann, 75–86. Princeton: Princeton University Press, 1992.

Wolin, Sheldon S. "Democracy, Difference, and Re-cognition." *Political Theory* 21, no. 3 (August 1993): 464–483.

———. "Political Theory: From Vocation to Invocation." In *Vocations of Political Theory*, edited by Jason A. Frank and John Tambornino, 3–22. Minneapolis: University of Minnesota Press, 2000.

———. *Politics and Vision: Continuity and Innovation in Western Political Thought*, exp. ed. Princeton: Princeton University Press, 2004.

———. "Postmodern Politics and the Absence of Myth." *Social Research* 52, no. 2 (Summer 1985): 217.

———. *The Presence of the Past: Essays on the State and the Constitution*. Baltimore: The Johns Hopkins University Press, 1989.

———. *Tocqueville between Two Worlds: The Making of a Political and Theoretical Life*. Princeton: Princeton University Press, 2001.

———. "What Time Is It?" *Theory & Event* 1, no. 1 (January 1997). [http://muse.jhu.edu/theory_&_event/v001/1.1wolin.html]

Young-Bruehl, Elisabeth. *Hannah Arendt: For Love of the World*. New Haven: Yale University Press, 1982.

Index

"Address to the Young Men's Lyceum"
(Lincoln), 98–100, 103
affirmative action, 50–51, 81
Africa, colonization of, 97
African Americans, 6, 15, 23, 80, 131–32.
  See also race and racism; slavery;
  American Indians compared to, 163–64;
  Black Power movement and, 118–19;
  Japanese American redress compared,
  62–65, 82; present disadvantages of,
  126–27; reparations sought by, 166–67;
  victim politics and, 168–69
Alaska Native Land Settlement (1971), 166
Aleinikoff, T. Alexander, 81
American Indians, 80. *See* Indian land
  claims; *specific tribal groups*; Trail of
  Tears and, 8, 63; in World War II, 6
American-Japanese Evacuation Claims Act
  (1948), 55, 61
American Revolution, 89–90, 94, 99;
  Oneida Indian role in, 30, 36, 145
Americans for Historical Accuracy, 60
Ancient Indian Land Claims Settlement
  Act (1982), 42
Anderson, Benedict, 21
anger, and vengeance, 147
apology, 83. *See also* national apologies; for
  Executive Order 9066, 56; forgiveness
  and, 10, 20; power and, 24, 151, 160–61;
  for slavery, 3, 17, 23, 164–65
Arendt, Hannah, 20, 121, 124, 134, 218n45;
  on collective guilt, 6, 117–19, 135, 169;
  on difference and plurality, 130;
  Eichmann in Jerusalem, 118, 119–20, 152,
  156–57; on forgiveness, 10, 147, 170; *The*

Human Condition, 148–50, 152, 158;
  Between Past and Future, 125–26; on
  political action, 127, 160; on political
  action and forgiveness, 152–59; on
  political membership, 131, 136;
  Thinking, 156; on totalitarianism,
  155–56; on tradition, 112;
  "Understanding and Politics," 155–56,
  170
Aristotle, 147, 148
Articles of Confederation, 29, 30, 196n9
Auden, W. H., 149
autonomy, 90–91. *See also* individual

Baker, Lillian, 60
Barber, Benjamin R., 175
Barkan, Elazar, 5
Beard, Charles, 182
Becker, Carl, 182
Bendetsen, Karl R., 141
Between Past and Future (Arendt), 125–26
Bible, 4, 20, 107, 108, 189n5; on
  forgiveness, 148, 151
Biddle, Francis, 52, 69
birth and birthright, 70, 90, 103–4, 108–12,
  122
Bitburg cemetery, 23
black colonization, 97. *See also* African
  Americans
Blackmun, Harry, 38
Black Power movement, 118–19
Blackstone, William, 39
Bloom, Allan, 182, 184
Boorstin, Daniel, 92
Brennan, William, 38